APMP for PRINCE2® Practitioners

London: TSO

information & publishing solutions

Published by TSO (The Stationery Office) and available from:

Online
www.tsoshop.co.uk

Mail, Telephone, Fax & E-mail
TSO
PO Box 29, Norwich NR3 1GN
Telephone orders/General enquiries: 0870 6005522
Fax orders: 0870 6005533
E-mail: customer.services@tso.co.uk
Textphone: 0870 240 3701

TSO Shops
16 Arthur Street, Belfast BT1 4GD
028 9023 8451 Fax 028 9023 5401
71 Lothian Road, Edinburgh EH3 9AZ
0870 606 5566 Fax 0870 606 5588

TSO@Blackwell and other Accredited Agents

The information contained in this publication is believed to be correct at the time of manufacture. Whilst care has been taken to ensure that the information is accurate, the publisher can accept no responsibility for any errors or omissions or for changes to the details given.

Graham Williams has asserted his moral rights under the Copyright, Designs and Patents Act 1988, to be identified as the author of this work.

Extracts from the *APM Body of Knowledge 5th edition, Project Risk Analysis and Management Guide 2nd edition* and *Directing Change: a Guide to the Governance of Project Management* have been reproduced with the kind permission of the Association for Project Management and APM Publishing Limited.

The Swirl logo™ is a Trade Mark of the Office of Government Commerce

PRINCE2® is a Registered Trade Mark of the Office of Government Commerce in the United Kingdom and other countries

The PRINCE2 Cityscape logo™ is a Trade Mark of the Office of Government Commerce in the United Kingdom and other countries

PRINCE® is a Registered Trade Mark of the Office of Government Commerce in the United Kingdom and other countries

A CIP catalogue record for this book is available from the British Library

A Library of Congress CIP catalogue record has been applied for

First published 2008

ISBN 9780113310951

Printed in the United Kingdom by The Stationery Office, London.

N5789872 c6 09/08

Contents

List of figures

List of tables

Foreword

The PRINCE2 method has probably been one of the most successful initiatives in the field of project management over the past 40 years. It certainly has if success is measured by the number of people who have passed examinations in the method, at both Foundation and Practitioner level. And even more so, when you consider the number of countries within which these examinations have taken place.

However, can PRINCE2 Practitioners, by virtue of their success in the PRINCE2 examinations, be considered to be fully rounded project managers? The answer is clearly 'No!' The PRINCE2 method does not cover a number of important project management topics, such as (and I quote from PRINCE2 here):

■ People management, such as motivation, delegation and team leadership
■ Generic planning techniques, e.g. Gantt charts and critical path analysis
■ Quality management and quality assurance mechanisms
■ Budgetary control and earned value analysis.

Such topics, and others, have for many years been considered to be essential personal competencies and skills that professional project managers should have and apply. The full range of topics is included within the Association for Project Management's *APM Body of Knowledge 5th Edition*, with a subset of these forming the syllabus for the Association's flagship qualification, the APMP.

That is where this book comes into its own. It provides a bridge for PRINCE2 Practitioners into an exploration of this broader range of topics, which will help them and their organization to become more successful in managing their projects. It does this by explaining every topic within the APMP syllabus in sufficient depth to meet the necessary learning outcomes for the qualification.

And so it gives me great pleasure, as Chairman of the Association for Project Management, to support this publication in the belief that Project Managers, who can demonstrate both an ability to apply the PRINCE2 method and an understanding of the fundamental knowledge areas covered by the APMP, can be considered to be fully rounded project management professionals.

I wish you well in your studies for the APMP examination and trust you will find the work involved both beneficial and rewarding.

Mike Nichols
Chairman, Association for Project Management

Acknowledgements

The Stationery Office (TSO) and the author, Graham Williams from GSW Consultancy, would like to thank David Atkinson for providing the exercise solutions, and the Association for Project Management and APM Publishing Limited for their kind permission to use extracts from the *APM Body of Knowledge 5th Edition*, *Project Risk Analysis and Management Guide 2nd Edition*, and *Directing Change: a Guide to the Governance of Project Management* (see Appendix D for full details).

In addition, TSO and Graham Williams would like to thank the following individuals for their help in reviewing this publication.

LEAD REVIEWER

Peter Simon from Lucidus Consulting

REVIEWERS

Graham Dixon, Oldham Metropolitan Borough Council

Catherine East, Audit Commission

Guy Eastoe, Snap-tech

Neil Franklin, Department of Health

Candice Hirons, Business Service Training and Development Group

Patrick Kennedy, HM Revenue & Customs

Eddie Lamont, Lothian Borders Police

Sue Mitchell, The Law Society

Tim Reeks, HM Revenue & Customs

Maturity mark

The TSO maturity mark (on the back cover) will help you decide if this publication is positioned at the appropriate level for your requirements, and provide a route map to progress with embedding the OGC best practice guidance.

This publication, *APMP for PRINCE2 Practitioners*, is level 2 and level 3.

Level 2 is Repeatable (process discipline) – OGC guidance is used repeatedly.

Level 3 is Defined (institutionalized) – OGC guidance is defined/confirmed as a standard business process.

For more information on the TSO maturity mark and how it can help you, please visit www.best-management-practice.com

Introduction

1 Introduction

1.1 PURPOSE

The purpose of this publication is to describe and explain the Association for Project Management's (APM's) fundamental project management knowledge areas and, more specifically, to provide a study guide for PRINCE2™ Practitioners to prepare for the APM's APMP examination.

The APMP examination is aimed at anyone who has worked in project management for up to two years, such as project office personnel, team members or recently appointed project officers, or anyone who has recently taken on project management responsibilities as part of their job.

The exam assesses a breadth of knowledge in all areas of project management, from the strategic and commercial implications of the Project Manager's role to the technical, commercial, organizational and people management skills required to successfully participate in a project team. There are 37 knowledge areas covered by the syllabus, each of which is defined in the *APM Body of Knowledge 5th Edition*. The APM Body of Knowledge itself contains 52 knowledge areas, with the 37 areas covered by the APMP being considered to be fundamental to the professional management of projects.

In contrast, PRINCE2 provides a proven project management method that incorporates a complete set of concepts and project management processes that are the minimum requirements for a properly run and managed project. It does not, however, cover all subjects relevant to project management. This is because the techniques and tools needed on a project will vary according to the project type and the corporate environment. Also, because certain aspects of project management are well covered by existing and proven methods, they are specifically excluded from the scope of PRINCE2.

Accordingly, by combining the structure provided by PRINCE2 with knowledge of the fundamental areas of project management covered by the APMP, Project Managers will be well equipped to meet the challenges of managing projects in any type of environment.

1.2 STRUCTURE OF THE GUIDE

Given that the prime audience for this guide consists of PRINCE2 Practitioners (or those working within a PRINCE2 environment), it has been structured to reflect the structure of PRINCE2.

- Chapter 2, Project management context, provides an introduction to project management and includes an explanation of how the PRINCE2 process model maps on to the APM's project lifecycle.
- Chapters 3–10 are each dedicated to one of the PRINCE2 components or themes. In each of these chapters, the PRINCE2 terminology is compared with that used within the APM Body of Knowledge (in the APMP exam it is important that the APM terminology is used). The PRINCE2 concepts are then summarized and finally the relevant APMP knowledge areas are described and explained.
- Chapters 11–13 then address aspects of project management that fall outside the scope of PRINCE2.

At the end of each chapter, there is a series of short exercises that reflect the types of question that could be asked as part of the APMP examination

1.3 APPENDICES

To support the main guide in this publication are four appendices (Table 1.1).

Table 1.1 Appendices included in this publication

Appendix A: Exercise solutions	This appendix provides solutions to the exercises provided at the end of each chapter in the main guide
Appendix B: APMP syllabus – 3rd edition	This appendix identifies the 37 (of the 52) APM Body of Knowledge areas and lists the topics and learning outcomes for each area
Appendix C: Mapping of guide to APMP syllabus	This appendix shows the alignment of the chapters within this guide to the APMP syllabus knowledge areas and provides a brief explanation for this alignment
Appendix D: Further reading	This appendix provides a short list of additional resources that would be useful for anyone wishing to expand their researches beyond the confines of the APMP syllabus

NB: A glossary has not been included in this publication, as both PRINCE2 and the APM Body of Knowledge contain extensive glossaries and the key terms from both are provided and compared at the start of each chapter in this guide. However, there are a number of terms that deserve special mention at this point. These terms do mean slightly different things in pure definition terms, but for the purposes of this guide they can be used interchangeably. These terms are:

- Time and Schedule and Delivery
- Cost and Budget
- Quality and Performance
- Product and Deliverable
- Success Criteria and Objectives
- Float and Slack
- Steering Group and Project Board
- Issue Log and Issue Register
- Risk Log and Risk Register
- Change Log and Change Register
- Procurement and Purchasing and Contracting.

1.4 USING THE GUIDE

While the guide has been structured to reflect the PRINCE2 Manual, the chapters can be studied in any order. However, a good place to start would be Chapter 2. Thereafter, even the topics within a chapter could be studied out of order as wherever possible the chapters are presented in sections, with each section covering one of the 37 APM knowledge areas.

Project management context

2

2 Project management context

2.1 PURPOSE

The purpose of this chapter is to:

- Introduce the topic of project management and describe some of its benefits and challenges (APMP topic 1.1)
- Distinguish between project management and the other types of management environment that may surround the project, namely:
  - Operational management or business-as-usual (BAU) (part of APMP topic 1.1)
  - Programme management (APMP topic 1.2)
  - Portfolio management (APMP topic 1.3)

- Provide a framework within which Project Managers can explore the various contexts within which projects may operate. This will consider some techniques that can be used to examine the environment within which the project is being undertaken (APMP topic 1.4)
- Consider the use of project lifecycles and explain why projects are split into lifecycle phases (APMP topic 6.1)
- Discuss the advantages of adopting a structured method and procedures (APMP topic 6.9).

2.2 DEFINITIONS

There are slightly different definitions of the key terms related to project management in PRINCE2, the APM Body of Knowledge and Managing Successful Programmes (MSP) (Tables 2.1 and 2.2).

Table 2.1 Comparison of the definitions of key terms related to project management context in PRINCE2 and the APM Body of Knowledge

	PRINCE2	APM Body of Knowledge
Project	A temporary organization that is created for the purpose of delivering one or more business products according to a specified Business Case	A unique, transient endeavour undertaken to achieve a desired outcome
	or	
	A temporary organization that is needed to produce a unique and predefined outcome or result at a predefined time using predetermined resources	
Project management	The planning, monitoring and control of all aspects of a project and the motivation of all those involved in it to achieve the project objectives on time and to the specified cost, quality and performance	The process by which projects are defined, planned, monitored, controlled and delivered so that agreed benefits are realized
Business-as-usual	Not defined	An organization's normal day-to-day operations

Table 2.2 Comparison of the definitions of key terms related to project management context in Managing Successful Programmes (MSP) and the APM Body of Knowledge

	MSP	APM Body of Knowledge
Programme	Temporary flexible organization structure created to coordinate, direct and oversee the implementation of a set of related projects and activities in order to deliver outcomes and benefits related to the organization's strategic objectives. A programme is likely to have a life that spans several years	A group of related projects, which may include related business-as-usual activities, that together achieve a beneficial change of a strategic nature for an organization
Programme management	The coordinated organization, direction and implementation of a dossier of projects and transformation activities (i.e. the programme) to achieve outcomes and realize benefits of strategic importance	The coordinated management of related projects that may include related business-as-usual activities, which together achieve a beneficial change of a strategic nature for an organization
Portfolio	All the programmes and standalone projects being undertaken by an organization, a group of organizations or an organizational unit	A grouping of an organization's projects, programmes and related business-as-usual activities taking into account resource constraints. Portfolios can be managed at an organizational, programme or functional level
Portfolio management	Not defined	The selection and management of all of an organization's projects, programmes and related business-as-usual activities, taking into account resource constraints

The APM Body of Knowledge definitions are extracts from the *APM Body of Knowledge 5th Edition*, reproduced with the permission of the Association for Project Management.

MSP refers to the Office of Government Commerce (OGC) guide *Managing Successful Programmes*.

2.3 PROJECT MANAGEMENT

Project management is the process by which projects are defined, planned, monitored, controlled and delivered so that agreed benefits are realized.

Source: *APM Body of Knowledge 5th Edition*, with permission of the Association for Project Management.

As can be seen from Tables 2.1 and 2.2, there are slightly different definitions for a project. However, there are some important similarities that form the main characteristics of any project:

■ **Uniqueness**: there will be some element of the project that has not been faced before. The extent of this uniqueness will vary from project to project, but regardless of the actual extent of uniqueness this feature does imply that there will be uncertainty surrounding the project, which in turn suggests that all projects involve an element of **risk**.

■ **Temporary or transient**: projects are not ongoing. They have a start, a middle and an end. This suggests that all projects have a defined lifespan in terms of **time** and that they follow some form of lifecycle. As time is defined, this also suggests that there will be defined resources used on the project and hence a defined **cost** for the project.

■ **Desired or predefined outcome**: the outcome of a project introduces change that can be considered in terms of a number of key elements:

● The set of products, deliverables or work content that the project will hand over to the operational environment – this is the **scope** of the project

● The extent to which the products or deliverables conform to the **quality** (or performance) specified

● The **benefits** that will be achieved by putting the products or deliverables into operational use and which justify the project investment as presented in the Business Case.

The outcomes also need to be considered from the viewpoint of the various **organizational stakeholders** in the project, as each stakeholder is likely to have slightly different objectives.

Figure 2.1 shows the inter-relationships between time, cost, quality and scope, how these all involve an element of risk, and how benefits will be realized once the output(s) of the project has been delivered.

Figure 2.1 Project characteristics

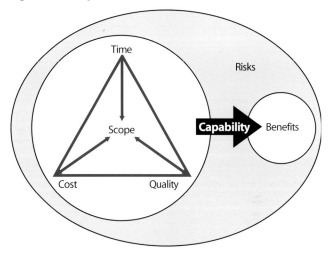

There are also differences between the definitions for project management, but again there are some important similarities in terms of:

■ **Planning**: the process of identifying the means, resources and actions necessary to accomplish the project's objectives.

■ **Monitoring**: the recording, analysing and reporting of project performance as compared with the plan, in order to identify and report deviations.

■ **Controlling**: the taking of corrective action in response to any deviations from plan.

The benefits of applying a project management approach to situations that have the above project characteristics can be described in terms of avoiding the potential causes for project failure. Some common causes and effects are shown in Table 2.3.

Table 2.3 Causes of project failure and their effects

Cause	Effect
▨ Insufficient attention to checking that a valid Business Case exists for the project	▨ Projects being undertaken that do not deliver business benefits
▨ Insufficient attention to quality at the outset and during development	▨ Products being delivered that are not fit for purpose
▨ Insufficient definition of the required outcomes	▨ Confusion over what the project is expected to achieve
▨ Lack of communication with stakeholders and interested parties	▨ Products being delivered that are not what the customer ordered or that the customer is not ready to use
▨ Inadequate definition and lack of acceptance of project management roles and responsibilities	▨ Lack of direction and poor decision-making
▨ Poor estimation of duration and costs	▨ Projects taking more time and costing more money than expected
▨ Inadequate planning and coordination or resources	▨ Poor scheduling
▨ Insufficient measurables and lack of control over progress	▨ Projects not revealing their exact status until too late
▨ Lack of quality control	▨ Delivery of products that are unacceptable or unusable

Whilst the above benefits are significant, there are likely to be a number of barriers or challenges to the implementation of a project management approach into organizations that are new to project management. These barriers include:

- Lack of organizational culture that appreciates the benefits of project management
- Immature project management practices
- Lack of project management support resources and time
- Lack of policies, processes and plans
- Lack of a senior management project management champion
- Lack of skills, training, knowledge and formal project management tools and techniques
- Lack of clear guidance to managers and staff involved in projects

- Lack of incentivization for those participating in project management.

2.4 OTHER MANAGEMENT ENVIRONMENTS

A further consideration of a project's context is where it fits alongside other management environments such as operational, programme and portfolio. As seen in Figure 2.2, a project may have direct links with any or all of these other management environments.

In the following sections, for each of the other perspectives, we will explore the characteristics, benefits and challenges faced.

2.4.1 Operational management

Operational management (or BAU) is in many ways the opposite to project management (see Table 2.4).

Figure 2.2 Inter-relationships between management environments

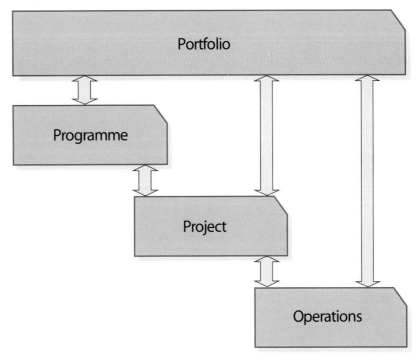

Table 2.4 Differences between project and operational management

Projects	Business-as-usual
▓ Are unique	▓ Is repetitive
▓ Are temporary and time needs to be managed	▓ Is ongoing and time needs to be optimized
▓ Introduce revolutionary change	▓ Improves by evolutionary change
▓ Create a disequilibrium	▓ Maintains equilibrium
▓ Have transient resources	▓ Has stable resources
▓ Require risk aware management	▓ Tends towards being risk averse

Projects will have close interfaces with BAU as the project will typically produce a product that is delivered into the operational environment, and as a result will create change within that operational environment.

Also, the project may have been established by management with operational responsibilities, in response to an operational problem or opportunity.

2.4.2 Programme management

> Programme management is the coordinated management of related projects that may include related business-as-usual activities, which together achieve a beneficial change of a strategic nature for an organization.
>
> Source: *APM Body of Knowledge 5th Edition*, with permission of the Association for Project Management.

As with the two definitions for project management, there are similarities between the definitions for programme management:

- **Coordination**: there will be various aspects of the programme that need to be managed in a coordinated fashion.
- **Projects and activities**: the programme will need to coordinate both projects and activities. The projects will deliver products or outputs. The activities will be undertaken within the BAU or operational environment in order to embed the products or outputs and deliver the required outcomes.

- **Strategic benefits**: the outcomes of the programme will enable the organization to realize benefits that are of strategic importance.

Business strategies, initiatives or policies are influenced and shaped from both the internal and external business environments. Programmes are then defined, scoped and prioritized to implement and deliver the outcomes required from those strategies, initiatives or policies.

Programmes differ from projects in several ways (Table 2.5).

A programme management approach should be adopted for implementing major change, where there will be complexity, risk and interdependencies to manage, and conflicting priorities to resolve. This is because organizations are unlikely to be successful in delivering change where:

- There is insufficient board-level support
- Leadership is weak
- There are unrealistic expectations of the organizational capacity and capability
- There is insufficient focus on benefits

Table 2.5 Differences between projects and programmes

Projects	Programmes
Tend to have a definitive start and finish point	Tend to be more loosely defined in terms of timescale
Aim to deliver a predetermined output or product	Aim to deliver organizational capability that in turn realizes benefits
Have a relatively clear development path	Often have no clear path of how to deliver these benefits
Require an intense and focused effort over a shorter period	Have a broader spread of activities over a longer period
Are best suited to closely bounded and scoped deliverables that can be relatively well defined	Are best suited to complex situations with changing inter-relationships in a wider, more dynamic and uncertain environment
Benefits are realized following the end of the project	Realize benefits both during and after conclusion of the programme

- There is no real picture of the future capability
- There is a poorly defined and poorly communicated vision
- The organization fails to change its culture
- There is insufficient engagement of stakeholders.

2.4.3 Portfolio management

> Portfolio management is the selection and management of all of an organization's projects, programmes and related business-as-usual activities taking into account resource constraints.
>
> Source: *APM Body of Knowledge 5th Edition*, with permission of the Association for Project Management.

This is usually the responsibility of the senior management of the organization, which seeks a mixture of projects and programmes to fulfil its strategic objectives, whilst constrained by limited resources. In such circumstances, prioritization is needed to allow the more important projects and programmes to access the required resources and to move forward in accordance with their plans.

Portfolio management can also be conducted at a functional level. Portfolio management involves:

- Establishing and reviewing the strategic objectives of the organization
- Assessing the extent to which prospective programmes and projects will contribute to these strategic objectives, and allocating priorities accordingly
- Assessing the organization's appetite and capacity for change, given the limited resources available to the organization
- Authorizing those programmes and projects with the highest priority whilst not exceeding the organization's resource availability
- Managing the interdependencies between programmes and projects within the portfolio

- Continually reviewing and realigning the organization's portfolio of programmes and projects in the light of changing circumstances.

Project and Programme Managers will contribute to the above by providing information to enable those responsible for portfolio management to:

- Undertake the initial and ongoing assessments of programmes and projects
- Monitor performance of programmes and projects within the authorized portfolio.

2.5 PROJECT CONTEXT

> The project context refers to the environment within which a project is undertaken. Projects do not exist in a vacuum and an appreciation of the context within which the project is being performed will assist those involved in project management to deliver a project.
>
> Source: *APM Body of Knowledge 5th Edition*, with permission of the Association for Project Management.

Awareness is required of both the internal and the external contexts. For example, there is a need to consider both the internal politics affecting a project and the influence that external governmental politics has on a project. The project context will also vary depending on whether it is standalone or one in a sequence of related projects, or forms part of a programme or corporate strategy.

A project will be managed differently according to the context within which it is being performed and accordingly it is important for the project management team to understand the project's context. The context covers both the external and internal environments and must consider the interests and influences of stakeholders.

Two common techniques used to investigate the context of a project are SWOT and PESTLE analyses.

2.5.1 SWOT analysis

SWOT is an acronym for Strengths, Weaknesses, Opportunities and Threats. The analysis brings together the results of both internal and external environmental analyses. The strengths and weaknesses generally arise in an organization's internal environment and include factors such as existing products and services, customers, staff and management expectations, and processes. The opportunities and threats arise in the organization's external environment and include factors such as political, economic, social and technological.

The results of a SWOT analysis are typically captured on a two-by-two grid (Figure 2.3).

Figure 2.3 SWOT analysis

	Strengths	Weaknesses
Internal		
	Opportunities	Threats
External		

2.5.2 PESTLE analysis

PESTLE is an acronym for Political, Economic, Sociological, Technical, Legal and Environmental. The analysis can be used to examine the organization's external environment, and from this draw out the opportunities for and threats to the organization.

A PESTLE analysis helps to bring together the broad range of issues that the project management team has to deal with as these issues may assist or restrict the achievement of the project's objectives. The project management team needs to give careful consideration to each of these areas and develop appropriate strategies to deal with them.

2.6 PROJECT LIFECYCLES

All projects follow a lifecycle and lifecycles will differ across industries and business sectors. A lifecycle allows the project to be considered as a sequence of distinct phases that provide the structure and approach for progressively delivering the required outputs (or products).

Source: *APM Body of Knowledge 5th Edition*, with permission of the Association for Project Management.

One possible lifecycle is described in Table 2.6.

All phases of the lifecycle are important and hence no phase should be omitted, but the phases may overlap. At the end of each phase (or stage within a phase) a 'Gate Review' (or End Stage Assessment) is undertaken where the project's expected worth, cost and execution plan are reviewed and a decision made whether to continue with the next phase or stage. These review points have the following benefits, in that they:

- Provide a 'fire-break' for the project by encouraging an assessment of the project viability at regular intervals, rather than letting it run on in an uncontrolled manner
- Ensure key decisions are made prior to detailed work needed to implement those decisions
- Clarify what the impact will be of an identified external influence, such as the corporate budget round
- Review a risky project at key moments when new information about those risks appears.

Table 2.6 Example project lifecycle

Lifecycle phase	Description (APM Body of Knowledge)	Alignment to PRINCE2 processes (see below)
Concept	During this phase the need, opportunity or problem is confirmed, the overall feasibility of the project is considered and a preferred solution identified	Starting up a Project (SU)
	Output: Business Case	Output: Project Brief which includes an outline Business Case
Definition	During this phase the preferred solution is further evaluated and optimized. Often an iterative process, definition can affect requirements and the project's scope, time, cost and quality objectives.	Initiating a Project (IP)
	Output: Project Management Plan	Output: Project Initiation Document
Implementation	Where the Project Management Plan is executed, monitored and controlled. During this phase the design is finalized and used to build the deliverables.	Controlling a Stage (CS); Managing Product Delivery (MP); and Managing Stage Boundaries (SB)
Handover and Closeout	During this phase final project deliverables are handed over to the sponsor and user. Closeout is the process of finalizing all project matters, carrying out final project reviews, archiving project information and redeploying the project team	Closing a Project (CP)
	Output: Post-Project Review	Output: End Project Report

The descriptions of the lifecycle phases are extracts from the *APM Body of Knowledge 5th Edition*, reproduced with the permission of the Association for Project Management.

Note that the Definition phase aligns to the PRINCE2 Initiation stage, and that the Implementation phases can be divided into a number of PRINCE2 stages.

(NB: In the APM Body of Knowledge, 'Post-Project Review' is the name given to a review that is undertaken after the project deliverables have been handed over but before final closeout. This review is intended to produce lessons learned that will enable continuous improvement. This is totally different from PRINCE2, where 'Post-Project Review' is the name given to a review held after project closure to determine if the expected benefits have been obtained. In the APM Body of Knowledge such a review is known as a 'Benefit Realization Review', and is described as a review undertaken after a period of operations of the project deliverables. It is intended to establish that the project benefits have or are being realized.)

Whilst the alignment of this lifecycle to the PRINCE2 processes is shown in Table 2.6, it should also be noted that in a PRINCE2 environment:

- The Concept phase would be considered to be pre-project
- The Definition phase aligns to the Initiation stage
- The Implementation phase may be divided into a number of stages
- The Handover and Closeout phase would form part of the last stage of the project.

The above lifecycle may be extended by including two more phases (see Table 2.7).

This extended lifecycle (also known as a product lifecycle or acquisition lifecycle) can be used as a basis for through life costing, i.e. from concept through to the disposal of the product. This is of particular relevance where the product of the project stands alone and has a defined lifespan, for example an offshore oil rig or power station. The value of having a structured approach to the through life or whole life costing is that it allows the additional cost of maintenance and disposal to be included in the project cost and balanced against the whole life benefits.

Project management should be applied throughout the project lifecycle. There are generic project management processes (see Figure 2.4) that need to be applied to each phase of the project lifecycle, which may be described as:

- Starting or initiation process – this secures agreement to begin a portion of work.
- Defining and planning process – this initially takes an input such as an approved Project Brief or Business Case and then turns it into a set of integrated plans against which to implement the project. As the project progresses there will be the need to re-plan in the light of progress made and changes to objectives.
- Monitoring and control process – monitoring is the measurement of progress of the project against a plan (typically in terms of performance against Time, Cost, Quality and Scope); control is the reaction to the information gathered during monitoring and enables decisions to be made to correct deviations from plan.
- Learning and closing process – learning takes input from a completed stage, phase or project and captures and disseminates lessons that can be learned for future stages, phases or projects; closing formally concludes a portion of work and hands it over to operations or BAU.

These project management processes are repeated during every phase of the project lifecycle, being concerned with the activity of project management rather than with the doing of the work.

Table 2.7 Further phases of an extended lifecycle

Lifecycle phase	Description (APM Body of Knowledge)	Alignment to PRINCE2 processes
Operations	Includes the ongoing support and maintenance of the project's products	Post-project
Termination	Concludes the operational life of the project's products and completes their disposal in an effective manner	Post-project

The descriptions of the lifecycle phases are extracts from the *APM Body of Knowledge 5th Edition*, reproduced with the permission of the Association for Project Management

Figure 2.4 Project management processes

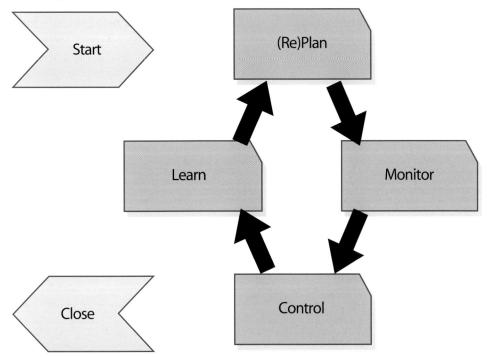

2.7 METHODS AND PROCEDURES

The final factor that could influence the running of the project is whether the organization has adopted any particular methods or procedures that should be applied to all projects within the organizations.

Methods and procedures detail the standard practices to be used for managing projects throughout a lifecycle.

- Methods provide a consistent framework within which project management is performed
- Procedures cover individual aspects of project management practice and form an integral part of the method.

Source: *APM Body of Knowledge 5th Edition*, with permission of the Association for Project Management.

A method can either be open (available in the public domain) or closed (developed for a particular organization either for internal use or for sale). An example of an open method is PRINCE2, which is owned by the OGC. Examples of closed methods are SUMMIT-D® developed by PricewaterhouseCoopers and Method One developed by Arthur Andersen. Methods typically consist of several elements (Table 2.8).

The benefits for an organization adopting a single, common, structured method with procedures for project management (such as PRINCE2) include:

- Having a method that is repeatable and therefore consistent
- Having a method that is teachable
- Building on experience

Table 2.8 Methods and procedures with examples from PRINCE2

Typical elements in methods (APM Body of Knowledge)	PRINCE2
▨ Process descriptions for each phase of a project lifecycle	Process Model and Process chapters
▨ Inputs and outputs for each process	Context diagrams within the Process chapters
▨ Document guidelines and templates for each input and output	Appendix A: Product Description Outlines
▨ Guidelines for organizational design, accountability, responsibility and communication	Organization Component
▨ Role definitions for all those involved in the project, including the project team	Appendix B: Project Management Team Roles
▨ Procedures to be used throughout the lifecycle, for example value management, project risk management and project quality management, issue management, change control and configuration management	Remaining Component chapters, e.g. Plans, Controls, Management of Risk, Quality in a Project Environment, Configuration Management and Change Control

List of typical elements of a method is an extract from the *APM Body of Knowledge 5th Edition*, reproduced with the permission of the Association for Project Management

- Ensuring that everyone knows what to expect, where, how and when
- Providing early warning of problems
- Being proactive, not reactive, and also able to accommodate sudden, unexpected events.

PRINCE2 provides organizations with:

- Controlled management of change, in terms of investment and return on investment
- Active involvement of users and stakeholders throughout the project to ensure that the products will meet business, functional, environmental, service and management requirements
- An approach which distinguishes the management of the project from the development of the products, so that the management approach is the same whether the project is to build a ship or to implement new working practices.

PRINCE2 provides a project with:

- A controlled and organized start, middle and end
- Regular reviews of progress against plan and against the Business Case
- Flexible decision points
- Automatic management control of any deviations from the plan
- The involvement of management and stakeholders at the right time during the project
- Good communication channels between the project management team and the rest of the organization
- Agreement on the required quality at the outset and continuous monitoring against those requirements.

Project Managers using PRINCE2 are able to:

- Establish terms of reference as a prerequisite to the start of a project
- Use a defined structure for delegation, authority and communication

- Divide the project into manageable stages for more accurate planning
- Ensure that resource commitment from management is part of any approval to proceed
- Provide regular but brief reports
- Keep meetings with management and stakeholders to a minimum but at the vital points in the project.

However, there are a number of potential drawbacks in adopting a structured method.

- The method may be applied too rigorously, particularly to short, low-risk projects. This could result in an overhead that is disproportional to the nature of the project.
- The method and associated procedures may be seen as bureaucratic, with the completion of templates treated as no more than form-filling exercises.
- Training is required to ensure that all staff understand how to apply the method. There is a danger that this training will not be provided to all staff with project management responsibilities, leading to inconsistencies of approach or even conflict between different parties involved in the project.
- Training only covering the method and as a result, team members may miss out on other key aspects of project management, such as the use of tools, techniques and people matters.

2.8 PROJECT MANAGEMENT CONTEXT – EXERCISES

(Sample answers are provided in Appendix A for the first question within each section. Answers to the remaining questions can be assessed against the relevant section within the chapter.)

APMP topic 1.1

1 Explain five differences between projects and business-as-usual.
2 Describe five challenges of using project management.
3 Describe five challenges that organizations face when using project management.
4 Explain the correlation between project management processes and the phases of the project lifecycle, making five relevant points.

APMP topic 1.2

1 Explain five typical responsibilities of the Programme Manager throughout the programme lifecycle.
2 Describe five differences between programme management and project management.
3 Describe five benefits of programme management.
4 Explain four challenges that an organization will face when using programme management.

APMP topic 1.3

1 Explain the principles of portfolio management, making four relevant points.
2 Describe five differences between portfolio management and project management.
3 Explain two situations where portfolio management would be appropriate.

APMP topic 1.4

1 Explain why it is important to consider a project's context, making five relevant points.
2 Describe what is meant by a project's context, making five relevant points.
3 Describe a tool or technique for ascertaining a project's context.

APMP topic 6.1

1 Describe five benefits of splitting a project into phases.

2 Describe a project lifecycle, making five relevant points.

3 Describe four differences between a project lifecycle and an extended lifecycle.

APMP topic 6.9

1 Explain the advantages and disadvantages of using a structured method, making five relevant points.

2 Describe the typical content of a structured method, making five relevant points.

Business Case

3

3 Business Case

3.1 PURPOSE

The purpose of this chapter is to consider:

- The purpose and typical content of the Business Case in terms of providing the business justification for the project (APMP topic 5.1)
- Various approaches that can be adopted for undertaking investment appraisal as part of the Business Case (APMP topic 5.1)
- The relationships between project success criteria, success factors and key performance indicators (KPIs) (APMP topic 2.1)
- Realization of the business benefits that form part of the justification for running the project (APMP topic 2.1).

3.2 DEFINITIONS

There are slightly different definitions of the key terms related to Business Case in PRINCE2 and the APM Body of Knowledge (Table 3.1).

3.3 BUSINESS CASE

The Business Case provides justification for undertaking a project, in terms of evaluating the benefit, cost and risk of alternative options and the rationale for the preferred solution. Its purpose is to obtain management commitment and approval for investment in the project. The Business Case is owned by the sponsor.

Source: *APM Body of Knowledge 5th Edition*, with permission of the Association for Project Management.

The purpose of the Business Case is to present the justification and strategic rationale for undertaking a project based on the estimated cost of development and implementation against the risks and the anticipated business benefits and savings to be gained. It should cover the entire scope of change to the organization that is affected by the project.

The Business Case is used to obtain management commitment and approval for the investment in the project. However, if a satisfactory Business Case does not exist, a project should not be started.

The Business Case is owned by the Project Executive (or Project Sponsor). However, responsibility for writing the Business Case may be delegated to the Project Manager, who in turn may call on others to provide the appropriate expertise where required.

As a minimum, a Business Case should contain information under the following headings.

3.3.1 Reasons

This section provides an explanation for the reasons why the end-product of the project is needed.

3.3.2 Options

This section should describe the various options that have been considered to deliver the required end-product. One option that should always be considered is the 'Do nothing' option, as this provides a starting option to act as a comparison for the other options.

Each of the options should be summarized to highlight the costs, benefits and risks associated with them, and the chosen option should be indicated. The remainder of the Business Case should then expand on this information for the chosen option.

Table 3.1 Comparison of the definitions of key terms related to Business Case

	PRINCE2	APM Body of Knowledge
Business Case	Information that describes the justification for setting up or continuing a project. It provides the reasons (and answers the question: 'Why?') for the project	Provides justification for undertaking a project, in terms of evaluating the benefit, cost and risk of alternative options and the rationale for the preferred solution. Its purpose is to obtain management commitment and approval for investment in the project. The Business Case is owned by the sponsor
Investment Appraisal	The balance between the development, operational, maintenance and support costs against the financial value of the benefits over a period of time	The appraisal of the value of a project
Benefit	The positive outcomes, quantified or unquantified, that a project is being undertaken to deliver and justifies the investment	The quantifiable and measurable improvement resulting from the completion of the project deliverables that is perceived as positive by a stakeholder. It will normally have a tangible value, expressed in monetary terms, that will justify the investment
Benefit Realization	The practice of ensuring that the outcome of the project produces the projected benefits claimed in the Business Case	The practice of ensuring that the outcome of the project produces the projected benefits

The APM Body of Knowledge definitions are extracts from the *APM Body of Knowledge 5th Edition*, reproduced with the permission of the Association for Project Management

3.3.3 Benefits

This section should identify each benefit that is claimed would be achieved by the end-product of the project. Each benefit should be described clearly in measurable terms, and ideally in financial terms. It is important to define the current status of each benefit so that measurable improvements can be assessed after the project has been completed. Consideration should also be given to defining how and when measurement of the improvements can be made.

Care should be taken to avoid defining benefits that cannot be measured. If a benefit cannot be measured, it cannot be managed. Likewise, care is needed when claiming intangible benefits such as 'happier staff' as these are difficult to substantiate. In this case, proxy measures, such as 'reduced absenteeism', may be required.

Benefits may be described using terms such as 'increased', 'faster', 'lower' and 'cheaper', but terms such as 'better' and 'improved' should be avoided, as these are unlikely to be specific enough.

An alternative way of assessing benefits is to consider what would happen if the project were not to be undertaken.

3.3.4 Risks

This section contains a summary of the key risks facing the project that, if they happen, would have a serious effect (either negative or positive) on the achievement of the project objectives in terms of costs versus benefits.

3.3.5 Costs

This section describes the development costs and will be based on the costs in the Project Plan.

3.3.6 Timescale

This section describes the timescale over which the investment cost will be expended (again based on the Project Plan) and the timescale over which the benefits (described earlier) will be realized.

3.3.7 Investment appraisal

This section illustrates the balance between the development, operational, maintenance and support costs against the financial value of the benefits over a period of time. This time period may be a fixed number of years or the useful life of the end-product. The most usual techniques for performing investment appraisal are Payback, Net Present Value (NPV) and Internal Rate of Return, each of which is described later in this chapter.

In addition to the heading described above, within the APM Body of Knowledge the sections listed in Table 3.2 are also considered to be part of the Business Case.

In PRINCE2, the list in Table 3.2 would initially form the Project Definition section of the Project Brief, and during initiation it would be incorporated into the Project Initiation Document.

Table 3.2 Additional sections of a Business Case

Project scope	The sum of the work content of the project
Assumptions	Statements that will be taken for granted as fact and upon which the project Business Case will be justified
Constraints	Things that should be considered as fixed or which must happen. Restrictions that will affect the project
Dependencies	Something on which the successful delivery of the project critically depends, which may often be outside the sphere of influence of the Project Manager, for example another project
Project success criteria	The qualitative or quantitative measures by which the success of the project is judged
Impact on BAU	How the project will affect the organization's normal day-to-day operations

List is an extract from the *APM Body of Knowledge 5th Edition*, reproduced with the permission of the Association for Project Management

3.4 DEVELOPMENT PATH

The Business Case should be updated and reviewed at key points throughout the lifecycle of a project (Table 3.3).

The Business Case should also be reviewed during the project lifecycle as part of assessing project issues, as new information may invalidate the justification for the project. Also, the Business Case will be used beyond the project lifecycle as part of the Post-Project Review (PRINCE2) or Benefit Realization Review (APM).

(NB: In the APM Body of Knowledge, 'Post-Project Review' is the name given to a review that is undertaken after the project deliverables have been handed over but before final closeout. This review is intended to produce lessons learned that will enable continuous improvement. This is totally different from PRINCE2, where 'Post-Project Review' is the name given to a review held after project closure to determine if the expected benefits have been obtained. In the APM Body of Knowledge such a review is known as a 'Benefit Realization Review', and is described as a review undertaken after a period of operations of the project deliverables. It is intended to establish that the project benefits have been or are being realized.)

All of these reviews are important, as even though the Business Case was valid at the start of the project, if this justification disappears once the project is under way, then the project should be stopped.

Finally, it should also be noted that a Business Case could form an input into a project having been produced as an output from an earlier feasibility project.

3.5 INVESTMENT APPRAISAL TECHNIQUES

A project represents a financial investment that is being made to benefit the organization. Investment appraisal techniques provide a means of analysing in quantitative terms the outcome of the investment to be made. This analysis will provide one of the criteria by which management will decide whether to go ahead with the project or not. It will also help decide which solution should be chosen from the possibilities available.

The three most common forms of Investment Appraisal are:

- Payback
- NPV
- Internal Rate of Return.

Table 3.3 Outputs of various phases of the lifecycle and comparison with the PRINCE2 process

PRINCE2 process	Output	APM lifecycle phases	Output
Starting up a Project	Outline Business Case as part of the Project Brief	Concept	Business Case
Initiating a Project	Initial Business Case as part of the Project Initiation Document	Definition	Updated Business Case as part of the Project Management Plan
Managing Stage Boundaries	Updated Business Case at the end of each stage	Implementation	Updated Business Case at project evaluation reviews
Closing a Project	Post-Project Review Plan	Handover and Closeout	Post-project review

Payback is the simplest to understand and the quickest to calculate. However, it does not take into account the time value of money, i.e. that £1 is worth more today than it will be worth in say a year's time. The other two methods take this into account by considering the value of money that will be received or expended in future periods.

All of the above methods can be used to undertake financial evaluations of project proposals based on the information contained in the Business Case. In this section each method is described, an example provided and the advantages and disadvantages listed.

3.5.1 Payback method

Description

The payback method calculates how long it takes to recover the initial project investment cost from the financial benefits that result from the project. Where the financial benefits are expected to be constant over a period of years, the payback period is calculated simply by dividing the project investment cost by the anticipated annual financial benefits. Where the financial benefits are expected to differ year by year, then the payback period is calculated by accumulating the anticipated financial benefits until they are equal to or greater than the project investment cost.

Examples

- Constant Financial Benefits. The organization is considering a proposal to invest £40,000 for which the estimated financial benefits are £8,000 per year. The expected payback period is:

  £40,000/£8,000 = 5 years

- Variable Financial Benefits. The organization is considering a proposal to invest £50,000 for which the estimated financial benefits are as shown in Table 3.4.

The expected payback period = 3 years (i.e. when the accumulated financial benefits equate to the investment cost).

Advantages

- The simplest and quickest method to calculate.
- The easiest to understand.

Disadvantages

- It ignores positive financial benefits received after the payback point. These benefits could be significant.
- It looks entirely at financial benefits in terms of cash flow and ignores profitability or return on investment.

Table 3.4 Estimated financial benefits over five years

Year	Expected pattern of financial benefits	Accumulated financial benefits
1	£22,000	£22,000
2	£18,000	£40,000
3	£10,000	£50,000
4	£10,000	£60,000
5	£ 8,000	£68,000

- It assumes that all money is of equal value no matter when it is spent or received (unless any financing costs are built into the anticipated net financial benefits).
- If a short payback period is required any worthwhile but longer-term proposals will be rejected.

3.5.2   Net Present Value method

Description

This method first considers the Net Value of a proposal by totalling up the financial benefits over an agreed period of years and then deducting the initial investment cost from the total financial benefit.

Example

Using the figures in Table 3.4, the Net Value is calculated as £18,000 (Table 3.5).

Then the Net Present Value (NPV) is calculated by applying a discount factor to all monies received or spent after completion of the project to reflect the time value of money (i.e. the fact that £1 in your pocket today is worth more than a £1 in your pocket in five years' time). The discount factor will usually be selected to reflect the returns available to the organization by investing surplus funds elsewhere or to reflect the cost of borrowing the investment costs.

Example

If a discount factor of say 10% is applied to the set of figures in Table 3.5, quite a different result will be seen (Table 3.6).

The discount factors for each year can either be found by reference to pre-prepared tables or they can be calculated. The formula for calculating the discount factor is:

$$DF = (1 + r/100)^{-n}$$

Where r is the chosen interest rate and n is the number of years into the future.

For example, with an interest rate of 10%, the discount factor in year 5 would be:

$$DF = (1 + 10/100)^{-5}$$

$$= (1 + 0.1)^{-5}$$

$$= 1.1^{-5}$$

Table 3.5 Calculating the Net Value

Year	Net financial benefits	Investment cost	Net Value
0		£50,000	
1	£22,000		
2	£18,000		
3	£10,000		
4	£10,000		
5	£ 8,000		
Totals	£68,000	£50,000	£18,000

Table 3.6 Effect of applying discount factors to calculate the NPV

Year	Net financial benefits	Investment cost	Discount factors (10%)	NPV
0		£50,000	1.000	(£50,000)
1	£22,000		0.909	£19,998
2	£18,000		0.826	£14,868
3	£10,000		0.751	£7,510
4	£10,000		0.683	£6,830
5	£ 8,000		0.621	£4,968
Totals	£68,000	£50,000		£4,174

To calculate 1.1^{-5} on a calculator, you need to divide 1 by 1.1, and progressively divide the result by 1.1 as follows:

1 $1/1.1 = 0.909$
2 $0.909/1.1 = 0.826$
3 $0.826/1.1 = 0.751$
4 $0.751/1.1 = 0.683$
5 $0.683/1.1 = 0.621$

The above calculation is not required for the APMP examination, as it is more usual to refer to tables! However, it is included here for sake of completeness.

Advantages

■ It reflects the full set of financial benefits over the agreed time period.
■ It reflects the time value of money.
■ It allows different cash flows to be compared on a like-for-like basis.

Disadvantages

■ It is difficult to use this method to compare proposals of different sizes, i.e. a proposal with an investment cost of £10,000 will almost certainly result in a much lower NPV than a proposal with an investment cost of £1,000,000.
■ It is more complicated to calculate and to understand.

3.5.3 Internal Rate of Return method

Description

This method calculates the rate of return to be obtained from the proposal, in order for the discounted value of the net financial benefits to exactly pay for the investment cost over a given period. In the case of the example above, we need to find the discount factor that, when applied to the net financial benefits, would give a value of exactly £50,000. The answer is found by trial and error using progressively higher discount rates until the NPV is reduced to zero, or near to zero.

This Internal Rate of Return (IRR) is an indication of the rate that would need to be obtained to achieve the same level of return as the proposed project. Organizations will often set a minimum IRR below which projects will not be approved, and will give priority to those projects that offer the highest IRR. If the IRR is greater than the set rate then the project will make a profit; conversely an IRR less than the set rate will show a loss. Organizations will often set a value for IRR much greater than the current level of interest rates, and will only approve projects whose IRR exceeds this figure. This helps to protect them from variations in the market.

Example

Using the example above, we could calculate the NPV based on a discount factor of say 15% (Table 3.7).

As this results in an NPV of minus £1,000 compared with an NPV of plus £4,000 when the discount rate of 10% is used, it appears that we might get closer to zero with a discount rate of 14%. In fact, applying a discount factor of 14% to the above figures gives a NPV of minus £24. Thus, the IRR in this example can said to be 14%.

Advantages

- It reflects the full set of financial benefits over the agreed time period.
- It reflects the time value of money.

- It enables projects of varying sizes to be compared on a like-by-like basis.

Disadvantages

- It is even more complicated to calculate and understand.
- It does not take into account the relative risk profiles of the options under consideration.

3.6 PROJECT SUCCESS CRITERIA

Project success is the satisfaction of stakeholder needs and is measured by the success criteria as identified and agreed at the start of the project.

Project success criteria are the qualitative or quantitative measures by which the success of the project is judged.

Source: *APM Body of Knowledge 5th Edition*, with permission of the Association for Project Management.

From the Project Manager's perspective, success is likely to equate to meeting the agreed time, cost, quality and scope objectives as defined in the Project Initiation Document (PRINCE2) or Project Management Plan (APM). However,

Table 3.7 Calculating the NPV based on a discount factor of 15%

Year	Net financial benefits	Investment cost	Discount factors (15%)	NPV
0		£50,000	1.000	(£50,000)
1	£22,000		0.870	£19,140
2	£18,000		0.756	£13,608
3	£10,000		0.656	£6,560
4	£10,000		0.572	£5,720
5	£ 8,000		0.497	£3,976
Totals	£68,000	£50,000		(£996)

other project stakeholders may have different views, for example those with operational responsibilities may require no/minimal disruption to business as usual (BAU).

One way of ensuring that stakeholders agree how success for the project is defined is by getting all stakeholders to agree on a set of Acceptance Criteria. These should first be established during Starting up a Project (PRINCE2) or as part of the Concept Phase (APM), and then agreed during the Initiation Stage (PRINCE2) or the Definition Phase (APM) of the project. Any changes to the criteria should then only be made through the project's change control process.

Acceptance Criteria define in measurable terms the characteristics required of the final product(s) of the project for it/them to be acceptable to the customer and staff who will be affected. The Acceptance Criteria will include many quality aspects of the final product such as:

- Appearance
- Performance levels
- Capacity
- Accuracy
- Availability
- Reliability.

However, the Acceptance Criteria can also contain references to time, cost and scope aspects of the project, for example the Acceptance Criteria could include:

- Target dates
- Development costs
- Running costs
- Major functions.

Having established these success/acceptance criteria, it is important for the Project Manager to track the progress towards achieving these criteria during the Implementation phase of the project. This can be achieved by establishing KPIs for each of the criteria. KPIs are measures that can be used throughout the project to ensure that it is progressing towards a successful conclusion. For example,

if the target date is an important project success criterion, then a KPI could be to assess progress at defined milestones. Similarly, if no disruption to BAU is another important criterion, then a KPI could be to assess the level of BAU production or output during the project.

As part of Closing a Project (PRINCE2) or the Handover and Closeout phase (APM), the criteria will be assessed to establish the extent to which they have been achieved.

Project success criteria should not be confused with project success factors. Success criteria are measures of project success, whereas success factors are factors that when present in the project environment are most conducive to the achievement of a successful project. The success factors that if absent or lacking, would cause the project to fail are sometimes termed the critical success factors or CSFs.

Research has indicated that there are five common project success factors:

- **Project Objectives**: must be clearly identified within the project plans and *kept to* throughout the work
- **Project Personnel**: the Project Manager and the project team must be competent
- **Support from Above**: the project must be supported by top management
- **Resources**: time, money, material and people must be sufficient to do the job
- **Communication and Control**: communications channels up, down and across the project are established with clear mechanisms for feedback on reports, deliverables and quality. Control must be in place and used such as milestones, plans, approvals, reviews etc. Contractors must be responsive to their clients.

3.7 BENEFITS MANAGEMENT

> Benefits management is the identification of the benefits (of the project) at an organizational level and the monitoring and realization of those benefits.
>
> Source: *APM Body of Knowledge 5th Edition*, with permission of the Association for Project Management.

Benefits can be defined as either:

■ The positive outcomes, quantified or unquantified, that a project is being undertaken to deliver and justify the investment (PRINCE2) or

■ The quantifiable and measurable improvement resulting from the completion of the project deliverables that is perceived as positive by a stakeholder. It will normally have a tangible value, expressed in monetary terms, that will justify the investment (APM Body of Knowledge).

Whereas the project success criteria can be assessed towards the end of a project, the benefits may not be realized until after the project has closed. Accordingly, ownership of benefit realization rests with the Project Executive or Project Sponsor rather than with the Project Manager.

The objectives of benefits management within the context of a project are to:

■ Ensure benefits are identified and defined clearly at the outset, and linked to strategic outcomes

■ Ensure business areas are committed to realizing their defined benefits with ownership and responsibility for adding value through the realization process

■ Drive the process of realizing benefits, including benefit measurement, tracking and recording benefits as they are realized.

Ideally benefits should be identified in quantifiable and measurable terms, preferably in financial terms. Benefits can be:

■ Tangible, such as reduced cost, increased sales, greater customer satisfaction, or legally compliant

■ Intangible, such as improved image.

An important aspect of benefits management is to ensure that the level of performance is measured prior to project delivery. This will provide a baseline against which subsequent improvements can be assessed.

An excellent way of gaining commitment to the realization of benefits is to get the business areas responsible for their realization to sign-up to Benefit Profiles. These are used to define each benefit and provide a detailed understanding of what will be involved and how the benefit will be realized.

For more information on benefits realization management see the OGC publication *Managing Successful Programmes*.

3.8 BUSINESS CASE – EXERCISES

(Sample answers are provided in Appendix A for the first question within each section. Answers to the remaining questions can be assessed against the relevant section within the chapter.)

APMP topic 5.1

1 Describe the typical contents of the Business Case.
2 Describe the purpose of a Business Case.
3 Explain which roles are responsible for authoring and ownership of the Business Case.
4 Explain the use of Payback, Net Present Value (NPV) and Internal Rate of Return (IRR) as investment appraisal techniques.

APMP topic 2.1

1 Explain the differences between success criteria and success factors.

2 Explain the differences between success criteria and key performance indicators (KPIs).

3 Explain the principles of benefits management and realization, making five relevant points.

Organization and governance

4

4   Organization and governance

4.1   PURPOSE

The purpose of this chapter is to consider five related topics:

- Organization structures: this topic looks at different types of organizational structures and the advantages and disadvantages of each from the perspective of running different types of project (APMP topic 6.7)
- Project Sponsorship: this topic looks at the specific role of the Project Sponsor or the project executive (APMP topic 1.5)
- Other organizational roles: this topic looks at the other roles and responsibilities of those involved in managing projects (APMP topic 6.8)
- Project Office: this topic looks at functions and benefits of having a project office to serve an organization's project management needs (APMP topic 1.6)
- Governance of project management: this topic looks at the principles involved in ensuring that an organization's project portfolio is aligned to the organization's objectives, is delivered efficiently and is sustainable (APMP topic 6.10).

4.2   DEFINITIONS

There are slightly different definitions of the key terms related to organization and governance in PRINCE2 and the APM Body of Knowledge (Table 4.1).

4.3   ORGANIZATION STRUCTURES

The organization structure is the organizational environment within which the project takes place. It defines the reporting and decision-making hierarchy of an organization and how project management operates within it.

Source: *APM Body of Knowledge 5th Edition*, with permission of the Association for Project Management.

Organizations have traditionally managed 'business-as-usual' by means of a functional hierarchical structure. However, as projects are temporary, they tend to be organized differently as they need to be more flexible and require a broad base of skills.

There are three basic types of project organization:

- Functional
- Project
- Matrix.

These types could be considered as lying on a continuum with functional at one extreme, project at the other and with matrix between the two. One aspect affected by the type of organization is the relative authority between the functional manager and the Project Manager (see Figure 4.1).

Table 4.1 Comparison of the key terms related to organization and governance

PRINCE2		APM Body of Knowledge	
Project Board	The Project Board is responsible for the overall direction and management of the project and has responsibility and authority for the project within the remit set by corporate or programme management. Comprises the Executive, Senior User and Senior Supplier roles	*Steering Group*	A group, usually comprising the sponsor, senior managers and sometimes key stakeholders, whose remit is to set the strategic direction of a project. It gives guidance to the sponsor and Project Manager. Often referred to as the Project Board
Project Executive	The Executive is ultimately responsible for the project and ensures that the project is focused on achieving its objectives and delivering a product that will achieve the forecast benefits. Owns the Business Case	*Project Sponsor*	The individual or body for whom the project is undertaken and who is the primary risk taker. The sponsor owns the Business Case and is ultimately responsible for the project and for delivering the benefits
Project Manager	The person given the authority and responsibility to manage the project on a day-to-day basis to deliver the required products within the constraints agreed by the Project Board	*Project Manager*	The individual responsible and accountable for the successful delivery of the project
Team Manager	A role that may be employed by the Project Manager or Senior Supplier to manage the work of project team members	*Team Leader*	The person responsible for leading a team
Project Support	An administrative role within the project management team. Project Support can be in the form of advice and help with project management tools, guidance, administrative services such as filing, and the collection of actual data	*Project Support Experts*	Individuals with expertise in particular aspects of project support such a scheduling, budgeting and cost management or reporting

PRINCE2		APM Body of Knowledge	
Project Support Office	A group set up to provide certain administrative services to the Project Manager. Often the group provides its services to many projects in parallel	*Project Office*	This serves the organization's project management needs. A project office can range from simple support functions for the Project Manager to responsibility for linking corporate strategy to project execution

The APM Body of Knowledge definitions are extracts from the *APM Body of Knowledge 5th Edition*, reproduced with the permission of the Association for Project Management

Figure 4.1 The organizational continuum (adapted from the APM Body of Knowledge 5th Edition)

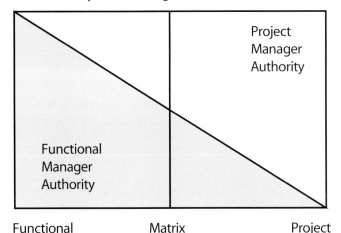

Functional   Matrix   Project

The type of project organization also affects aspects such as how the project team is managed, what forms of communications are needed and the areas of the project that the Project Manager should emphasize.

In practice, many project organizations do not fall neatly into one of these types, but may combine elements of each type.

4.3.1 Functional organization

A functional organization is one where work is carried out within functionally organized groups as illustrated by the example in Figure 4.2.

In organizations where functional divisions are rigid, project work tends to be handed from one functional team to another in order to complete the work. For example a project to develop a new training course may start in Product Development where the idea was conceived, pass to Marketing to test the level of interest in the new course, then on to Finance to develop the Business Case, who then pass it back to Product Development to arrange for the course to be written, and finally it goes to Operations to deal with all aspects of course delivery. This is often referred to as 'baton passing' using the analogy of a relay race, and for each leg of the relay a new manager is appointed to manage that aspect of the project.

Managing projects in this type of organization requires that the overall Project Manager (if there is one) has an oversight of the entire project to ensure that each functional team hands over work to its successor team in such a state that the successor team can carry on with minimal problems. The Project Manager is really undertaking a coordination role and as such needs to ensure that there is effective communication between

Figure 4.2 Functional organizational structure

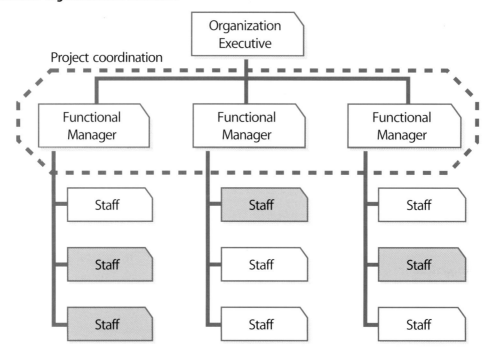

(Shaded boxes represent staff engaged in project activities)

the various teams. However, they may have no authority over any of the functional teams involved in the project. Table 4.2 lists the advantages and disadvantages of having a functional organizational structure.

4.3.2 Project organization

A project organization brings together all of the skills needed to complete the project under the leadership of the Project Manager (Figure 4.3). So, in the case of the project to develop a new training course, the team will consist of people with product development, marketing,

finance and operational skills and the Project Manager has direct authority over all of these people. Such teams will often stay together to work on subsequent projects, and is most common where an organization is engaged repeatedly in projects of a similar nature.

The closeness of such teams should lead to fewer communication issues within the team. However, it may lead to communication breakdowns with other stakeholders as teams of this nature can become introspective (Table 4.3).

Table 4.2 Advantages and disadvantages of having a functional organizational structure

Advantages	Disadvantages
▦ Lowest administrative costs	▦ Coordination and communication across functional areas is difficult
▦ Reasonably successful	▦ Inflexible
▦ Offers job security and a well-defined career path	▦ Long and slow chain of command
▦ Pools technical and professional expertise	▦ Tends to push decision-making upwards
▦ Handle routine work well	▦ Difficult to deal with non-routine matters
▦ Allows training and development within departments	▦ Limits career development outside recognized paths
▦ Line managers have control over projects	▦ Tends to dampen creativity
▦ Easy to set up and terminate projects	▦ Project Manager has limited authority

Figure 4.3 Project organization

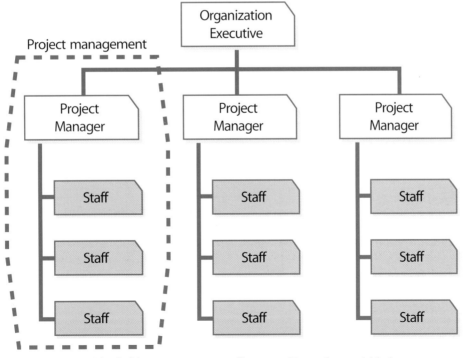

(Shaded boxes represent staff engaged in project activities)

Table 4.3 Advantages and disadvantages of project organization

Advantages	Disadvantages
■ Greater authority and control	■ High administrative costs
■ Team contribute to and share objectives	■ Project Manager more involved in administration
■ Good for team building and communication	■ Difficult to graft on to established organizations
■ Quick decisions	■ Projects tend to be more difficult to terminate
■ High degree of management skills development	■ Potential lack of job security, and undefined career path
■ Easier for top management to coordinate and influence	■ Slow to mobilize
■ Can give career development/change for team members	■ Often limited number of good project people available
■ Builds synergy within the team	
■ Clear responsibilities	

Figure 4.4 Matrix organization structure

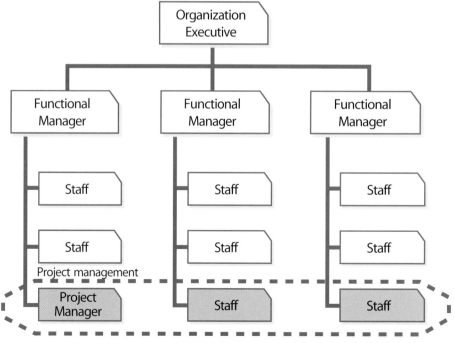

(Shaded boxes represent staff engaged in project activities)

4.3.3 Matrix organization

A matrix organization structure is one where staff report to different managers for different aspects of their work. Staff will be responsible to a functional line manager for the 'business-as-usual' aspects of their work and to the Project Manager for their work on the project. The functional line manager also tends to be responsible for the appraisal, training and career development of their staff. An example of how this would apply to the development of a new training course is shown in Figure 4.4.

In this type of organization, staff are loaned from various functional areas and seconded to work on projects. This may be on either full-time or part-time basis. This means that the Project Manager has a clear team that he or she is responsible for. The greatest challenge with this type of structure is the fact that staff have dual reporting lines.

This requires good interpersonal relationships with team members and regular communications. It also requires good resource management to ensure that any individual member of staff is not being overloaded. Table 4.4 lists the advantages and disadvantages of matrix organization.

4.4 PROJECT SPONSORSHIP

Project sponsorship is an active senior management role, responsible for identifying the business need, problem or opportunity. The sponsor ensures the project remains a viable proposition and that benefits are realized, resolving any issues outside the control of the Project Manager.

Source: *APM Body of Knowledge 5th Edition*, with permission of the Association for Project Management.

Table 4.4 Advantages and disadvantages of matrix organization

Advantages	Disadvantages
Acceptable to traditional managers	Dual reporting lines for project staff
Retains functional strengths and control of administration	Staff appraisal and performance measurement is difficult
Some planning power in the project team	Can cause conflict of priorities for staff
Faster to start up	Wider skills required of Project Manager
Top management retain control over projects but are relieved of day-to-day decisions	Project Manager may not be able to influence who is assigned to the project
Flexible	Dilutes the resource available in those functional areas contributing personnel
Reasonable interface with clients and customers	
Some team building is possible	

Within PRINCE2, project sponsorship is provided by the Executive role. Throughout this section, wherever the term 'Executive' is used, this is interchangeable with the term Project Sponsor.

The Executive is described as being the single individual with overall responsibility for ensuring that a project meets its objectives and delivers the projected benefits. This individual should ensure that the project maintains its business focus, that it has clear authority and that the work, including risks, is actively managed. The Executive is the chairperson of the Project Board (PRINCE2) or Steering Group (APM), representing the customer, and is the owner of the Business Case.

Thus the Executive will direct the project with a clear focus on realizing the anticipated objectives, whereas the Project Manager will manage the project focused on delivering a set of products that are capable of achieving those benefits.

The specific responsibilities of the Executive are to:

- Oversee the development of the Project Brief and Business Case
- Ensure that there is a coherent project organization structure and logical set of plans
- Authorize customer expenditure and set stage tolerances
- Monitor and control the progress of the project at a strategic level, in particular reviewing the Business Case continually
- Ensure that any proposed changes of scope, cost or timescale are checked against the possible effects on the Business Case
- Ensure that risks are being tracked and responded to as effectively as possible
- Brief corporate or programme management about project progress
- Recommend future action on the project to corporate or programme management if the project tolerances are exceeded

- Approve the reports issued at the closure of the project
- Ensure that the benefits have been realized by holding a Post-Project Review (PRINCE2) or Benefits Realization Review (APM).

The responsibilities of the Executive during the project lifecycle can be summarized as follows.

Concept phase

During concept the Executive should establish, with the Project Manager (if appointed), the context of the project, including consideration of the political, economic, sociological, technical, legal and environmental aspects of the project. This will help the Project Manager to design the team, which the Executive should confirm and make sure that adequate resources are made available. During concept the Business Case for the project must be prepared and this will require the Executive to state the benefits and contribute to its production. Upon completion, the Executive will sign off the Business Case and make application to the corporate body for agreement to proceed into the Definition phase.

Definition phase

During definition, the Project Initiation Document (PRINCE2) or Project Management Plan (APM) will be produced and this will incorporate fundamental decisions on risk, schedules, budgets and stakeholder management. The Executive will make these decisions and provide guidance throughout. It is very important that the Executive is involved and 100% committed to the project and this will be demonstrated by his or her involvement during definition/initiation. At the end of definition, the Executive will make an application to the corporate body for the funding to cover the project and sign off the Project Initiation Document (PRINCE2) or Project Management Plan (APM).

Implementation phase

During implementation, the Executive will receive the regular progress reports, resolve issues, chair Steering Group meetings, and provide advice, guidance and support to the Project Manager. The Executive will be required to authorize the Project Manager to proceed with the work in the next stage of the implementation phase. Another important facet of the Executive involvement in implementation will be making decisions about change requests received and analysed by the Project Manager. Finally, the Executive must make sure that arrangements are made to realize the benefits, and that the benefits are benchmarked during the implementation stage.

Handover and Closeout phase

In this final phase of the project, the Executive must accept the project's deliverables after checking and being confident that they have met their Acceptance Criteria. The Executive must ensure that they understand the amount of outstanding work and the arrangements that have been made to have it completed. Project resources may need to be handed back to business-as-usual. During this phase the Executive must complete the arrangements for benefits realization with the business areas concerned. The Executive must take part in the Post-Project Review (APM) and sign off the final project reports.

(NB: In the APM Body of Knowledge, 'Post-Project Review' is the name given to a review that is undertaken after the project deliverables have been handed over but before final closeout. This review is intended to produce lessons learned that will enable continuous improvement. This is totally different from PRINCE2, where 'Post-Project Review' is the name given to a review held after project closure to determine if the expected benefits have been obtained. In the APM Body of Knowledge, such a review is known as a 'Benefit Realization Review', and is described

as a review undertaken after a period of operations of the project deliverables. It is intended to establish that the project benefits have or are being realized.)

4.5 ORGANIZATIONAL ROLES

> Organizational roles are the roles performed by individuals or groups in a project. Both roles and responsibilities within projects must be defined to address the transient and unique nature of projects and to ensure that clear accountabilities can be assigned.
>
> Source: *APM Body of Knowledge 5th Edition*, with permission of the Association for Project Management.

Organizational roles have different names in PRINCE2 and APM. However, both have a project management team structure consisting of three levels, and the responsibilities associated with the roles within these structures are broadly similar.

4.5.1 The three levels

Table 4.5 shows the responsibilities of the three levels of the project management team structure (Figure 4.5).

4.5.2 Project Board

The Project Board represents the business, user and supplier interests of the project at managerial level. The Project Board members must have authority because they must be able to:

■ Make decisions relating to the project
■ Commit resources to the project.

Given that their Project Board responsibilities will be in addition to their normal work, the Project Board members are expected to 'manage by exception', i.e. they are kept informed by regular reports but are only asked to make joint decisions at key points in the project.

Table 4.5 Responsibilities associated with the roles within a project management team structure

Responsibilities	PRINCE2 roles	APM roles
Direction of the project	Project Board, Chaired by the Project Executive	Steering Group, chaired by the Project Sponsor
Day-to-day management of the project	Project Manager	Project Manager
Team management and product delivery	Team Manager	Team Members

Figure 4.5 Project management team structures

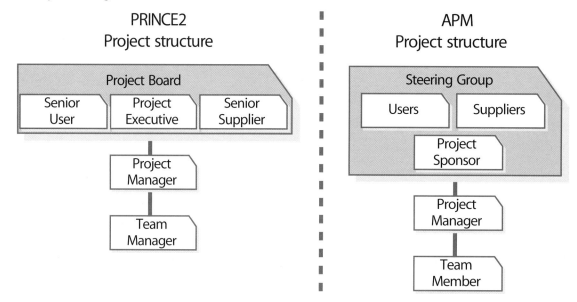

The Project Board itself consists of three roles:

■ **Executive**. This role is ultimately accountable for the success of the project, and as such is the key decision-maker. The Executive's role is to ensure that the project is focused throughout its lifecycle on achieving its objectives and delivering a product that will achieve the forecast benefits. The Executive is responsible for the Business Case and commits the financial resources required by the project.

■ **Senior User**. This role is responsible for specifying the needs of those who will use the final product, for user liaison with the project team and for monitoring that the solution will meet those needs within the constraints of the Business Case, in terms of quality, functionality and ease of use. The Senior User role commits user resources to the project.

Table 4.6 Members of the Steering Group

Project Sponsor	Owns the Business Case and is ultimately accountable for the project and for delivering the benefits
Users	Represent the group of people who will benefit from the project. Users may also be subject matter experts who contribute to defining requirements and acceptance criteria
Suppliers	Represent the people or organizations that will provide resources to the project. Suppliers can be internal or external to the organization. They are responsible for producing the project's deliverables

Role descriptions are extracts from the *APM Body of Knowledge 5th Edition*, reproduced with the permission of the Association for Project Management

- **Senior Supplier**. This role represents the interests of those designing, developing, facilitating, procuring, implementing and possibly operating and maintaining the final product. This role is accountable for the quality of the products delivered by the suppliers and must have the authority to commit or acquire supplier resources required.

The above roles may be shared (e.g. where there are several users involved in the project) or may be combined (e.g. where one person could represent both business and user interests in the project).

4.5.3 Steering Group

The Steering Group (Table 4.6) is chaired by the Project Sponsor and consists of representatives from the users and suppliers.

Other stakeholders may also be represented on the Steering Group. These may be other individuals or groups who have an interest in the project and who will contribute to defining fitness for purpose for the project.

4.5.4 Project Manager

The Project Manager provides the single focus for day-to-day management of the project, managing the project on behalf of the Project Board or Steering Group within the constraints laid down.

The prime responsibility of the Project Manager is to ensure that the project:

- Produces the required *scope* of products
- To the required standard of *quality*
- Within the specified constraints of *time* and *cost*.

The Project Manager is also responsible for the project delivering a final product or deliverable that is capable of achieving the benefits defined in the Project Initiation Document.

4.5.5 Team Manager

The Project Manager may find that it is beneficial to delegate the authority and responsibility for planning the creation of certain products and for managing a team of specialists to produce those products. Reasons for using Team Managers include the size of the project, the particular specialist skills or knowledge needed, and the geographical location of some of the team members.

The Team Manager's prime responsibility is to ensure production of those products defined by the Project Manager to an appropriate quality, in a timescale and at a cost acceptable to the Project Board. The Team Manager reports to and takes direction from the Project Manager.

4.5.6 Project team members

Project team members are accountable to the Project Manager for ensuring that the work assigned to them by the Project Manager is performed either by themselves or by others within a working group.

Table 4.7 Definitions of project office

▓ Project office (PO) ▓ Project support office (PSO)	PO and PSO are synonymous and typically refer to an office that provides project support to a single project
▓ Project and programme support office (PPSO)	This is typically an office that provides project support to all of the projects within a programme in addition to providing support to the programme
▓ Project management office (PMO)	This is typically an office that provides project support to all projects within an organization or to a part of an organization
▓ Enterprise programme management office (EPMO)	This is typically an office that provides both project and programme support across the entire organization. It may also have responsibility for some aspects of portfolio management

Table 4.8 Project office roles

Where the project office is the functional home for Project Managers	The project office allocates project management resources to projects and is responsible for the professional development of project management professionals. (As part of this role, the project office can provide the infrastructure to support communities of practice, i.e. informal networks of individuals within an organization who have an interest in learning and the best practice of a particular area of project management)
Where the project office contains project support experts	It provides a service to projects by ensuring they have the tools, techniques and information they need. This can be in the form of either coaching and mentoring Sponsors and Project Managers or by doing the support work for them
Where the project office instigates improvements to the way the organization runs projects	It enables and drives lessons learned from projects to be implemented on future projects
Where the project office is responsible for excellence in project execution	This frees the Sponsor and the organization's senior management (or Project Board members) to make business decisions and concentrate on exception management for the projects
Where the project office has a strategic role	It is responsible for the execution of corporate strategy through projects and programmes. This project office acts as developer and repository of the standards, processes and methods that improve individual project performance. It also facilitates the organization's ability to manage its entire collection of projects and programmes as one or more portfolios, and serves as a single source of information on project-based activity and data across the enterprise. This type of project office can be referred to as an enterprise project management office (or centre of excellence).

Description of additional roles are extracts from the *APM Body of Knowledge 5th Edition*, reproduced with the permission of the Association for Project Management

4.5.7 Project Assurance

An important aspect of project management is project assurance. In PRINCE2 this is seen as an integral part of each of the Project Board roles. Here, it refers to the Project Board's responsibility to assure itself that the project is being conducted correctly. Project Assurance monitors all aspects of the project's performance and products independently of the Project Manager.

In the APM Body of Knowledge, Project Assurance is the independent monitoring and reporting of the project's quality and deliverables. Here, this role may report directly to the Project Sponsor or to the Steering Group.

4.5.8 Other roles

Other organizational roles that may be required, depending on the nature of the project, include:

- Configuration Manager
- Cost Manager
- Project Accountant
- Project Planner
- Procurement Manager
- Quality Manager
- Resource Manager.

4.6 PROJECT OFFICE

A project office serves the organization's project management needs. A project office can range from simple support functions for the Project Manager to responsibility for linking corporate strategy to project execution.

Source: *APM Body of Knowledge 5th Edition*, with permission of the Association for Project Management.

The project office function can be known by a range of titles (Table 4.7).

Within this section we shall use the term project office as a general term to refer to all of the definitions in Table 4.7.

As a minimum the project office should:

- Support Project Managers in administrative work
- Provide support skills in such areas as expertise in planning and control tools and risk management
- Ensure correct and efficient use of PRINCE2 standards across all projects.

In addition to the above, a project office can fulfil a number of additional roles (Table 4.8).

The main advantages of establishing a project office are that it enables the organization to:

- Learn from the experience of many projects
- Provide guidance to those with project management roles
- Develop its project management expertise.

4.7 GOVERNANCE OF PROJECT MANAGEMENT

Governance of project management (GoPM) concerns those areas of corporate governance that are specifically related to project activities. Effective governance of project management ensures that an organization's project portfolio is aligned to the organization's objectives, is delivered efficiently and is sustainable.

Source: *APM Body of Knowledge 5th Edition*, with permission of the Association for Project Management.

The term corporate governance can be defined as the ongoing activity of maintaining a sound system of internal control by which the directors and officers of an organization ensure that effective management systems have been put in place to protect the assets, earnings capacity and the reputation of the organization.

Table 4.9 Project management governance principles

1	The (organization's) board has overall responsibility for governance of project management
2	The roles, responsibilities and performance criteria for the governance of project management are clearly defined
3	Disciplined governance arrangements, supported by appropriate methods and control, are applied throughout the project lifecycle
4	A coherent and supportive relationship is demonstrated between the overall business strategy and the project portfolio
5	All projects have an approved plan containing authorization points at which the Business Case is reviewed and approved. Decisions made at authorization points are recorded and communicated
6	Members of delegated authorization bodies have sufficient representation, competence, authority and resources to enable them to make appropriate decisions
7	The project Business Case is supported by relevant and realistic information that provides a reliable basis for making authorization decisions
8	The board or its delegated agents decide when independent scrutiny of projects and project management systems is required, and implement such scrutiny accordingly
9	There are clearly defined criteria for reporting project status and for the escalation of risks and issues to the levels required by the organization
10	The organization fosters a culture of improvement and of frank disclosure of project information
11	Project stakeholders are engaged at a level that is commensurate with their importance to the organization and in a manner that fosters trust

Principles are extracts from the *APM Body of Knowledge 5th Edition*, reproduced with the permission of the Association for Project Management

Figure 4.6 Governance of project management context (reproduced from the **APM Body of Knowledge 5th Edition***)*

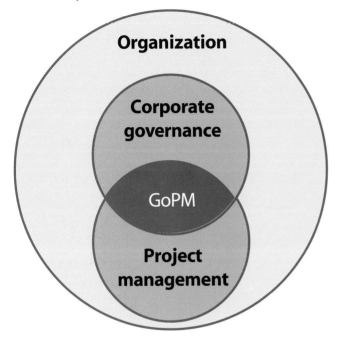

The governance of project management is a subset of the activities involved in corporate governance and most activities involved with the management of projects lie outside the direct concern of corporate governance (see Figure 4.6).

Source: *APM Body of Knowledge 5th Edition*, with permission of the Association for Project Management.

The main components to be addressed are: portfolio direction, project sponsorship, project management effectiveness and efficiency, and disclosure and reporting. These can be best addressed by the intelligent application of the 11 principles for the governance of project management (Table 4.9).

Effective governance of project management involves aligning the interests of the organization's board of directors, project teams and wider stakeholders and will contribute towards:

- Optimizing the organization's portfolio of projects
- Avoiding many common failures in project performance
- Motivating staff, customers and suppliers through better communication
- Minimizing threats to the organization arising from projects
- Maximizing benefits to be realized from projects
- Assuring the continued development of the organization.

4.8 ORGANIZATION AND GOVERNANCE – EXERCISES

(Sample answers are provided in Appendix A for the first question within each section. Answers to the remaining questions can be assessed against the relevant section within the chapter.)

APMP topic 6.7

1 Explain the strengths and weaknesses of managing a project in a matrix type of organizational structure. Make five relevant points.
2 Explain the strengths and weaknesses of managing a project in a functional type of organizational structure. Make five relevant points.
3 Explain the strengths and weaknesses of managing a project in a project type of organizational structure. Make five relevant points.
4 Describe the differences between functional, matrix and project organizational structures.

APMP topic 1.5

1 Explain the typical responsibilities of the Project Sponsor in the Concept, Definition, Implementation and Handover and Closeout phases of the project lifecycle.

2 Explain why Project Sponsorship is important in project management.

APMP topic 6.8

1 Explain the main responsibilities of five key project management roles.

2 Explain the differences between the role and responsibilities of the Project Manager and the Project Sponsor (Executive).

3 Describe the role of users on a project.

4 Describe the roles of project team members.

APMP topic 1.6

1 Explain the role of a project office, making four relevant points.

2 Describe five functions that a project office may perform.

3 Describe five benefits of having a project office.

APMP topic 6.10

1 For two distinct principles of governance of project management, explain the possible effects of *not* practising them.

2 State six principles of the governance of project management that would help avoid common causes of project failure.

Planning 5

5 Planning

5.1 PURPOSE

The purpose of this chapter is to describe a generic planning process and explain a number of techniques used during this process, in the areas of:

- Scope management (APMP topic 3.1)
- Scheduling (APMP topic 3.2)
- Resource management (APMP topic 3.3)
- Budgeting and cost management (APMP topic 3.4)
- Estimating (APMP topic 4.3).

5.2 DEFINITIONS

There are slightly different definitions of the key term related to planning in PRINCE2 and the APM Body of Knowledge (Table 5.1).

5.3 THE PLANNING PROCESS

Planning provides the Project Manager and Executive (PRINCE2) or Project Sponsor (APM) with the basis for assessing:

- Whether the targets for the project (in terms of time, cost, quality and scope) are achievable
- The resources needed to achieve those targets
- The activities needed to ensure that quality can be built into the products
- The issues and risks associated with trying to achieve the targets and stay within the constraints.

Once the plan has been produced and approved, it will then act as the basis against which to monitor actual progress.

A common planning process can be used for each level of plan, which consists of identifying and understanding the plans:

1 Products
   - Establishing what products are needed for the plan
   - Describing those products and their quality criteria
   - Determining the sequence in which each of the products should be produced

2 Activities
   - Identifying the activities needed to produce the products

Table 5.1 Comparison of the definition of plan in PRINCE2 and the APM Body of Knowledge

	PRINCE2	APM Body of Knowledge
Plan	A document, framed in accordance with a predefined scheme or method, describing how, when and by whom a specific target or set of targets is to be achieved	The project management plan brings together all the plans for a project. [Its purpose] is to document the outcomes of the planning process and to provide the reference document for managing the project. The project management plan is owned by the project manager.

The APM Body of Knowledge definition is an extract from the *APM Body of Knowledge 5th Edition*, reproduced with the permission of the Association for Project Management

Table 5.2 The levels of plan

Level of plan	Description
Project Plan	Used by the Project Board (PRINCE2) or Steering Group (APM) to monitor actual cost and project progress stage by stage
Stage Plan	Used by the Project Manager as the basis for day-to-day control for each stage of the project
Team Plan	Used by the Team Manager (where present) as the basis for day-to-day control of their Work Packages

- Deciding when the activities should be done and by whom
- Estimating how much effort each activity will consume
- Estimating how long the activities will take
- Agreeing what quality control activities are needed

3 Resources
- Identifying all of the resources needed to undertake the activities to produce each of the products and to undertake the quality control activities

4 Time schedule
- Producing a time-based schedule of activities using information from the previous steps

5 Costs
- Calculating how much the overall effort will cost
- Producing the budget from the cost of the effort plus any materials and equipment that must be obtained

6 Controls
- Assessing the risks contained in the plan
- Identifying the management control points needed
- Agreeing tolerance levels for the plan.

Whilst the above steps are presented in a sequence, in practice several iterations of this process are usually needed.

An overview of the total project is needed, and this is provided for by the Project Plan. This plan can then be broken down into lower-level plans containing more detail, and reflecting the needs of the different levels of management involved in the project (Table 5.2).

In addition, should any of the above plans be forecast to exceed their tolerances, an Exception Plan may be required. This plan replaces the existing plan by picking up from the current plan actuals and continuing to the end of that plan.

Tolerance refers to the permissible deviation from plan without bringing this deviation to the attention of the next higher authority. The two standard elements of tolerance are time and cost.

5.4 SCOPE MANAGEMENT

Scope management is the process by which the deliverables (or products) and the work (or activities) to produce these are identified and defined. Identification and definition of the scope must describe what the project will include and what the project will not include, i.e. what is in and out of scope.

Source: *APM Body of Knowledge 5th Edition*, with permission of the Association for Project Management.

The initial high-level definition of scope will first be documented as part of the project's Business Case, which will describe the breadth of the scope. The scope will then be refined and described to increasing levels of detail in the Project, Stage and Team Plans.

Scope is identified and defined by using a Product Breakdown Structure (PBS) and a Work Breakdown Structure (WBS). These diagrams can then be supplemented with a Cost Breakdown Structure (CBS), and an Organizational Breakdown Structure (OBS). Also, the OBS and WBS can be combined to form a Responsibility Assignment Matrix (RAM). These are described below.

5.4.1 Product Breakdown Structure

A PBS is a hierarchical structure that breaks down the final product of a plan into its constituent sub-products. Breaking down products into a lower level of detail makes it easier to:

- Estimate the effort, resources and timescale needed
- Apply quality criteria more specifically
- Avoid omitting products.

The PBS starts with the final product of the plan, breaks this down into intermediate products, and continues with this breakdown until the simple products are identified at the lowest level of the breakdown. This lowest level will vary, depending on the level of detail required by the plan, i.e. the simple products in the Project Plan may be broken down further in the Stage Plans and the simple products in the Stage Plans may be broken down further in any Team Plans.

Figure 5.1 provides an example of a Product Breakdown Structure at project level showing the products needed for a Conference to launch this book.

Figure 5.1 Product Breakdown Structure

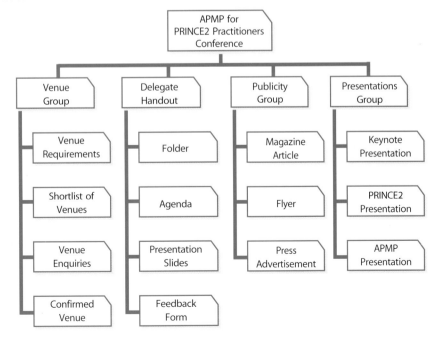

PRINCE2 goes on to recommend that for each simple product, a Product Description should be written, which provides a clear, complete and unambiguous description for each product. They include information regarding the purpose, composition, derivation, format, quality criteria and other quality aspects of each product.

PRINCE2 also recommends a third step in the technique, which is to show the simple products in the form of a Product Flow Diagram. This shows the sequence of development of the products of the plan and any dependencies between them. By including the 'external products', it also shows dependencies on any products outside the scope of the plan.

5.4.2 Work Breakdown Structure

A WBS is a hierarchical structure that breaks down the work required to deliver the products of a project. Major categories are broken down into smaller components. These are sub-divided until the lowest required level of detail is established. The lowest level units of the WBS are generally referred to as Work Packages. The Work Packages may then be further divided into the activities needed to perform the Work Package.

The Product Flow Diagram can be helpful in identifying the activities required to take one product (or set of products) and turn it into the next product (or set of products).

Some guidelines to consider when preparing a WBS are listed below.

- The split of work into Work Packages should be logical and compatible with the other breakdown structures, e.g. a Work Package could correspond to one or more simple products on the PBS.
- It should be possible to test whether the Work Package is complete; this can be done by testing for the quality criteria detailed in each of the Product Descriptions that form part of the Work Package.
- At the very lowest level, the activities should be well-defined tasks for an individual to perform within a reasonable period of time; this may only be achievable for a WBS for the Stage or Team Plans.

Figure 5.2 Work Breakdown Structure

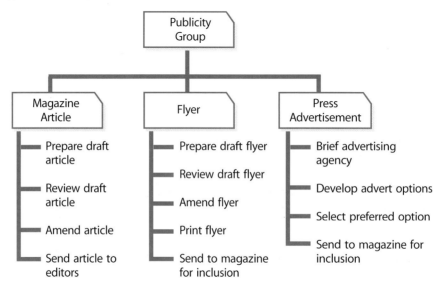

Breaking the work down in this way will help those responsible for undertaking the work to prepare input to estimating and scheduling.

Figure 5.2 provides an example of a WBS at project level showing the expanded Publicity Group to include the activities necessary to produce the products. (In practice all of the other groups would be expanded in the same way.)

5.4.3 Organizational Breakdown Structure

The OBS is a hierarchical structure that shows project management team structure for the project together with the communication routes and reporting lines. This will reflect the structure as described in Chapter 4. An OBS often resembles an organization chart, and it shows the project organization in enough detail for the work of the project to be allocated to teams or individuals.

Figure 5.3 provides an example of an OBS at project level showing the project resources that would be required for the Conference project.

5.4.4 Responsibility Assignment Matrix

The OBS can be combined with the PBS or WBS to create a Responsibility Assignment Matrix (RAM). This is a diagram or chart showing assigned responsibilities for elements of work. It is usually a grid with the PBS products or WBS activities down the left hand side, and the OBS resources across the top. Ticks in the appropriate intersections indicate who is doing what.

This approach can be developed further by using letters in the matrix to create a RACI Diagram. RACI is an acronym formed from the four participatory roles that it describes, i.e.:

- **R**esponsible – those who will actually do the work
- **A**ccountable – the person who must ensure that the work is completed successfully (note: only one person can be accountable)
- **C**onsult – those whose opinions are sought
- **I**nform – those who are kept up-to-date on progress.

Figure 5.3 Organizational Breakdown Structure

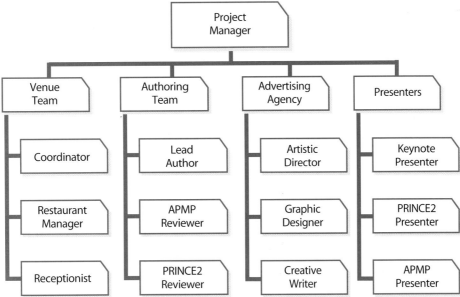

The RACI Diagram can be expanded to RACI-VS, which adds two further roles:

- **V**erifies – those who check whether the product meets its quality criteria
- **S**igns-off – the person who approves the V decision.

Figure 5.4 provides an example of a RACI Diagram at project level showing the activities involved in the creation of the Press Advertisement.

5.4.5 Cost Breakdown Structure

The CBS is another hierarchical structure that is a breakdown of a project into cost categories. It identifies in one document all cost categories in an arrangement that suits the purpose of the project.

The CBS is usually completed when the PBS or WBS and OBS have been outlined as it is helpful to have a view of the products and/or activities in order to estimate time and materials, and the OBS is useful when allocating a value to the resources working on the product and/or activity. For example, the costs of labour could be cross-referenced to the WBS, while the capital cost categories could be related to products within the PBS.

It is also possible, however, for the hierarchy within the CBS to differ significantly from the other structures where there is an organizational requirement for the categories to be aligned with those used by the accounts department. In this case possible categories are (Figure 5.5):

- Labour costs (direct and indirect)
- Materials
- Services
- Overheads.

Figure 5.4 RACI Diagram

Press Advertisement	PERSON					
ACTIVITY	Lead Author	PRINCE2 Reviewer	APMP Reviewer	Artistic Director	Graphic Designer	Creative Writer
Brief advertising agency	A	R	C	I		
Develop advert options	I	I	I	A	R	C
Select preferred option	A	R	C	C		
Send to magazine for inclusion	I			A	R	C

R = Responsible
A = Accountable
C = Consult
I = Inform

Figure 5.5 Cost Breakdown Structure

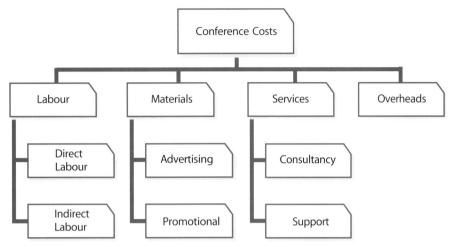

Alternatively, the cost breakdown may relate to the different types of cost incurred by the project. For example:

- Labour
- Materials
- Services
- Plant and equipment
- Subcontract
- Management
- Administration
- Fees and taxation.

For each activity detailed on the WBS, figures will be allocated against each of the items. These are then allocated a cost code/cost centre. Often organizations will use an accounting system, such as SAP, to record this data. The staff then book time to the various activities using these codes, which enables various analyses to be produced. This could include Earned Value data (see Chapter 6).

5.5 SCHEDULING

Scheduling is the process used to determine the overall plan duration and when activities and events are planned to happen. This includes identification of activities and their logical dependencies, and estimation of activity durations, taking into account requirements and availability of resources.

Source: *APM Body of Knowledge 5th Edition*, with permission of the Association for Project Management.

There is a direct link here with the WBS, as scheduling needs to identify the activities within the plan and these can be drawn from the work packages defined in the WBS. Having identified all of the activities, the next step is to define the logical dependencies between the activities.

There are four types of dependency (Table 5.3).

These dependencies can be shown in a number of formats.

Table 5.3 Types of dependency

Finish to start (FS)	The start of an activity depends on the finish of a preceding activity, either immediately or after a lapse of time
Finish to finish (FF)	The finish of an activity depends on the finish of a preceding activity, either immediately or after a lapse of time
Start to start (SS)	The start of an activity depends on the start of a preceding activity, either immediately or after a lapse of time
Start to finish (SF)	The finish of an activity depends on the start of a preceding activity, either immediately or after a lapse of time

5.5.1 Dependency Table

The Dependency Table is a list of all of the activities with additional columns showing the predecessors and/ or successors for each activity. See Table 5.4 which, for simplicity purposes, only includes FS dependencies.

Table 5.4 Dependency Table

Activity	Predecessor
A	–
B	A
C	B
D	B
E	C
F	E
G	D
H	G
J	F and H
K	G
L	K and J
M	L

5.5.2 Network Diagram (or activity network)

The Network Diagram is a pictorial representation of the dependencies between the activities. These dependencies can be presented in one of two forms:

- Activity-on-Arrow, in which the arrows symbolize the activities
- Activity-on-Node, in which the nodes symbolize the activities.

The most common format nowadays is the Activity-on-Node diagram, an example of which is shown in Figure 5.6, based on the information contained in the above Dependency Table.

5.5.3 Critical Path Analysis

> Critical Path Analysis is a procedure that calculates the critical path and floats in a network, and analyses this information to predict project duration.
>
> Source: *APM Body of Knowledge 5th Edition*, with permission of the Association for Project Management

The critical path is a sequence of activities through the activity network from start to finish, the sum of whose durations determines the overall plan duration. This is the shortest time within which a project can be completed.

Figure 5.6 Simple Activity-on-Node Network Diagram

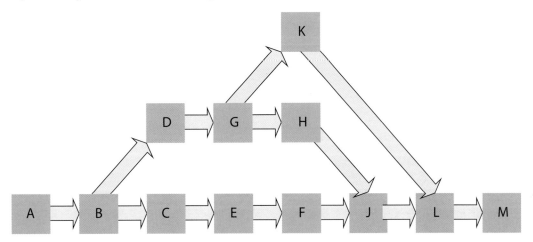

There are two types of float:

■ Free Float– the time by which an activity may be delayed or extended without affecting the start of any succeeding activity

■ Total Float– the time by which an activity may be delayed or extended without affecting the total plan duration or violating the target finish date.

Having drawn a network, the next step is to estimate the duration for each of these activities. (See below for more guidance of formulating estimates.) These estimates can then be added to the Dependency Table (Table 5.5).

The estimates can also be added to the Network Diagram and used to calculate the early start and early finish, and the late start and late finish of the activities within the network. In turn, this information can be used to calculate the floats and critical path.

This is very powerful as it enables the Project Manager to explore many different options by undertaking what-if analysis, based on different assumptions regarding the durations and logical dependencies of the activities.

Table 5.5 Dependency Table showing estimates of duration for each activity

Activity	Predecessor	Duration (e.g. weeks)
A	–	4
B	A	1
C	B	5
D	B	3
E	C	6
F	E	4
G	D	2
H	G	8
J	F and H	1
K	G	7
L	K and J	2
M	L	3

In order to undertake these calculations, the activity node is divided into seven internal boxes (Figure 5.7). The top three segments contain the early start, duration and early finish, respectively. The bottom three contain the late start, total float and late finish, respectively. The central segment contains a description of the activity. Finally, whilst the dependencies connecting the activities usually have zero duration, they can be given a duration to indicate either:

■ A lag, indicated by a positive duration. A lag is the minimum necessary lapse of time between the finish of one activity and the finish of an overlapping activity, or the delay incurred between two activities

■ A lead, indicated by a negative duration. A lead is the minimum necessary lapse of time between the start of one activity and the start of an overlapping activity.

There are five steps involved, which are known as:

■ Add estimated durations to the Network Diagram
■ Forward Pass
■ Back Pass
■ Calculate Float
■ Identifying the Critical Path.

Figure 5.7 Activity-on-Node Notation

ES	D	EF
Activity ID		
LS	TF	LF

ES = Early Start   LS = Late Start
D = Duration   TF = Total Float
EF = Early Finish   LF = Late Finish
    Activity ID = Activity identifier

Network Diagram

Figure 5.8 is the Network Diagram for the activities listed in Table 5.4 with the estimated duration added.

Forward Pass

Early start and finish are calculated by conducting a forward pass through the network. The early start of the first activity is zero and the early finish is calculated by adding the duration. The early finish is transferred to the subsequent activities as the early start, adding or subtracting any lead or lag (assuming a finish to start dependency.) Where an activity has two or more preceding activities the largest number is transferred. This process is repeated throughout the network.

Figure 5.9 shows the Network Diagram with the Forward Pass completed.

Backward Pass

The late start and finish and float are calculated by conducting a backward pass. The early finish of the last activity becomes its late finish. The duration is subtracted to calculate the late start. The late start is transferred back to the late finish of preceding activities. Where an activity has two or more succeeding activities, it is the smallest number that is transferred (after adding lags or subtracting leads). The process is repeated throughout the network.

Figure 5.10 shows the Network Diagram with the Backward Pass completed.

Figure 5.8 Network Diagram with durations

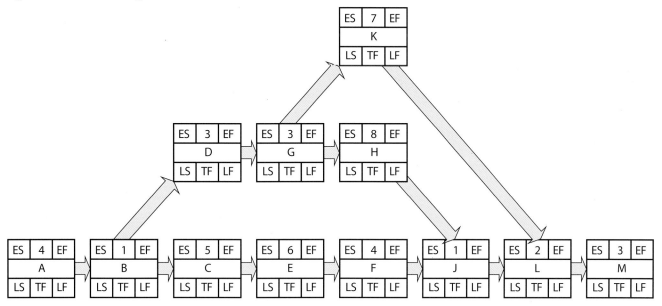

Figure 5.9 Forward Pass

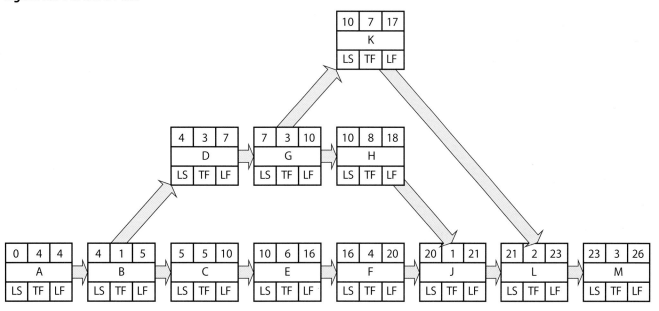

Figure 5.10 Backward Pass

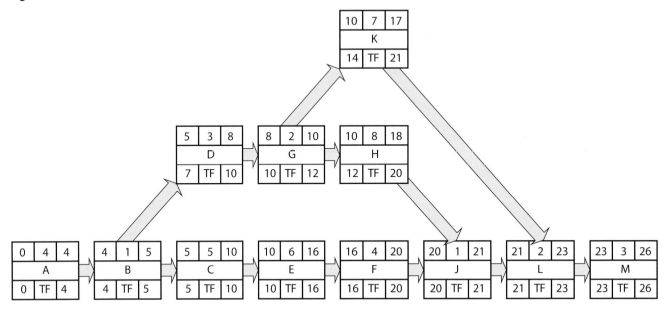

Figure 5.11 Total Float and Free Float

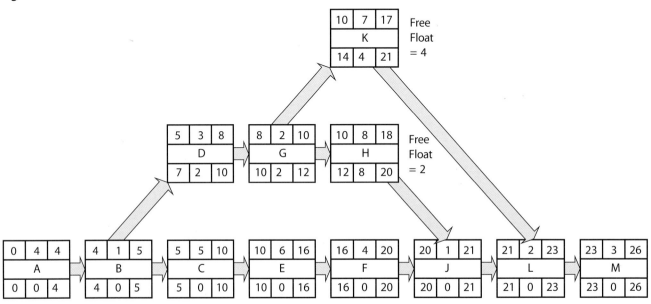

Calculation of Float

There are two types of float that can be calculated:

- Total Float – this is the time by which an activity may be delayed or extended without affecting the total project duration or violating a target finish date. The total float of each activity is calculated using one of the following formulae:

  Total Float = Late Finish – Early Start – Duration

  Total Float = Late Finish – Early Finish

  Total Float = Late Start – Early Start

- Free Float – this is the time by which an activity may be delayed or extended without affecting the start of any succeeding activity. The Free Float is calculated using the following formula:

Free Float = Early Start of next activity – Early Finish of activity in question

Figure 5.11 shows the Network Diagram with the floats calculated.

Identifying the Critical Path

This is the sequence of activities through a project network from start to finish, the sum of whose durations determines the overall project duration. The Critical Path is identified by all of those activities in the network having zero float.

In Figure 5.12, the critical path is represented by activities A, B, C, E, F, J, L and M. The duration of the project is 26 time units.

Figure 5.12 Completed Activity Network

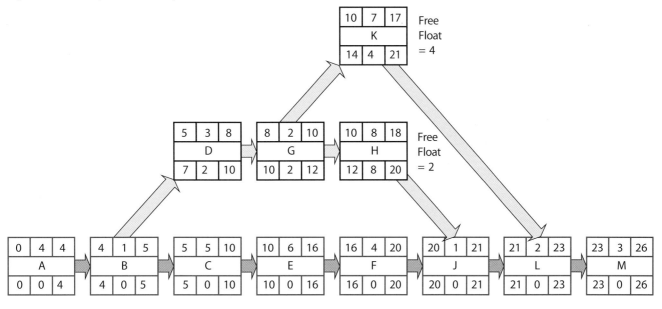

5.5.4 Gantt charts

Having completed the above steps and calculations, the information can be shown more visually on a Gantt chart (named after the American engineer Henry Gantt [1861–1919]). A Gantt chart is a particular type of bar chart showing the planned activities against time (Figure 5.13). Activities are listed with other tabular information on the left side of the chart with the time intervals over the bars. Activity durations are shown in the form of horizontal bars.

5.5.5 Milestone progress chart

A milestone progress chart is formed by plotting 'plan time' across the top of the chart and 'real time' down the side shown as monitoring periods. In the example in Figure 5.14, the monitoring periods occur every four weeks. By plotting the monitoring period against plan time the completion line is created. This represents time in the project. The milestones are scheduled at the top of the chart and for each monitoring period the date for the milestone is plotted. The points in the future are shown with a different symbol.

Figure 5.13 Gantt chart

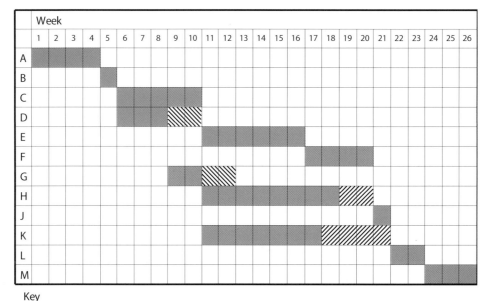

Key

▨ Total Float

▨ Free Float

Figure 5.14 Milestone progress chart

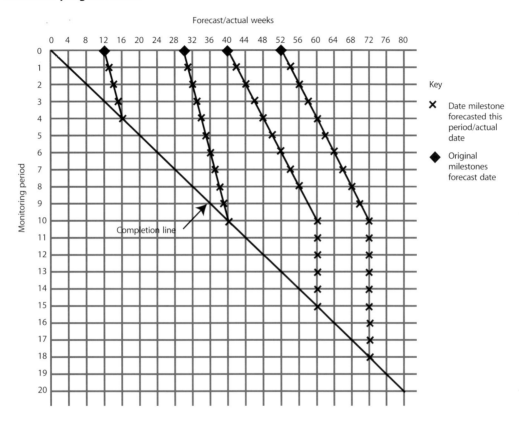

The resulting charts can be extremely useful for senior management as they provide, at a glance, a view of how well the project is progressing. For a project that is forecast to be on schedule, the plotted lines will be vertical, whereas if a delay is forecast the plotted lines will become diagonal going from left to right. The forecast completion date can also easily be seen, from where the plotted lines cross the completion line.

5.5.6 Program Evaluation Review Technique

Program Evaluation Review Technique (PERT) is a variation on Critical Path Analysis that takes a slightly more realistic view of time estimates. It involves the use of three point estimates:

- Optimistic – the shortest possible time each activity will take
- Most likely length of time
- Pessimistic – the longest time that might be taken if the activity takes longer than expected.

Assuming a statistical normal distribution, the following formula is used to calculate the time to use for each activity:

(optimistic time + 4 × most likely time + pessimistic time)/6

This duration is then used in place of the single point estimate and this helps to bias time estimates away from the unrealistically short timescales usually assumed.

5.6 RESOURCE MANAGEMENT

> Resource management is a process that identifies and assigns resources to activities so that the project is undertaken using appropriate levels of resources and within an acceptable duration. Resource allocation, smoothing, levelling and scheduling are techniques used to determine and manage appropriate levels of resources.
>
> Source: *APM Body of Knowledge 5th Edition*, with permission of the Association for Project Management.

Having established the necessary activities required to produce the defined products, the next step in the planning process is to consider the resource requirements. So far, the network diagrams and schedules that have been produced have been done on the basis that the resources needed to perform the activities would be available when required. However, in most projects this is unlikely to be the case as there will be some constraints on the availability of these resources. Accordingly, it will be necessary to schedule activities, not based on their early start date, but at a time that makes the best use of the available resources.

Resources, here, include all those items required to undertake a project such as people, finance and materials. Within any project, two particular types of resource need to be considered (as defined in the *APM Body of Knowledge 5th Edition*):

■ Replenishable – these are resources where, when they are absent or have been used up, fresh supplies can be obtained. Common examples are raw materials and money.

■ Re-usable – these are resources where, when no longer needed, they become available for other uses. Common examples are accommodation, machines, equipment and people.

The main techniques used to determine and manage the appropriate levels of resources are resource allocation, resource smoothing and resource levelling. The use of resource smoothing and resource levelling reflect two potential extreme situations.

The first is where resources are unlimited but the plan timescale is fixed (or limited), in which case resource smoothing would be applied. This situation is also known as time-limited scheduling.

The second extreme is where resources are fixed (or limited) but the plan timescale is flexible (or unlimited), in which case resource levelling would be applied. This situation is also known as resource-limited scheduling.

5.6.1 Resource allocation

> This is the process by which resources are mapped against activities which are often shown as aggregated resource histograms against a timescale.
>
> Source: *APM Body of Knowledge 5th Edition*, with permission of the Association for Project Management.

Expanded on the earlier example, Table 5.6 shows the resources requirements for each of the activities in our plan.

This information can be mapped against the activities in the Gantt chart and then added together to calculate the resources requirements week by week. These can

Table 5.6 Dependency Table with duration estimates

Activity	Predecessor	Durations	Staff resources
A	–	4	8
B	A	1	4
C	B	5	5
D	B	3	18
E	C	6	18
F	E	4	4
G	D	2	8
H	G	8	16
J	F and H	1	2
K	G	7	21
L	K and J	2	10
M	L	3	6

then be combined to calculate the cumulative resource requirements over the duration of the plan. Figure 5.15 shows the resources mapped against the activities.

This information is often shown in the form of an aggregated resource histogram against the timescale of the plan. Such histograms can be used to show resource requirements, usage and availability using vertical bars against a horizontal timescale (Figure 5.16).

The same information can also be presented graphically in the form of a cumulative S curve, so-called because of the shape of the line (Figure 5.17).

5.6.2 Resource smoothing (or time-limited scheduling)

This is a process applied to projects to ensure that resources are used as efficiently as possible. It involves utilizing float within the project or increasing or decreasing the resources required for specific activities, such that any peaks and troughs of resource usage are smoothed out. This does not affect the plan duration. It is also known as time-limited scheduling.

Source: *APM Body of Knowledge 5th Edition*, with permission of the Association for Project Management.

Figure 5.15 Gantt chart showing resource allocation

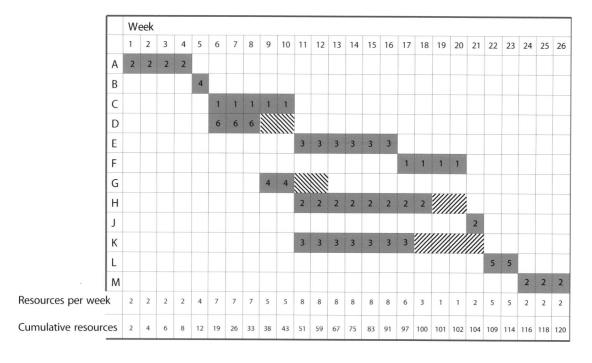

Figure 5.16 Resource histogram

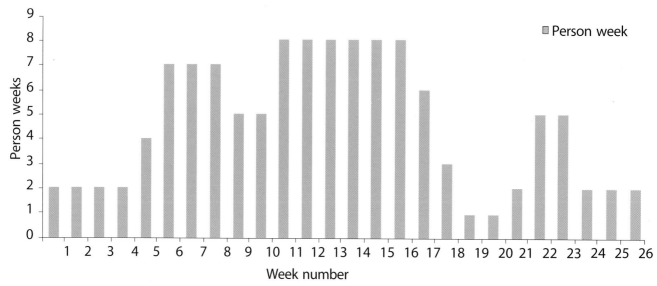

Figure 5.17 Cumulative 'S' curve

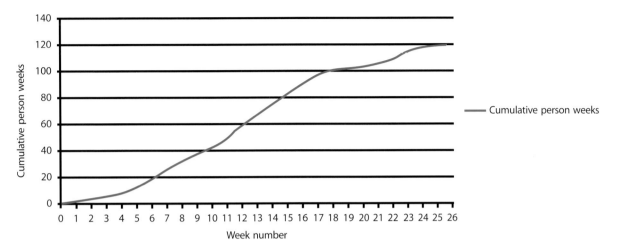

The objectives of scheduling in the time-limited situation are:

- To calculate the resource requirements so that they are made available at the right time
- To schedule each activity so that the resource loading is as smooth as possible (hence the phrase resource smoothing).

This is achieved by using serial scheduling, which is a method of drawing up a schedule by positioning one activity at a time. All of the activities are listed in order of, say, increasing float and then each activity is dealt with consecutively.

Using the information in Table 5.7, the resource histograms in Figures 5.18 and 5.19 show the result of applying resource smoothing.

Table 5.7 Serial scheduling

Activity	Dependency	Resource	Duration	Early start time	Total Float	Late start time
A	–	4	1	0	0	1
B	A	2	12	1	0	13
E	B and C	4	10	13	0	23
F	D and E	3	10	12	0	33
H	F and G	3	1	33	0	34
C	A	2	8	1	4	13
G	B and C	1	5	13	15	33
D	A	1	4	1	18	23

Figure 5.18 Resource histogram prior to smoothing

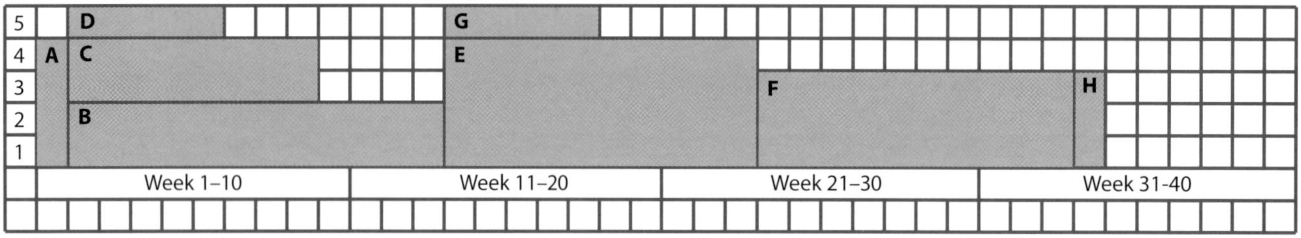

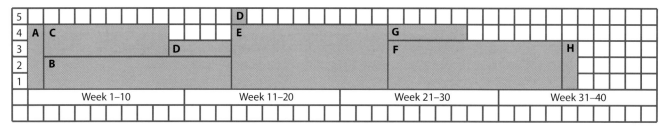

Figure 5.19 Resource histogram smoothed

As can be seen in Figure 5.19 the histogram has been smoothed by delaying activity D by eight weeks and activity G by 10 weeks. This has resulted in a smoother resource profile but has not delayed the project end date.

5.6.3 Resource levelling (or resource-limited scheduling)

Resource levelling can be applied to projects when there are resource constraints. Resource levelling forces the amount of work scheduled not to exceed the limits of resources available. This results in either activity durations being extended or entire activities being delayed to periods when resources are available. This often results in a longer project duration. It is also known as resource-limited scheduling.

Source: *APM Body of Knowledge 5th Edition*, with permission of the Association for Project Management.

The objectives of scheduling in the resource-limited situation are:

■ To calculate the resource requirements so that they are made available at the right time

■ To schedule each activity so that the resource loading is as level as possible with the given constraints (hence the phrase resource levelling).

This is achieved by using parallel scheduling. This is a method of drawing up a schedule that starts at the beginning of the plan and considers all eligible activities in parallel. Eligible activities are those that could be started if there were available resources, taking into account the dependencies. If insufficient resource is available, then decision rules are applied to decide which activities can start and which need to be delayed. Examples of such rules could be:

Figure 5.20 Resource histogram levelled

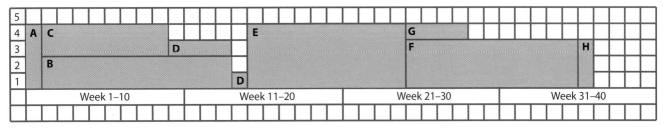

Rule 1: Start with the activity with the earliest date for the latest start date.

Rule 2: Continue with an activity until it has been finished.

Rule 3: Do not allow a resource to stand idle if an eligible activity could be started.

Rule 4: Do not allow an activity to start with partial resources.

Using the same information as before, Figure 5.20 shows the impact of resource levelling. As can been seen, the resource has been constrained to a maximum of four. This has meant that activity D had to be completed before E could start, resulting in the project being delayed by one week.

5.6.4 Software-based scheduling tools

A wide range of software packages can be used to undertake either resource smoothing or resource levelling. These will enable the Project Manager to perform the steps involved very quickly, and as a result, allow what-if analysis to be undertaken considering many different options. However, it is worth noting that judgement still needs to be exercised.

5.7 BUDGETING AND COST MANAGEMENT

Budgeting and cost management is the estimating of costs and the setting of an agreed budget, and the management of actual and forecast costs against that budget.

Source: *APM Body of Knowledge 5th Edition*, with permission of the Association for Project Management.

Having produced a time schedule based on an understanding of the scope of the plan (i.e. the set of products to be produced), and the activities and resources required to produce those products, the next step is to produce a cost plan and budget. A cost plan shows the amounts and expected dates of incurring costs on the plan. A budget is the agreed total cost of the plan.

Budgeting involves the Project Manager calculating the costs that will be incurred over the life of the plan. This can be derived from the time schedule if costs can be attributed to each of the resources specified in that plan. The Project Manager may also need to consider income generated by the project. Based on this information the Project Manager will be able to produce a cash flow forecast (a prediction of the difference between cash received and payments made during a specific period or for the duration of the project). This can be displayed in tabular or graphical format.

Where a project does not receive any income, the cash flow forecast will equate to the cost plan. Once approved, the cash flow forecast and/or cost plan can be used as a baseline against which to monitor expenditure during the life of the project.

As part of cost management it is important to recognize that expenditure goes through a number of distinct stages.

■ Planned Cost – the estimated cost which forms part of the budget. This is the anticipated cost of an item, prior to placing an order.

■ Committed Cost – the costs that are legally committed even if delivery has not taken place with invoices neither raised nor paid. This reflects the placement of an order for work to be done and is the amount of money removed from the budget represented by this order. This is the confirmed cost of an item, having placed an order.

■ Accrued Cost – the costs that are earmarked for the project and for which payment is due, but has not been made. This is typically when the item has been delivered but has not yet been paid for or work that is part of an ongoing contract that has been done but not paid for e.g. design or programming.

■ Actual Cost – the incurred costs that are charged to the project budget and for which payment has been made. This is when the item has been paid for and the money has been withdrawn from the organization's bank account.

Therefore, at any time during a project some costs will be planned, others will be committed, some will be accrued and some will actually have been paid. The sum total of these four elements is known as the forecast out-turn cost:

Forecast out-turn cost = Planned Costs + Committed Costs + Accrued Costs + Actual Costs

This distinction is important as:

■ Whilst planned costs are estimates, the other three are known costs. At the beginning of a project all costs will be planned and therefore estimates. As the project proceeds more costs will become known, until the end of the project when all costs will be known

■ Planned costs can be avoided simply by making a decision not to proceed with the project or an element of the project

■ Committed costs may be avoided, but there are likely to be some costs incurred in cancelling the work that has been ordered

■ Accrued costs can no longer be avoided as the work has already been carried out

■ Actual costs reflect the fact that money has now left the organization.

Accordingly, it is important when setting up reporting systems to capture information about expenditure that reflects these four elements of the forecast out-turn costs.

5.8 ESTIMATING

Estimating uses a range of tools and techniques to produce estimates. An estimate is an approximation of project time and cost targets that is refined throughout the project lifecycle.

Source: *APM Body of Knowledge 5th Edition*, with permission of the Association for Project Management.

The refinement of estimates over the project lifecycle is reflected in the different levels of plan. There are three basic approaches to estimating, namely bottom-up, comparative and parametric. Whilst each has its advantages and disadvantages, and requires certain circumstances to be of any use, it is worthwhile using more than one of these approaches when arriving at an estimate for a plan.

Various aspect of the planning process rely to some extent on the Project Manager's ability to estimate. Estimating is necessary for a number of reasons:

- To assess the viability of the project – estimates will be required for the cost, time and benefit sections of the project Business Case
- To obtain funding – there needs to be an understanding of the funding requirements of the project over its lifecycle i.e. the cash flow forecast
- To allocate resources – the work content needs to be established so that resources can be made available to the project as and when required
- To form the basis for control – once estimates have been established and agreed, these become the baseline against which progress can be assessed.

5.8.1 Estimates across the project lifecycle

At the very beginning of the project lifecycle, the estimates that are produced are at their most uncertain due to the lack of detailed information. The level of certainty increases throughout the lifecycle, until at the very end of the project lifecycle total certainty is achieved. This is reflected in Table 5.8.

It is worth considering some of the factors that can result in errors being made when estimates are produced.

- Psychological factors – such as optimism or pessimism. The usual bias is to be optimistic over the time it takes to do anything. But there are those whose tendency is to be pessimistic. Hence the Project Manager needs to know their own bias and that of others providing information for estimates.

Table 5.8 Level of accuracy in the project lifecycle

Lifecycle Phase	PRINCE2 process	Level of plan	Comments	Level of accuracy (increases as lifecycle progresses)
Concept	Starting up a Project (SU)		Very high level plan estimates form part of the Business Case	Uncertain ± 30%
Definition	Initiating a Project (IP)	Project Plan	High level estimates still, but refined based on a better understanding of the project objectives and approach	Less uncertain, say ± 15%
Implementation	Managing Stage Boundaries (SB)	Stage Plan	Lower level and more detailed estimates are now possible based on a good understanding of the products to be produced	Even less uncertain, say ± 10%
	Managing Product Delivery (MP)	Team Plan	The lowest level and most detailed estimates are now possible based on an excellent understanding of the products to be produced	Least uncertain, say ± 5%
Handover and Closeout	Closing a Project (CP)		Actual times and costs are confirmed	Certain

- Social and political factors – pressure from senior management or from a client may result in over-optimistic estimates.
- Lack of estimating experience – the accuracy of estimates does tend to improve as people learn from experience.

5.8.2 Bottom-up estimating

Bottom-up estimating is an estimating technique based on making estimates for every work package (or activity) in the Work Breakdown Structure and summarizing them to provide a total estimate of cost or effort required. This technique uses the project Work Breakdown Structure derived to a level of detail that allows estimates of cost and time for the project activities to be provided. Once estimates for each work package (or activity) have been agreed, these can be totalled together and the overall project estimate can be established.

Source: *APM Body of Knowledge 5th Edition*, with permission of the Association for Project Management.

5.8.3 Comparative estimating

Comparative estimating is an estimating technique based on the comparison with, and factoring from, the cost of a previous similar project or operation. This technique uses historic data from similar projects to determine the most appropriate cost and time. The data is compared by scaling of size, complexity and type of technology employed to determine a more informed estimate of the project's budget and schedule parameters.

Source: *APM Body of Knowledge 5th Edition*, with permission of the Association for Project Management.

5.8.4 Parametric estimating

Parametric estimating is an estimating technique that uses a statistical relationship between historic data and other variables (for example, square metreage in construction, lines of code in software development) to calculate an estimate. This technique uses defined parameters by which a project can be measured, for example the cost or time to build a single deliverable, with this figure then being multiplied depending on the number of such parameters required. This method of estimating is typically used in statistical modelling.

Source: *APM Body of Knowledge 5th Edition*, with permission of the Association for Project Management.

5.8.5 Three-point estimates

A three-point estimate is an estimate in which the most likely mid-range value, an optimistic value and a pessimistic, worst case value are given.

Source: *APM Body of Knowledge 5th Edition*, with permission of the Association for Project Management.

The definition above reflects the fact that all estimates are uncertain. It is also useful in terms of helping to reduce the natural bias towards producing over-optimistic estimates. Three-point estimates are used in PERT (see section 5.5).

5.9 PLANNING – EXERCISES

(Sample answers are provided in Appendix A for the first question within each section. Answers to the remaining questions can be assessed against the relevant section within the chapter.)

The questions for sections 3.2 and 3.3 below are slightly longer than any you could expect to get in an APMP exam. Also, in the exam, candidates are unlikely to be asked to draw a network. However, the questions are intended to let you practise the techniques, and if you can do these then you can do any in the exam. It is expected that they will take between 20 and 30 minutes to complete.

APMP topic 3.1

1 Explain how a Work Breakdown Structure will be constructed and its purpose in a project.
2 Explain the purpose of a Product Breakdown Structure.
3 Explain the purpose of a Cost Breakdown Structure.
4 Explain the purpose of an Organizational Breakdown Structure.
5 Explain why a Responsibility Assignment Matrix would be used on a project.

APMP topic 3.2

1 Using the information given in Table 5.9, draw a network, and identify the critical path, total and free floats. Use the network to draw a Gantt chart. Indicate the free and total floats on the chart.
2 Explain how a project schedule is created and maintained.
3 Explain how a milestone chart is constructed and used. Include an appropriately labelled diagram.
4 Describe three advantages and three disadvantages of using software tools for scheduling.

Table 5.9 Estimates of duration for each activity

Activity	Predecessor	Duration (weeks)
A	–	2
B	A	4
C	A	6
D	C	3
E	D	3
F	B	1
G	F	4
H	G and E	6
J	H	3
K	H	2
L	K	4
M	J and L	2

APMP topic 3.3

1 Using the information given in Table 5.10 draw a network, and identify the critical path, total and free floats. Use the network to draw a Gantt chart. Indicate the free and total floats on the chart.

   Derive a resource histogram and cumulative resource curve ('S' curve) from the Gantt chart. Table 5.10 gives the resources per activity.

   What could be done to reduce the peak resource demand on day 9?

2 Explain the difference between resource smoothing and resource levelling and give an example of when each might be used.

APMP topic 3.4

1 Explain the difference between commitment and accrual, and state four benefits of cost management.
2 State four benefits of budgeting and cost management.
3 Explain the difference between planned expenditure, commitments, accruals and actual expenditure.

APMP topic 4.3

1 Explain bottom-up estimating. Include a diagram to illustrate your answer.
2 Explain comparative estimating.
3 Explain parametric estimating.
4 Explain three-point estimating.
5 Describe five practical problems of estimating across the project lifecycle.

Table 5.10 Resources per activity

Activity	Predecessor	Duration (weeks)	Resources
A	–	3	3
B	–	4	2
C	A	2	4
D	C	1	4
E	B	4	1
F	E	5	2
G	E	2	3
H	D	3	3
J	G and F	1	2
K	J and H	4	4
L	J	6	1
M	L and K	3	3

6

Controls

6 Controls

6.1 PURPOSE

The purpose of this chapter is to describe project controls from three perspectives:

- Controlled Start – to ensure that only viable projects are undertaken and that appropriate plans are put in place at the beginning of the project. This is achieved by having a well-documented Project Initiation Document (PRINCE2) or Project Management Plan (APMP) (APMP topic 2.4)
- Controlled Progress – to ensure that the project remains viable against its Business Case, is producing the required products in line with defined quality criteria, and is being carried out to schedule and in accordance with its resource and cost plans. Approaches to help achieve this include Earned Value Management and Information Management and Reporting (APMP topics 3.6 and 3.7)
- Controlled Close – to ensure that all the agreed products have been delivered and accepted, arrangements are in place to support and maintain the product in its useful life (Handover and Closeout), and that any useful statistics or lessons for later projects are passed to the relevant body and that a plan has been made to check on the achievement of the benefits claimed in the project's Business Case (Project Reviews) (APMP topics 6.5 and 6.6).

6.2 DEFINITIONS

There are slightly different definitions of the key terms regarding controls in PRINCE2 and the APM Body of Knowledge (Table 6.1).

6.3 CONTROLLED START

The Controlled Start of the project covers the first two processes within the PRINCE2 process model or the first two phases of the project lifecycle (Table 6.2).

6.3.1 Starting up a Project/Concept

Starting up a Project (or Concept phase) establishes the need, problem or opportunity for the project. The project's feasibility is investigated and a preferred solution identified; if supported, the project continues to Initiation (or Definition) phase.

According to PRINCE2, the main outputs of this process are the:

- **Project Brief**. This establishes the initial Project Definition (including the project objectives, scope and constraints), includes the outline Business Case, identifies the initial risks, and records the Customer's Quality Expectations and the related Acceptance Criteria. Its purpose is to provide a full and firm foundation for the initiation of the project
- **Project Approach**. This defines the type of solution to be developed by the project and/or the method of delivering that solution. It should also identify any environment into which the solution must fit.

According to the APM Body of Knowledge, the output of this process is the:

- **Business Case**. This provides justification for undertaking a project, in terms of evaluating the benefit, cost and risk of alternative options and the rationale for the preferred solution. Its purpose is to obtain management commitment and approval for the investment in the project. The Business Case is owned by the Sponsor/Executive of the Project Board.

Table 6.1 Comparison of the definitions of key terms regarding controls

PRINCE2	Definition	APM Body of Knowledge	Definition
Project Initiation Document (PID)	A logical document that brings together the key information needed to start the project on a sound basis and to convey that information to all concerned with the project	Project Management Plan (PMP)	A plan that brings together all the plans for a project. The purpose of the PMP is to document the outcome of the planning process and to provide the reference document for managing the project. The PMP is owned by the Project Manager
Checkpoint Report	A progress report of the information gathered at a checkpoint meeting, which is given by a team to the Project Manager and provides data as defined in the Work Package	Progress Report	A regular report to senior personnel, sponsors or stakeholders, summarizing the progress of a project including key events, milestones, costs and other issues
Highlight Report	Time-driven report from the Project Manager to the Project Board on stage progress		
Exception Report	Description of the exception situation, its impact, options, recommendation and impact of the recommendation to the Project Board	Exception Report	A focused report drawing attention to instances where planned and actual results are expected to be, or are already, significantly different
End Stage Assessment	The review by the Project Board and Project Manager of the End Stage Report to decide whether to approve the next Stage Plan	Gate Review	A formal point in a project where its expected worth, progress, cost and execution plan are reviewed and a decision made whether to continue with the next phase or stage of the project

PRINCE2	Definition	APM Body of Knowledge	Definition
Post-Project Review	One or more reviews held after project closure to determine if the expected benefits have been obtained	Post-Project Review	Undertaken after the project deliverables have been handed over and before final closeout, this review is intended to produce lessons that will enable continuous improvement
		Benefit Realization Review	A review undertaken after a period of operation of the project deliverables. It is intended to establish that project benefits have or are being realized

The APM Body of Knowledge definitions are extracts from the *APM Body of Knowledge 5th Edition*, reproduced with the permission of the Association for Project Management

Table 6.2 Processes and phases covered by the controlled start

	PRINCE2 processes	APM project lifecycle phases
Controlled Start	Starting up a Project (SU)	Concept
	Initiating a Project (IP)	Definition

Although the two approaches use different terms to describe the outputs of this process/phase, the information contained in the outputs is very similar.

6.3.2 Definition/Initiating a Project

Initiating a Project undertakes further evaluation of the preferred solution and the options to meet that solution, and prepares the plans necessary for the implementation of the project.

According to PRINCE2, the main output of this phase is the **Project Initiation Document** (PID). This defines the project to form the basis for its management and the assessment of overall success. It gives the direction and scope of the project and forms the contract between the Project Manager and the Project Board. The purpose of the PID is to provide a sound basis for the Project

Board to make a major commitment to the project and to act as a baseline against which to assess progress. The PID is the responsibility of the Project Manager.

According to the APM Body of Knowledge, the output of this phase is the **Project Management Plan** (PMP).

This is a plan that brings together all of the plans for a project. The purpose of the PMP is to document the outcome of the planning process and to provide the reference document for managing the project. The Project Management Plan is owned by the Project Manager.

Source: *APM Body of Knowledge 5th Edition*, with permission of the Association for Project Management.

It confirms the agreements between the Project Sponsor and other stakeholders and the Project Manager.

Again, although the two approaches use different terms to describe the output of this process/phase, each documents how the project will be managed in terms of why, what, how (and how much), who, when and where. Also, the information contained in the PMP and PID is very similar (Table 6.3).

6.4 CONTROLLED PROGRESS

The Controlled Progress of the project covers three overlapping processes in the PRINCE2 process model, which correspond to the third phase of the project lifecycle (Table 6.4).

This phase of the project implements the project strategy and plan. It is often divided into two or more stages. At the end of each stage, an End Stage Assessment (PRINCE2) or a Gate Review (APM Body of Knowledge) is held to review the expected worth, progress, cost and execution plan, and to decide whether to continue with the next stage of the project. Accordingly, the focus during the controlled middle is on the controlled production of the agreed products:

- To stated quality standards
- Within cost, effort and time agreed
- Ultimately to achieve defined benefits.

Two important aspects of Controlled Progress are Earned Value Management and Information Management, each of which are described in the following sections.

6.4.1 Earned Value Management

Earned Value Management is a project control process based on a structured approach to planning, cost collection and performance measurement. It facilitates the integration of project scope, time and cost objectives and the establishment of a baseline plan for performance measurement.

Source: *APM Body of Knowledge 5th Edition*, with permission of the Association for Project Management.

A key concept in PRINCE2 is tolerance. Tolerance is the permissible deviation from plan without bringing the deviation to the attention of the next higher authority. It reflects the reality that all plans are based on estimates and, by definition, that it is unlikely that actual outcomes will exactly correspond to these estimates. To avoid the Project Manager having to report to the Project Board every time it is forecast that the estimates will not be achieved (which would probably be a daily occurrence), tolerance levels are agreed. Having agreed these tolerances, however, the Project Manager must advise the Executive whenever it is forecast that the tolerances may be exceeded.

The question that this poses the Project Manager is whether the plan performance is within or outside of the tolerance bounds. Earned Value Management provides one means of answering this question.

Table 6.3 Information contained in the Project Initiation Document and the Project Management Plan

	Project Initiation Document	Project Management Plan (APM)
WHY	Initial Business Case	Business Case
WHAT	Project Definition:	
	▨ Project objectives	Objectives
	▨ Project scope	Scope
	▨ Project deliverables	Deliverables with acceptance criteria
	▨ Exclusions	Project success criteria and key performance indicators
	▨ Constraints	Constraints
	▨ Interfaces	Assumptions
	▨ Assumptions	Dependencies
HOW	Project Approach	Strategies for:
	Project controls and tolerances	▨ Project Management
	Communication Plan	▨ Handover
	Project Quality Plan, which includes:	▨ Monitoring and Control
	▨ Change Control approach	▨ Reporting
	▨ Configuration Management Plan	▨ Quality Management
		▨ Communication
		▨ Change Control
		▨ Configuration Management
		▨ Governance
		▨ Health, safety and environmental matters
		▨ Procurement
		▨ Risk Management
HOW MUCH	Project Plan, which includes:	Project budget
	▨ Project schedule	Budgeting and cost management process
	▨ Project financial budget	
	▨ Table of resources required	

Table 6.3 *continued*

	Project Initiation Document	Project Management Plan (APM)
WHEN		Project schedule
WHO	Project organization structure	Project roles and responsibilities
		Resource plan
WHERE		Geographical location(s) where the work will be performed

Table 6.4 Processes and phases covered by Controlled Progress

	PRINCE2 processes	APM project lifecycle phases
Controlled Progress	Controlling a Stage (CS); Managing Product Delivery (MP); Managing Stage Boundaries (SB)	Implementation

The earned value approach is based on assigning a value to achievement of project work:

- Achievement relates to the achievement of a milestone or the completion of products
- Value is usually measured in monetary terms but can be expressed in any appropriate unit of effort, e.g. person-hours
- The value to be earned when a specific milestone is achieved (or product completed) is based on the planned cost of achieving that milestone (or producing the product).

Earned Value Management replaces the traditional approach of simply comparing planned to actual costs as a means of assessing progress. However, the approach does require a plan that clearly specifies when milestones or products are to be achieved. The milestones/products must have the following characteristics:

- They must represent well-defined events
- There must be a clear relationship between the milestones/products and activities within the plan

- There must be quantifiable criteria for assessing achievement of the milestones/products
- The achievement must be defined at a specific point in time.

Figure 6.1 is a graphical representation of a plan showing the planned duration and budgeted cost. The line shows the planned cost or cumulative cost curve.

Figure 6.1 Budgeted Cost and Planned Duration

BAC = Budget at completion
PC   = Planned cost

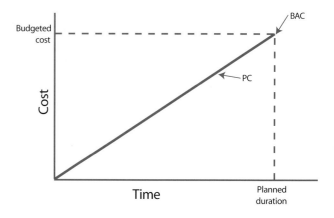

Figure 6.2 Actual Cost and Earned Value

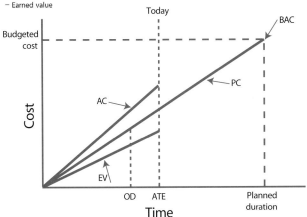

BAC = Budget at completion
PC = Planned cost
OD = Original duration planned
ATE = Actual time expended
AC = Actual cost
EV − Earned value

Figure 6.3 Cost and Schedule Variances

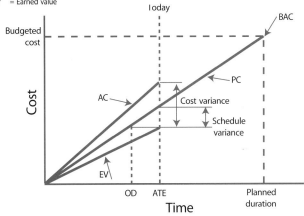

BAC = Budget at completion
PC = Planned cost
OD = Original duration planned
ATE = Actual time expended
AC = Actual cost
EV = Earned value

After a period of monitoring it will be possible to assess progress in terms of:

- The Actual Cost of the work that has been performed (AC)
- The Budgeted Cost of the work that has been performed or Earned Value (EV).

Figure 6.2 shows this information plotted against the original plan.

Based on the above information, performance analysis can be undertaken (Table 6.5).

- Positive cost or schedule variances are favourable in that they suggest that the plan is either under-spent or ahead of schedule.
- Negative cost or schedule variances are unfavourable in that they suggest that the plan is either over-spent or behind schedule.

Figure 6.3 shows these calculations in graphical form.

Table 6.5 Analysis of Cost and Schedule Variances

Analysis	Calculation	Explanation
Cost Variance (CV)	CV = EV − AC	Earned Value (EV) can be established from the plan by multiplying the budget for the activities by the percentage complete. Actual Cost (AC) needs to be obtained from the person responsible for each of the activities.
Schedule Variance (SV)	SV = EV − PC	Planned Cost (PC) can be established from the plan.

Table 6.6 Calculation of performance indices

Analysis	Calculation	Explanation
Cost Performance Index (CPI)	CPI =EV/AC	This provides a direct comparison of what has been achieved (Earned Value) to what has been paid for (Actual Cost).
Schedule Performance Index (SPI)	SPI =EV/PC	This provides a direct comparison of what has been achieved (Earned Value) to what had been expected to have been achieved in the same time (Planned Cost)

The same data used in Figure 6.3 can be expressed as ratios that provide an indication of the value for money achieved to date. These ratios are known as performance indices and may be arrived at as shown in Table 6.6.

■ Ratios equal to or greater than 1 are favourable in that they suggest that the work is proceeding to plan, or better than planned.

■ Ratios less than 1 are unfavourable in that they suggest that the work is proceeding worse than planned.

The performance indices in Table 6.6 can also be used to assess the efficiency and effectiveness of the team:

Efficiency = CPI × 100%

Effectiveness = SPI × 100%

A useful way to use Earned Value data to show trends, is to plot CPI and SPI over a period of time (Figure 6.4). The lines drawn should reveal very accurately the direction of the plan. This diagram may also be used to demonstrate the effect of any recovery action.

Figure 6.4 Trend analyses of Cost Performance Index (CPI) and Schedule Performance Index (SPI)

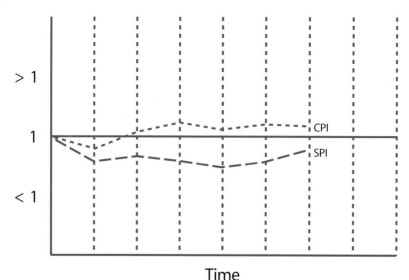

Table 6.7 Calculation of plan completion cost

Analysis	Calculation	Explanation
Estimated Cost at Completion (EAC)	EAC = BAC/CPI	BAC stands for budget at completion, i.e. the total planned cost of work. The EAC figure can be used to assess whether the plan is likely to be completed within the agreed cost tolerances
Estimated Time at Completion (ETC)	ETC = OD/SPI	Again, the ETC figure can be used to assess whether the plan is likely to be completed within the agreed time tolerances

The information can also be used to forecast plan completion cost and time (Table 6.7).

Figure 6.5 shows this information graphically.

Finally, the same information can be used to calculate the percentage complete figure, where:

Percentage complete = (Earned Value/Budget at Completion) × 100

Whilst there are clear advantages from using Earned Value analysis to assess progress of a plan care should be exercised as:

- The data derived is only as good as the data entered
- If new to the principles of Earned Value, the project team may resist its introduction
- The visibility of data produced could reinforce an existing blame culture which itself could be counter-productive

Figure 6.5 Estimated Cost and Time at Completion

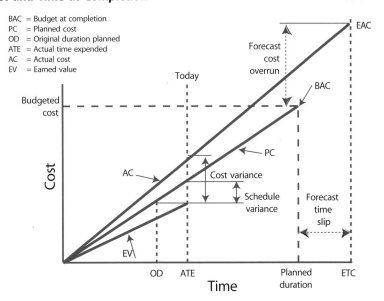

- Used on its own, it could result in the Project Manager missing other important indicators, for example:
  - Earned Value does not take into account the Critical Path
  - A low value item may not register any concerns in Earned Value calculations but could be hindering progress across a range of subsequent activities.

6.4.2 Information management

Information management is the collection, storage, dissemination, archiving and appropriate destruction of project information.

Source: *APM Body of Knowledge 5th Edition*, with permission of the Association for Project Management.

Over the lifecycle of a project a great deal of information is received, analysed and produced. Accordingly, there needs to be a suitable process to manage this information. This process must be aligned to the project's Communication

Table 6.8 Essential elements of an information management process

Collection	Information is collected from a number of sources and the flow of this information needs to be actively managed. Information may be either: ▨ Acquired, i.e. information that already exists elsewhere is acquired from the available sources for use within the project ▨ Created, i.e. information that has to be created by some intellectual and/or automated means within the project A decision needs to be taken as to the level of detail of information that requires collection (and subsequently storage and archiving)
Storage	Once information has been collected, decisions need to be made regarding: ▨ What information should be stored ▨ How this information will be stored so that it can be readily accessed and retrieved
Dissemination	This may involve: ▨ Distributing information in its existing format ▨ Converting information into reports for distribution to members of the project management team and other stakeholders
Archiving	This should be done throughout the lifecycle of a project. Archiving means that information is removed to a secure location but is no longer immediately accessible. This provides a repository for historic records, an audit trail for any future audit, a record of planned and actual performance, and details of any lessons learned
Destruction	After a period of time, information that has been archived can be destroyed in accordance with organizational procedures

Plan and to the organization's own information management process, e.g. consideration may need to be given to commercial confidentiality and statutory obligations such as information security and freedom of information.

The essential elements of an information management process are given in Table 6.8.

Information management changes during the project lifecycle in terms of:

- What information needs to be collected and stored
- Who the information need to be disseminated to
- When to archive and when to destroy information

6.4.3   Information reporting

Information reporting takes information and presents it in an appropriate format which includes the formal communication of project information to stakeholders.

Source: *APM Body of Knowledge 5th Edition*, with permission of the Association for Project Management.

Some reports will be produced during the phase or stage, and others will be produced towards the end of a phase or stage. Table 6.9 shows the PRINCE2 reports that are usually produced as part of Controlled Progress.

Table 6.10 shows a further report that may need to be produced.

6.4.4   Project reviews

Project reviews take place throughout the project lifecycle to check the likely or actual achievement of the objectives specified in the Project Management Plan (or Project Initiation Document) and the benefits detailed in the Business Case. Additional reviews will take place following handover and closeout to ensure that the benefits are being realized by the organization.

Source: *APM Body of Knowledge 5th Edition*, with permission of the Association for Project Management.

Reviews should be undertaken throughout the project lifecycle. They enable the project management team to assess and review the work undertaken so far. In the APM Body of Knowledge these are known as Gate Reviews or project evaluation reviews, and in PRINCE2 they are known as End Stage Assessments, but the nature and objectives of each are broadly the same.

A Management Stage is a PRINCE2 concept. Management Stages are partitions within the Definition and Implementation Phases of the project with decision points. A Management Stage is a collection of activities and products whose delivery is managed as a unit. As such, a stage is a subset of the project and in PRINCE2 terms is the element of work that the Project Manager is managing on behalf of the Project Board at any one time. The use of stages in a PRINCE2 project is mandatory and every PRINCE2 project should consist of at least two stages, Initiation (or the Definition Phase) and one other (or the Implementation and Handover and Closeout Phases).

Table 6.9 PRINCE2 reports produced as part of Controlled Progress

Checkpoint Report	A checkpoint is a time-driven control when the status of work in a team is ascertained. It involves the people doing the work and is carried out by the Team Manager. This could be undertaken by way of a formal meeting or more informally. The information gathered at a checkpoint is recorded in a Checkpoint Report for submission to the Project Manager. The typical contents of a Checkpoint Report are:

- Date and period covered
- Follow-ups from previous reports
- Activities during the period
- Products completed during the period
- Quality work carried out during the period
- Tolerance status
- Update on risks and issues
- Work planned for the next period
- Products to be completed during the next period

Highlight Report	A Highlight Report is a time-driven report on the status of a stage's progress from the Project Manager to the Project Sponsor and other stakeholders (or the Project Board). The Project Manager will use the information received from the Checkpoint Reports as a basis for the Highlight Report. The typical contents of a Highlight Report are:

- Date and period covered
- Budget status
- Schedule status
- Tolerance situation
- Update on risks and issues
- Products completed during the period
- Products to be completed during the next period

End Stage Report	An End Stage Report provides a summary of progress to date, the overall project situation and sufficient information to ask for a Project Board or Steering Group decision on what to do next. The typical contents of an End Stage Report are:

- Current Stage Plan with actuals
- Performance against stage tolerances
- Project Plan outlook
- Business Case review
- Risk review

Table 6.10 Other PRINCE2 reports produced as part of Controlled Progress

Exception Report	An Exception Report is a warning to the Project Sponsor and other stakeholders (or the Project Board) that a serious problem exists that needs a decision such as a Stage or Project Plan deviating outside its tolerance margins. The typical contents of an Exception Report are: ▓ Description of the cause of a deviation from the plan ▓ Consequences of the deviation ▓ Available options ▓ Effect of each option on the Business Case, risks and tolerances ▓ Project Manager's recommendation

The process of defining where stages should be placed during the Implementation phase is fundamentally a process of balancing:

■ Where the key decision points need to be in the project

■ The amount of risk within a project

■ How far ahead in the project it is sensible to plan

■ Too many small stages versus too few big ones.

The purpose of a Gate Review or End Stage Assessment is to approve the work to date and provide authority to proceed to the next stage. A stage should not be considered complete until it has received this formal approval.

The specific objectives of a Gate Review or End Stage Assessment are to:

■ Review the project against its Business Case and ensure that the project is still viable

■ Review the results of the stage against the Stage Plan

■ Satisfy the Project Board about the quality of the products delivered

■ Establish that the current stage has been completed satisfactorily

■ Check whether any external event has changed the project's assumptions

■ Perform a risk analysis and management review of the project and the next Stage Plan and incorporate the results into the next Stage Plan and Project Plan

■ Review overall project status against the Project Plan (which may now have been revised)

■ Review the next Stage Plan against the Project Plan

■ Ensure that a complete and consistent baseline is established for the next stage

■ Review the tolerances set for the next stage

■ Ensure that the specialist aspects of the project are still sound

■ Confirm the resource availability for the next stage

■ Authorize the passage of the project into the next stage (if the Business Case continues to be viable).

Within a PRINCE2 project, the preparation work for an End Stage Assessment is carried out by the Project Manager by undertaking the 'Managing Stage Boundaries' process and producing an End Stage Report. The typical contents of an End Stage Report are:

■ Current Stage Plan with actuals

■ Performance against tolerances

■ Project Plan outlook

■ Business Case review

■ Risk review

■ Project Issue situation

■ Quality statistics

■ Project Manager's report on any events that affected stage performance.

Table 6.11 Process and Phases covered by Controlled Close

	PRINCE2 processes	APM project lifecycle phases
Controlled Close	Closing a Project (CP)	Handover and Closeout

6.4.5 Audits

> Audits are reviews undertaken by a group outside of the project management team. This can be an independent project office, internal audit or a third-party organization. The purpose of an audit is to provide an objective evaluation of the project.
>
> Source: *APM Body of Knowledge 5th Edition*, with permission of the Association for Project Management.

6.5 CONTROLLED CLOSE

The Controlled Close of the project covers the Closing a Project process, which corresponds to the final phase of the project lifecycle (Table 6.11).

> Handover and closeout is the fourth and final phase in the project lifecycle. During this phase final project deliverables (or products) are handed over to the sponsor and users (or the Project Board). Closeout is the process of finalizing all project matters, carrying out final project reviews, archiving project information and redeploying the project team.
>
> Source: *APM Body of Knowledge 5th Edition*, with permission of the Association for Project Management.

6.5.1 Handover

The Handover process broadly aligns to the PRINCE2 sub-process of 'Decommissioning a Project', the key outputs of which are:

- Configuration Audit – confirmation that all of the component products have been approved
- Customer Acceptance – confirmation that the customer accepts the products
- Operational and Maintenance Acceptance – confirmation that the product can be operated and supported
- Project Closure Recommendation – stating that the project is about to close and that supporting facilities and resources will no longer be needed
- Archived project information.

6.5.2 Closeout

The Closeout process broadly aligns to the PRINCE2 sub-processes of 'Identifying Follow-on Actions' and 'Evaluating a Project', key outputs of which are:

- Post-Project Review Plan – a suggested plan for the Post-Project review for ratification by the Project Board. The purpose of the Post-Project Review is to establish whether the expected benefits have been realized and whether the product has caused any problems in use
- Follow-on Action Recommendations – recommendations for further work, which the Project Board must direct to the appropriate audience for attention
- Lessons Learned Report – to pass on any lessons that can be usefully applied to other projects
- End Project Report – the Project Manager's report on how well the project has performed against the PID, including the original planned costs, schedule and tolerances, the revised Business Case and final version of the Project Plan.

Table 6.12 Reported figures after 10 months (budget £1 million)

Cost type	Amount
Planned Costs	£600,000
Actual Costs	£500,000
Earned Value	£460,000

Table 6.13 Reported figures after 10 months (budget £1.6 million)

Cost type	Amount
Planned Costs	£700,000
Actual Costs	£800,000
Earned Value	£850,000

(NB: In the APM Body of Knowledge, the 'Post-Project Review' is the name given to a review that is undertaken after the project deliverables have been handed over but before final closeout. This review is intended to produce lessons learned that will enable continuous improvement. This is totally different to PRINCE2, where the 'Post-Project Review' is the name given to a review held after project closure to determine if the expected benefits have been obtained. In the APM Body of Knowledge such a review is known as a 'Benefit Realization Review', and is described as a review undertaken after a period of operations of the project deliverables. It is intended to establish that the project benefits have or are being realized.)

6.6 CONTROLS – EXERCISES

(Sample answers are provided in Appendix A for the first question within each section, except for section 3.6, where answers are provided for the first three questions. Answers to the remaining questions can be assessed against the relevant section within the chapter.)

APMP topic 2.4

1 List and briefly describe 10 fundamental parts of the Project Management Plan.
2 Explain the purpose of the Project Management Plan.
3 Describe the authorship, ownership and audience of the Project Management Plan.

APMP topic 3.6

1 Consider a project with a budget of £1 million (BAC). It has a planned duration of 18 months. Table 6.12 shows the reported figures after 10 months.

   Calculate the CPI, CV, SPI, SV, Final Cost, Final Planned Duration and % Complete. Comment on the figures you have calculated.

2 Consider a project with a budget of £1.6 million (BAC). It has a planned duration of 24 months. Table 6.13 shows the reported figures after 10 months.

   Calculate the CPI, CV, SPI, SV, Final Coat, Final Planned Duration and % Complete. Comment on the figures you have calculated.

3 Complete Table 6.14, calculating the Earned Value (EV), the Efficiency and the % Complete for weeks 4, 8, 12, 16 and 20. What can you conclude from the results?

   NB: This question will take more than 15 minutes – it provides practice of the calculations and interpretation of results.

4 Describe how Earned Value Management can be used.
5 Explain three advantages and three disadvantages of Earned Value Management.

APMP topic 3.7

1 Explain the purpose of archiving project documentation, making five relevant points.
2 Explain project reporting.

Table 6.14 Calculating the Earned Value (EV), Efficiency and % Complete (all figures for Budget and Actual Costs in man/hours)

Activity	Budget	Week 4				Week 8				Week 12				Week 16				Week 20			
		% Complete	Actual Costs	EV	Efficiency	% Complete	Actual Costs	EV	Efficiency	% Complete	Actual Costs	EV	Efficiency	% Complete	Actual Costs	EV	Efficiency	% Complete	Actual Costs	EV	Efficiency
A	300	20	65			30	85			50	130			80	180			100	240		
B	400	15	70			25	120			40	180			60	250			100	420		
C	500	10	90			20	200			50	450			70	600			90	750		
D	200	5	12			10	23			20	45			50	110			70	155		
E	350	0	0			5	20			15	58			40	150			50	180		
F	240	0	0			5	14			10	30			30	90			40	115		
TOTALS	1,990		237				462				893				1,380				1,860		
BAC	1,990																				

APMP topic 6.5

1 Explain five benefits of formally closing a project.
2 Explain a process for project handover describing five major elements.
3 Describe why project handover is important, making five relevant points.
4 Describe why project closeout is important, making five relevant points.

APMP topic 6.6

1 Explain five types of project review.
2 Explain gate reviews.
3 Describe audits.
4 Describe post-project reviews.
5 Describe benefit realization reviews.
6 Explain five benefits of project reviews.

Management of Risk 7

7 Management of Risk

7.1 PURPOSE

Project risk management is a structured process that allows individual risk events and overall project risk to be understood and managed proactively, optimizing project success by minimizing threats and maximizing opportunities.

Source: *APM Body of Knowledge 5th Edition*, with permission of the Association for Project Management.

The purpose of this chapter is to describe a project risk management process, explain each step within this process and explain the benefits of project risk management (APMP topic 2.5). This is achieved by considering:

- A project risk management approach
- A risk management process
- The benefits of risk management.

This chapter also explains the importance of health, safety and environmental management, as these can be considered as specialist aspects of risk management (APMP topic 2.7).

Whereas the previous chapters have been based on PRINCE2, this chapter is based on the OGC publication *Management of Risk: Guidance for Practitioners* (M_o_R) because with effect from the next refresh of PRINCE2, it will be aligned to the M_o_R guide. A comparison is also provided of M_o_R to the APM publication *Project Risk Analysis and Management Guide 2nd Edition* (PRAM).

7.2 DEFINITIONS

There are slightly different definitions of the terms related to the management of risk in M_o_R and the APM Body of Knowledge (Table 7.1).

7.3 RISK MANAGEMENT

The purpose of risk management is to ensure that the project makes cost-effective use of a risk management process that includes a series of well-defined steps. The aim is to support better decision-making through a good understanding of risks and their likely impact.

The term risk management refers to the systematic application of processes to the tasks of identifying and assessing risks, and then planning and implementing risk responses. This provides a disciplined environment for proactive decision-making.

For risk management to be effective, risks need to be:

- Identified – this includes risks being considered that could affect the achievement of the project's objectives, and then described to ensure that there is a common understanding of these risks
- Assessed – this includes ensuring that each risk can be ranked in terms of estimated likelihood, impact and immediacy; and understanding the overall level of risk associated with the project
- Controlled – this includes identifying appropriate responses to risks, assigning owners and then executing, monitoring and controlling these responses.

7.4 PROJECT RISK MANAGEMENT APPROACH

A major factor determining how risk management is undertaken within any given project will be the way in which risks are managed across the organization. A starting point, therefore, will be to review the organization's Risk Management Policy and/or Risk Management Process Guide (or similar documents).

Table 7.1 Comparison of the definitions of key terms related to Management of Risk

Management of Risk (M_o_R)		APM Body of Knowledge	
Risk	An uncertain event or set of events that, should it occur, will have an effect on the achievement of objectives. A risk is measured by a combination of the probability of a perceived threat or opportunity occuring and the magnitude of its impact on objectives	Project Risk	The exposure of stakeholders to the consequences or variation in outcome
		Risk event	An uncertain event or set of circumstances that should it or they occur would have an effect on the achievement of one or more of the project objectives
Risk Management Strategy	Describes the goals of applying risk management to the project, a description of the process that will be adopted, the roles and responsibilities, risk thresholds, the timing of risk management interventions, the deliverables, the tools and techniques that will be used and reporting requirements	Risk Management Plan	A document defining how risk management is to be implemented in the context of the particular project concerned.
Risk Register	A record of all identified risks relating to a project, including their status and history. Also called a Risk Log	Risk Log	A document that provides identification, estimation, impact evaluation and countermeasures for all risks to the project. Also called a Risk Register

The APM Body of Knowledge definitions are extracts from the *APM Body of Knowledge 5th Edition*, reproduced with the permission of the Association for Project Management

The organization's Risk Management Policy communicates how risk management will be implemented throughout the organization to support the realization of its strategic objectives. This will include information such as the organization's risk appetite and capacity, risk tolerance thresholds, procedures for escalation, and defined roles and responsibilities. The Risk Management Process Guide describes the series of steps and their respective associated activities necessary to implement risk management. This guide should provide a best practice approach that will support a consistent method of risk management across the organization. Such a process is placed into a project context below.

The project approach to risk management will consist of its own strategy, processes (including planning for implementation), and means of delivery (such as the Risk Register).

7.4.1 Project Risk Management Strategy (or Plan)

Having reviewed the organizational level documents, and before embarking on any risk management activities, a Risk Management Strategy (or Plan) should be developed for the project. The purpose of this strategy/plan is to describe the specific risk management activities that will be undertaken to support effective risk management within the project.

The strategy/plan will typically include:

- Introduction – states the purpose and owner of the strategy/plan.
- Outline of the project – provides a summary of the project to which the strategy/plan relates.
- Roles and responsibilities – describes the main roles and responsibilities within the project.
- The process – this will be based on the Risk Management Process Guide but may be adapted as necessary depending on the nature of the project.
- Scales for estimating probability and impact – these should be developed for each project to ensure that the scales for cost and time (for instance) are relevant to the cost and timeframe of the project. These may be shown in the form of probability impact grids giving the criteria for each level within the scale, e.g. for 'very high', 'high', 'medium', 'low', and 'very low'.
- Expected value – provides guidance on calculating expected value, which is done by multiplying the average impact by the probability percentage of each risk. By totalling the expected values for all the risks

associated with a project, an understanding of the total risk exposure faced by the project can be calculated.

- Proximity – provides guidance on how this time factor for risks is to be assessed. Proximity reflects the fact that risks will occur at particular times and the severity of their impact will vary according to when they occur.
- Risk response category – the responses available will depend on whether the risk is a perceived threat or an opportunity. Table 7.4 below describes the alternative responses for a threat and Table 7.5 describes those for an opportunity.
- Budget required – describes the budget required to support risk management throughout the life of the project.
- Tools and techniques – refers to any preferred techniques to be used for each step of the process described above.
- Templates – these might include a Risk Register.
- Early warning indicators – these will be selected for their relevancy to the project.
- Timing of risk management activities – will state when formal risk management activities are to be undertaken, as part of End Stage Assessments.
- Reporting – describes the reports that are to be produced and record their purpose, timing and recipients.

7.4.2 Risk Register

The purpose of the Risk Register is to capture and maintain information on all of the identified threats and opportunities relating to the project. The typical content of a Risk Register will be:

- Risk identifier
- Risk category
- Risk cause

- Risk event (threat or opportunity)
- Risk effect (description in words of the impact)
- Probability (pre-response action)
- Probability (post-response action)
- Impact (pre-response action)
- Impact (post-response action)
- Expected Value (pre-response action)
- Expected Value (post-response action)
- Proximity
- Risk response categories
- Risk response actions
- Residual risk
- Risk status
- Risk owner
- Risk actionee.

7.5 RISK MANAGEMENT PROCESS

This section describes the risk management process. The M_o_R risk management process (Figure 7.1) is divided into four primary risk management processes and four secondary processes known as:

- Identify
  - Identify – Context
  - Identify the Risks
- Assess
  - Assess – Estimate
  - Assess – Evaluate
- Plan
- Implement.

This compares with the PRAM Guide process, which has six processes (Figure 7.2; reproduced with the kind permission of the Association for Project Management).

Figure 7.1 The project risk management process

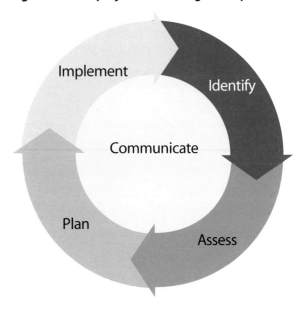

Figure 7.2 The PRAM risk management process (reproduced from Project Risk Analysis and Management Guide 2nd Edition)

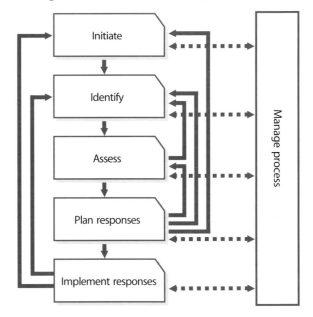

Table 7.2 Comparison of the M_o_R and PRAM processes

M_o_R Process	PRAM Process	Comments
Steps:	Phases:	
▨ Identify – Context	▨ Initiate	Both gather information about the project as a starting point for risk management and define how risk management will be undertaken within the particular project
▨ Identify the Risks	▨ Identify	Both identify the threats and opportunities that could impact on the achievement of the project's objectives
▨ Assess	▨ Assess	Both include estimating the probability and impact of individual risks and then combining these to evaluate the overall risk exposure of the project
▨ Plan	▨ Plan responses	Both consider a range of possible response types to help plan specific responses to the risks identified
▨ Implement	▨ Implement responses	Both implement the planned responses and monitor and review the effectiveness of these responses

The M_o_R process is very similar to the PRAM process (Table 7.2).

The M_o_R project risk management processes are described in the following sections.

7.5.1 Identify – Context

The primary process goal of the Context step within the Identify process is to obtain information about the project. This will include understanding:

■ What the project's objectives are
■ What the scope of the project is
■ What assumptions have been made
■ How complete the information is

■ Who the stakeholders are and what their objectives are
■ Where the project fits in relation to the organizational structure
■ The organization's own environment (industry, markets, products and services etc.)
■ The organization's approach to risk management as described by the Risk Management Policy.

It is also within the process step that the Risk Management Strategy/Plan for the project is prepared to describe how risks will be managed on the project.

7.5.1 Identify – Identify the risks

The primary goal of this step within the Identify process is to identify the threats to the project that would reduce or remove the likelihood of the project reaching its objectives, while maximizing the opportunities that could lead to improved performance. This will include:

■ Identifying the threats and opportunities to the project
■ Preparing a Risk Register
■ Preparing key performance indicators
■ Understanding the stakeholders' view of the risks.

Risks can be identified using a number of approaches such as:

■ Risk Checklists
■ Risk Prompt Lists
■ Risk Breakdown Structure
■ Risk Identification Workshops
■ Brainstorming
■ Assumption analysis
■ Constraints analysis
■ Interviews.

An important aspect of identifying risk is being able to provide a clear and unambiguous expression of each risk. A useful way of expressing risk is to consider the following aspect of each risk:

■ **Risk cause**. This should describe the source of the risk, i.e. the event or situation that gives rise to the risk. These are often referred to as risk drivers. They are not risks in themselves, but the potential trigger points for risk. These may be either internal or external to the project.
■ **Risk event**. This should describe the area of uncertainty in terms of the threat or the opportunity.
■ **Risk effect**. This should describe the impact/s that the risk would have on the project should the risk materialize.

This could be expressed as follows: Because it has been raining heavily (risk cause), there is a risk that the river flowing through the farmer's field might overflow (risk event), which would severely damage his crop (risk effect).

Or: Because the weather has been particularly mild this winter (risk cause), there is an opportunity that fewer people will be hospitalized with influenza (risk event), which will mean that there will be less disruption to planned routine operations (risk effect).

7.5.3 Assess – Estimate

The primary goal of the Estimate step within the Assess process is to assess the threats and the opportunities to the project in terms of their probability and impact. The risk proximity will also be of interest to gauge how quickly the risk is likely to materialize if no action was taken. This will require an understanding of:

■ The probability of the threats and opportunities in terms of how likely they are to occur
■ The impact of each threat and opportunity in terms of the project objectives. For example, if the objectives are measured in time and cost, the impact should also be measured in units of time and cost
■ The proximity of these threats and opportunities with regard to when they might materialize.

A useful way of summarizing the set of risks and their estimations is to plot them onto a Summary Risk Profile, based on a previously agreed Probability Impact Grid.

An example of a Probability Impact Grid is shown in Figure 7.3. As can be seen, the ranking priority order for risks is weighted towards impact rather than probability. Thus, a very high-impact/very low-probability risk is considered to be of more concern than a very low-impact/ very high-probability risk. This weighting is likely to be appropriate to most projects, as high impacts are often disproportionately severe in comparison with low impacts, and because the highest impact band in any scale is usually classified as having no upper limit.

Applying such rankings, each risk can then be plotted on a Summary Risk Profile, an example of which is shown in Figure 7.4. Here a number of risks have been plotted based on their estimated impact and probability.

From Figure 7.4 it is relatively easy to identify the most important risks. The top 10 risks in the above example are shown in Table 7.3.

7.5.4 Assess – Evaluate

The primary goal of the Evaluate step within the Assess process is to understand the net effect of the identified threats and opportunities on a project when aggregated together. This may include preparing, for example, the following:

- An estimated monetary value (EMV) calculation, which records the weighted average of the anticipated impact
- A risk model, which aggregates the risks together using a simulation technique
- A net present value (NPV) calculation using an accepted discount rate.

Figure 7.3 Probability Impact Grid

Probability	0.9	Very high 71–90%	0.045	0.09	0.18	0.36	0.72
	0.7	High 51–70%	0.035	0.07	0.14	0.28	0.56
	0.5	Medium 31–50%	0.025	0.05	0.10	0.20	0.40
	0.3	Low 11–30%	0.015	0.03	0.05	0.12	0.24
	0.1	Very low up to 10%	0.005	0.01	0.02	0.04	0.08
			Very low	Low	Medium	High	Very high
			0.05	0.1	0.2	0.4	0.8
			Impact				

Figure 7.4 Summary Risk Profile

Probability					
Very high		19	10	21	7
High	5	3, 13	17, 18	9	11
Medium		14	28	27, 29	12, 20
Low	2	22, 25	1, 15		8
Very low	24	30	16	6, 23	4, 26
	Very low	Low	Medium	High	Very high

Impact

Table 7.3 Top risks in Summary Risk Profile shown in Figure 7.4

Rank	Risk number
1	7
2	11
=3	12, 20
5	21
6	9
7	8
=8	27, 29
10	10

7.5.5 Plan

The primary goal of the Plan process is to prepare specific management responses to the threats and opportunities identified ideally to remove or reduce the threats and to maximize the opportunities. Attention to this step ensures as far as possible that the organization and its staff are not taken by surprise if a risk materializes.

The types of response defined in M_o_R are listed in Tables 7.4 and 7.5.

In PRAM a much wider set of responses are considered, with corresponding responses defined for threats and opportunities. These are summarized in Figure 7.5 and Table 7.6.

Table 7.4 Threat responses

Reduction	Proactive actions taken to reduce: ■ The probability of the event occurring, by performing some form of control ■ The impact of the event should it occur
Removal	Typically involves changing some aspect of the project, i.e. changing the scope, procurement route, supplier or sequence of activities
Transfer	A third party takes on responsibility for an aspect of the threat. (For example through insurance or by means of appropriate clauses in a contract.)
Retention	A conscious and deliberate decision is taken to retain the threat, having discerned that it is more economical to do so than to attempt a risk response action, for example. The threat should continue to be monitored to ensure that it remains tolerable
Sharing	Modern procurement methods commonly entail a form of risk sharing through the application of a pain/gain formula: both parties share the gain (within pre-agreed limits) if the cost is less than the cost plan; or share the pain (again within pre-agreed limits) if the cost plan is exceeded. Several industries include risk-sharing principles in their contracts with third parties

Table 7.5 Opportunity responses

Realization	*Identifying and seizing an opportunity*: The realization of an opportunity ensures that potential improvements to the project are delivered. For example, if there is an opportunity to complete a project early and reduce the headcount, the realization of the opportunity would be to achieve the reduced costs made possible through a lower-than-planned headcount
Enhancement	*Seizing and improving on an identified opportunity*: Enhancement of an opportunity refers to both the realization of an opportunity and achieving additional gains over and above the opportunity. An example may be negotiating a lower rental figure for existing occupied premises and restructuring the organization to reduce the floor space required. Or it may include achieving financial gain from finishing a project early and gaining additional revenue from deploying the released resources on another project
Exploitation	*Identifying and seizing multiple benefits*: Exploitation refers to changing the project's scope, supplier or specification to achieve a beneficial outcome without changing the objectives or specification. An example is where a contractor on a fixed-price contract manages to obtain a lower price from an alternative supplier on *multiple* subcontracts, while maintaining the desired specification

Reproduced with the permission of the Association for Project Management.

Figure 7.5 Mirror-imaged summary of PRAM risk responses (reproduced from **Project Risk Analysis and Management Guide 2nd Edition***)*

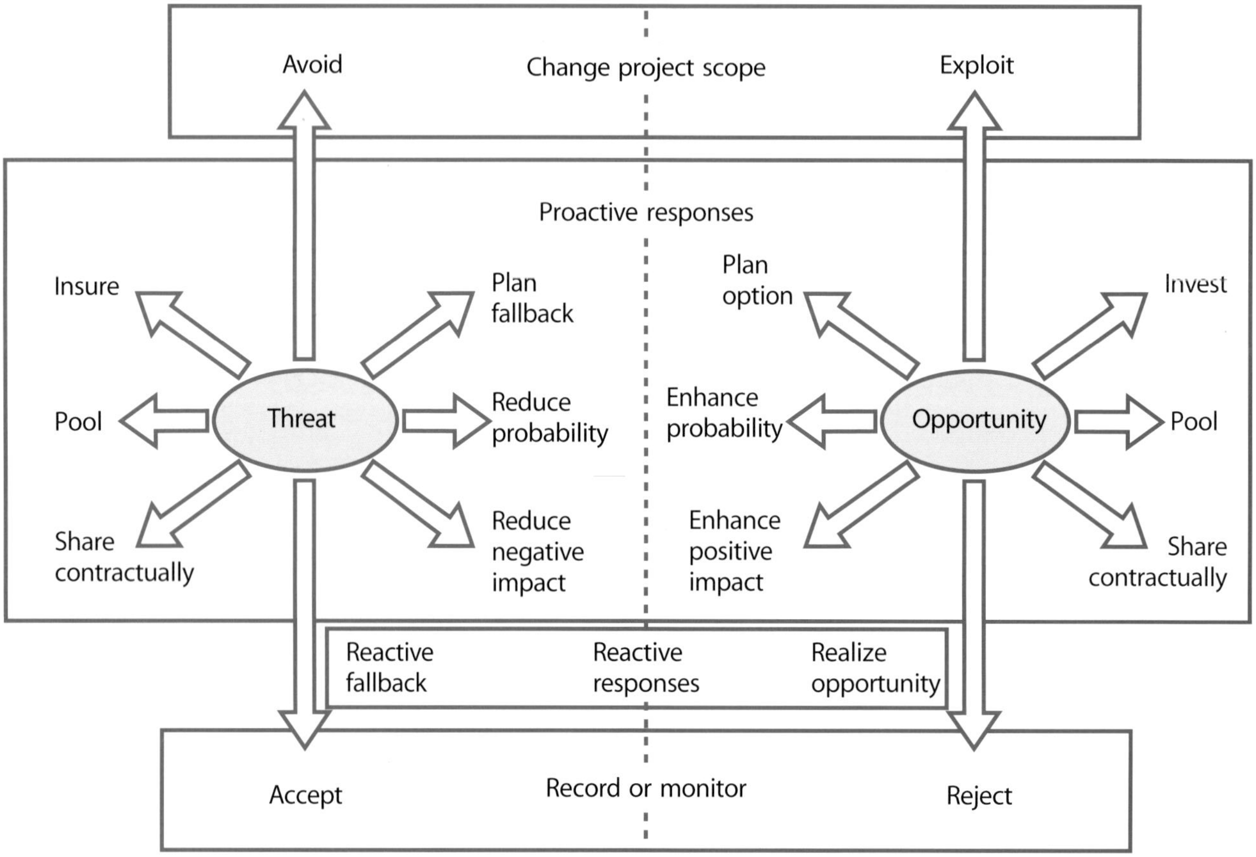

It is common for risk responses not to be fully effective, in that they do not remove the risk in its entirety. This leaves a residual risk remaining. If the original risk was significant and the risk response was only partially successful, the remaining risk can be considerable.

It is also possible that the responses to risks, once implemented, will change some aspect of the project. This in turn may lead to secondary risks, i.e. risks that may occur as a result of invoking a risk response. It is essential that these risks are identified, assessed and controlled in the same way as the primary risk.

7.5.6 Implement

The primary goal of the Implement process is to ensure that the planned risk management actions are implemented and monitored as to their effectiveness, and corrective action is taken where responses do not match expectations.

An important part of this is to ensure that there are clear roles and responsibilities allocated. The main roles in this respect are:

Table 7.6 PRAM Risk Responses (adapted from Figure 8.1 in *Project Risk Analysis and Management Guide 2nd Edition*)

Threat responses	Comments	Opportunity responses	Comments
Avoid	By changing objectives or practices	Exploit	By changing the project scope
Plan fallback	A plan of action implemented if the threat occurs	Plan option	A plan of action implemented if the opportunity occurs
Reduce probability	By tackling the risk at source	Enhance probability	By identifying improved methods for project delivery
Reduce negative impact	By proactive or reactive means	Enhance positive impact	By proactive or reactive means
Accept	Where there is no other appropriate response	Reject	Where there is no other appropriate response
Share contractually	Could include liquidated damages, warranties or performance bonds	Share contractually	For example by way of a risk-sharing joint venture
Pool	Self-insurance against threats by setting aside funds in the form of a risk pool	Pool	Any unexpected opportunities are used to help fund the risk pool
Insure	Taking out insurance, typically for low-probability but high-impact threats	Invest	Making an investment, typically in low-probability but high-return opportunities

- Risk owner – a named individual who is responsible for the management and control of all aspects of the risks assigned to them, including the implementation of the selected actions to address the threats or to maximize the opportunities.

- Risk actionee – the individual assigned the implementation of a risk response action or actions to respond to a particular risk or set of risks. They support and take direction from the risk owner.

7.5.7 Communicate

Rather than being a distinct stage in the risk management process, communication is an activity that is carried out throughout the whole process. A number of aspects of communication should be recognized and addressed if risk management is to be effective.

A project's exposure to risk is never static: effective communication is key to the identification of new threats and opportunities or changes in existing risks. Horizon scanning in particular depends on the maintenance of a good communications network, including relevant

Table 7.7 Characteristics of hard and soft benefits (reproduced from *Project Risk Analysis and Management Guide 2nd Edition*)

Hard benefits	Soft benefits
■ Enable better informed and more believable plans, schedules and budgets	■ Improve corporate experience and general communication
■ Increase the likelihood of a project adhering to its schedules and plans	■ Lead to a common understanding and improved team spirit
■ Lead to the use of the most suitable type of contract	■ Help distinguish between good luck/good management and bad luck/bad management
■ Allow a more meaningful assessment of contingencies	■ Help develop the ability of staff to assess risks
■ Discourage the acceptance of financially unsound projects	■ Focus project management attention on the real and most important issues
■ Contribute to the build up of statistical information to assist in better management of future projects	■ Facilitate greater risk-taking, thus increasing the benefits gained
■ Enable a more objective comparison of alternatives	■ Demonstrate a responsible approach to customers
■ Identify, and allocate responsibility to, the best risk owner	■ Provide a fresh view of the personnel issues in a project

contacts and sources of information to facilitate the identification of changes that may affect the project's overall risk exposure.

The implementation of risk management is dependent on participation, and participation, in turn, is dependent on communication. It is important for management to engage with staff across the project as well as wider stakeholders.

7.6 BENEFITS OF RISK MANAGEMENT

The main benefits of adopting a structured approach to risk management can be summarized as (Table 7.7):

■ Hard benefits – that is, contingencies, decisions, control, statistics and the like
■ Soft benefits – that is, people issues which are implicit in some of the 'hard' benefits but which are not usually expressed as benefits in their own right.

7.7 HEALTH, SAFETY AND ENVIRONMENTAL MANAGEMENT

Health, safety and environmental management is the process of determining and applying appropriate standards and methods to minimize the likelihood of accidents, injuries or environmental damage both during the project and during the operation of the deliverables.

Source: *APM Body of Knowledge 5th Edition*, with permission of the Association for Project Management.

Health, safety and environmental management is an important aspect of project management, and accordingly the Project Manager needs to have a sound understanding of the legal and organizational polices and procedures that may need to be applied to the project. This is particularly so in sectors which operate under strict regulatory control, for example construction, communications, energy, nuclear, food, pharmaceutical and waste.

7.7.1 Responsibilities of a Project Manager

The Project Manager has a responsibility and duty of care towards the people working within the project team. For example, the Project Manager needs to ensure that nature of the physical environment does not cause discrimination against any individual within the team.

These responsibilities are laid down in legislation and by regulations, and a number of these are summarized below.

7.7.2 Legislation and regulations

Environmental legislation tends to be subject specific. For example, there are requirements relating to noise, dust, protection of flora and fauna, waste and sustainability.

UK and EU legislation demands that health and safety risk assessment and management are carried out for most commercial activities, including projects, in order to reduce health and safety risk to an acceptable level. A number of techniques and processes cover these activities, including:

- Hazard and Operability (HAZOP)
- Hazardous Condition (HAZCON)
- Defect Reporting and Corrective Action (DRACAS)
- As Low As Reasonably Practical (ALARP).

The various regulations and sets of legislation include:

- Workplace regulations such as the Health and Safety at Work etc Act (HSWA) 1974
- Control of Substances Hazardous to Health Regulations (COSHH) 1974
- Building-related regulations (for example Electricity at Work Regulations covering ergonomics, lighting, noise levels and air quality)
- Fire Precautions

- Working Time Regulations (based on the EU Working Time Directive)
- EU Part-time Working Directive
- The Health and Safety Executive (HSE) produces much guidance in this area, including links to expert guidance, risk assessment steps and specific guidance and information on health and safety, the law and management.

The Health and Safety at Work etc Act 1974 sets out the responsibilities of employers and employees with regard to safety in the workplace. It provides the legal umbrella for the various safety regulations that have been developed for specific industries and activities. The HSWA sets out in broad terms the duties of those persons with responsibilities for health, safety and welfare within the workplace.

The Act is also an 'enabling Act', allowing Regulations on specific subjects to be made under the HSWA. These Regulations, and their accompanying Approved Codes of Practice and Guidance, add detail to the legislation that is set out in broad statements in the HSWA. Both employers and employees have duties under HWSA:

- Duties of employers:
  - Provide and maintain a safe workplace, plant and equipment
  - Provide safe systems of work
  - Provide the information, instruction, training and supervision necessary so that employees endanger neither themselves nor their colleagues
  - Provide and maintain a safe and healthy environment
  - Provide suitable facilities and arrangements for the welfare of employees.
- Duties of employees:
  - To take reasonable care while at work for his or her own health and safety and for that of persons who may be affected by his or her acts or omissions at work
  - To cooperate with the employer on safety matters

- Not to misuse or damage safety equipment provided by the employer.

7.7.3 Reporting

There are also statutory responsibilities for reporting.

- The Reporting of Injuries, Diseases and Dangerous Occurrences Regulations (RIDDOR) 1995 states that all of the following must be reported by law:
  - A death or major injury
  - An over-three-day injury
  - A work-related disease
  - A dangerous occurrence (that didn't cause a major injury, but might have done).
- The Environmental Protection Act 1996 and associated EU legislation highlights the thresholds where pollution incidents must be reported.
- Other reports that may be required are:
  - Reports about time lost due to safety-related incidents
  - Reports about costs associated with safety, health and environmental issues.

7.8 RISK MANAGEMENT – EXERCISES

(Sample answers are provided in Appendix A for the first question within each section. Answers to the remaining questions can be assessed against the relevant section within the chapter.)

APMP topic 2.5

1 Explain how a probability impact grid can be used to assess the importance of a risk to a project. Make four relevant points and include a diagram that fully illustrates the use of the technique.
2 Describe a risk management process making five relevant points.
3 List and explain four responses that can be applied to threats.
4 List and explain four responses that can be applied to opportunities.
5 Describe five benefits of project risk management.

APMP topic 2.7

1 Explain four specific duties of employers or employees regarding the Health and Safety at Work Act.
2 Explain why project health and safety is important.
3 Explain why project environmental management is important.

Quality management

8

8 Quality management

8.1 PURPOSE

The purpose of this chapter is to explore the topic of quality as it applies to the project environment (APMP topic 2.6). It also describes the related topic of requirements management (APMP topic 4.1).

8.2 DEFINITIONS

There are slightly different definitions for some of the key terms related to quality management in PRINCE2 and the APM Body of Knowledge (Table 8.1).

8.3 QUALITY MANAGEMENT PROCESSES

Project quality management is the discipline that is applied to ensure that both the outputs (or products) of the project and the process by which the outputs (or products) are delivered meet the required needs of stakeholders. Quality is broadly defined as fitness for purpose or more narrowly as the degree of conformance of the outputs (or products) and process.

Source: *APM Body of Knowledge 5th Edition*, with permission of the Association for Project Management.

The foundations for quality management for a project are the requirements for quality expressed in measurable terms in the form of Acceptance Criteria.

Quality management covers four processes (Table 8.2).

8.4 THE PRINCE2 PATH TO QUALITY

This section summarizes the elements of PRINCE2 that contribute towards achieving quality in a project environment.

8.4.1 Customer's Quality Expectations

These are the quality aspirations of the customer. These are likely to be loosely defined and quite subjective, but do reflect the standard of quality that is expected. A higher standard may be expected for certain types of product, compared with other types of product.

8.4.2 Acceptance Criteria

These are based on the customer's quality expectations, but now provide a definition in measurable terms of the characteristics required of the final product(s) for it/them to be acceptable to the customer and staff who will be affected. These may reflect the balance reached between the customer's quality expectations with time and cost constraints and the ability to realize business benefits.

8.4.3 Project Approach

The Project Approach defines the type of solution to be developed by the project and/or the method of delivering that solution. Typical approaches would include:

- Build from scratch by the customer's own staff
- Build from scratch using staff from an external supplier
- Modify an existing product to meet new needs
- Buy a product off-the-shelf.

The quality control methods and responsibilities will vary according to the approach chosen.

8.4.4 Project Quality Plan

The Project Quality Plan forms part of the Project Initiation Document (or Project Management Plan) and defines in general terms how the project will meet the customer's quality expectations.

Table 8.1 Comparison of the definitions of key terms related to quality management

	PRINCE2	APM Body of Knowledge
Quality	The totality of features and characteristics of a product or services that bear on its ability to satisfy stated needs. Also defined as 'fitness of purpose' or 'conformance to requirements'	The fitness for purpose or the degree of conformance of the outputs of the process
Quality Planning	Establishes the objectives and requirements for quality and lays out the activities for the application of the quality system	The process of determining which quality standards are necessary and how to apply them
Quality Assurance	Creates and maintains the quality system and monitors its application to ensure that the quality system is operated and is effective	The process of evaluating overall project performance on a regular basis to provide confidence that the project will satisfy the relevant quality standards
Quality Control	The means of ensuring that products meet the quality criteria specified for them	The process of monitoring specific project results to determine if they comply with relevant standards and identifying ways to eliminate causes of unsatisfactory performance
Continuous Improvement	Not defined	A business philosophy popularized in Japan, where it is known as Kaizen. Continuous Improvement creates steady growth and improvement by keeping a business focused on its goals and priorities. It is a planned systematic approach to improvement on a continual basis
Acceptance Criteria	A prioritized list of criteria that the final product(s) must meet before the customer will accept them; a measurable definition of what must be done for the final product to be acceptable to the customer	The requirements and essential conditions that have to be achieved before project deliverables are accepted
Quality Criteria	The quality specification that the product must be produced to and the measurements that will be applied by those inspecting the finished product	The characteristics of a product that determine whether it meets certain requirements

The APM Body of Knowledge definitions are extracts from the *APM Body of Knowledge 5th Edition*, reproduced with the permission of the Association for Project Management

Table 8.2 Processes in quality management

Quality Planning	Prepares to achieve those requirements, enabling the Project Manager to manage the trade-off between scope, time, cost and quality. Outputs and products can only be fit for purpose if the purpose is understood
Quality Assurance (QA)	Provides confidence to stakeholders that requirements for quality will be achieved. QA validates the consistent use of procedures and standards, supported by independent reviews and quality audits. QA will also be a source of lessons learned and ideas for improvement
Quality Control (QC)	Consists of inspection, testing and quality measurement, and verifies that the project deliverables conform to specification, are fit for purpose and meet stakeholder expectations
Continuous Improvement	Is focused on specifying requirements tightly and meeting them without wasting time or resources in the process

Extracted from the *APM Body of Knowledge 5th Edition*, reproduced with the permission of the Association for Project Management

The typical contents of the Project Quality Plan are:

- Customer's Quality Expectations
- Acceptance Criteria (including any quality tolerances)
- Quality responsibilities
- Reference to any standards that need to be met
- Quality control and audit processes to be applied to project management
- Quality control and audit process requirements for specialist work
- Change Control procedures
- Configuration Management Plan
- Any tools to be used to ensure quality.

8.4.5 Stage/Team Quality Plan

This is not a separate document, but each Stage or Quality Plan should contain a quality plan that will identify the method(s) and resources to be used to check the quality of each product.

8.4.6 Product Descriptions

A Product Description provides a clear, complete and unambiguous description of each product that is to be produced. It is given to the creator to explain what quality is required of the product when built. It is later given to the quality checkers to identify how the presence of that quality will be tested and to help establish if the required quality has been built into the product.

The typical contents of a Product Description are:

- Product identifier
- Title
- Purpose
- Composition
- Derivation
- Format and presentation
- Allocated to
- Quality criteria (including any quality tolerances)
- Quality method
- Quality check skills and/or people required.

8.4.7 Quality Log

A Quality Log is a record of all the quality checking done in the project. The details of all the quality checking activities are entered in the log as they are planned. The Team Manager or individual team member charged with the development and testing of the product subsequently updates the log with the results and dates of that quality checking. As such, it forms an audit trail of the quality work done in the project.

The typical contents of a Quality Log are:

- Reference number
- Product
- Method of quality checking
- Staff responsible
- Planned date
- Target sign-off date
- Actual date
- Result
- Number of action items
- Actual sign-off date.

8.4.8 Quality Techniques

A range of techniques are used in quality planning and assurance. Some of the most popular techniques are described below.

Audit

This is a review of the project, and its management, standards and procedures. An internal body, such as the project support office, or an external auditor, can undertake the audit depending on the situation. The aim of the audit is to assist the team to undertake the project in a controlled manner that will aid the project to deliver 'right first time'. The auditor will prepare a report documenting the results of the audit, and if non-conformances are noted will usually give a date by which they should be rectified. This will often include a date for a reassessment.

This is normally used as part of the regular project review cycle – perhaps at the end of a stage or phase.

Ishakawa Diagrams (Cause and Effect Analysis)

These are also known as fishbone diagrams where there is an effect, and a range of possible causes 'sorted' into categories with factors on each 'bone' emanating from the central backbone. Variants include Influence Diagrams and Mind Maps. In a quality situation the quality problem would be the 'head' and factors that contribute to the problem would be categorized and added to the 'bones'.

Once this has been completed a further analysis will be required to see which 'bone' or group of 'bones' would have the most effect if fixed. This could be achieved using a Pareto analysis (see Figure 8.1).

This tool could be used when quality problems are being experienced – perhaps a series of complaints about installation problems are being received from customers and it is necessary to get to the root cause.

Pareto Analysis

Vilfredo Pareto was an Italian economist who, in 1906, observed that 20% of the Italian population owned 80% of the country's total wealth. Ever since then, Pareto's observation has been used in a variety of ways, and is often referred to as the 80–20 Rule, the 'Vital Few and Trivial Many Rule' or simply Pareto's Principle.

It is of particular use when there are a number of causes and a need to establish where to apply efforts to solve the majority of the problems quickly and efficiently. It is often used in conjunction with fishbone diagrams. Thus it is possible to identify those problems (the 20%), which if fixed will have the most effect (the 80%).

Figure 8.1 Ishakawa Diagram

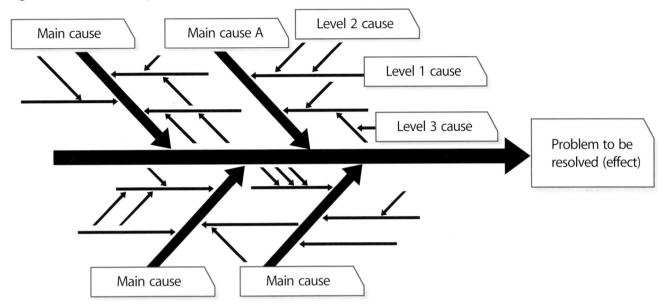

This information can be presented in the form of a Pareto Diagram (Figure 8.2), which is a type of histogram, ordered by frequency of occurrence and shows how many defects were generated by each cause. The diagram provides a rank ordering of the problems that cause the greatest number of defects and should, therefore, be fixed first.

Figure 8.2 Pareto Diagram

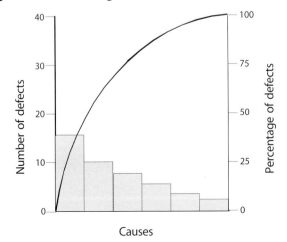

Control Charts

These can be used to monitor a process over a period of time to determine whether it is performing within acceptable limits. For example, a control chart can be used to evaluate whether the number of defects found during testing are acceptable or not in relation to an organization's standards for quality.

Control Charts (see Figure 8.3) usually have three common lines:

- A centre line, designated with an x, which provides an average of the process data
- An upper line designated the upper control limit (UCL)
- A lower line designated the lower control limit (LCL).

Figure 8.3 Control Chart

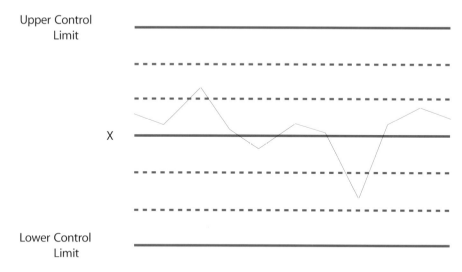

Sampling

This is a quality control technique and is used to check that products meet the quality criteria specified. For example, in a manufacturing environment the products will be checked every 100 runs.

100% testing

This quality control technique does exactly what it says – everything is tested. For example an installation of telephone sockets in a large building may mean that 10,000 outlets are installed. The client may want all to be tested. However, as this number includes a number of spares and allows for growth it may be that sampling may be a more cost-effective and adequate approach.

8.4.9 The cost of quality

Applying the above techniques costs money, and this cost needs to be justified against the benefits of achieving higher quality. One way of providing this justification is to consider the cost of quality as being made up of three elements:

- The cost of failure, i.e. the costs associated with rework following the handover of the product to the customer, and any consequential losses
- The cost of appraisal, i.e. the costs related to undertaking quality control activities to check for errors before the product has been handed over to the customer
- The cost of prevention, i.e. those costs incurred to ensure that the work is done right first time, for example by applying techniques such as Ishakawa Diagrams and Pareto Analysis.

If nothing is done, then the only cost will be the cost of failure. However, this cost can be very high.

Investing in techniques such as Ishakawa Diagrams and Pareto Analysis will certainly increase the cost of prevention, but it should lead to a reduction in the number of failures. That has a direct effect on the cost of failures and, as the number of failures fall, the need for appraisal also falls. As a result the total cost of quality (i.e. the cost of failure plus the cost of appraisal plus the cost of prevention) can be less than the cost of failure alone.

8.5 REQUIREMENTS MANAGEMENT

> Requirements management is the process of capturing, analysing and testing the documented statement of stakeholder and user wants and needs. Requirements are a statement of the need that a project has to satisfy, and should be comprehensive, clear, well structured, traceable and testable.
>
> Source: *APM Body of Knowledge 5th Edition*, with permission of the Association for Project Management.

As mentioned above, the foundations for quality management for a project are the requirements for quality expressed in measurable terms in the form of Acceptance Criteria. In a PRINCE2 project the requirements could be documented in the form of a Product Description for the final product of the project. Alternatively, having a requirements definition document in another format could negate the need for a separate Product Description.

High-level requirements are documented during the Concept phase (as part of the Project Brief) and are further developed and agreed during the Definition phase (as part of the Project Initiation Document or Project Management Plan). The preferred solution that meets the defined wants and needs is then produced during the Implementation phase and tested against the Acceptance Criteria as part of the Handover and Closeout phase.

The requirements management process consists of three steps (Table 8.3).

Requirements are the basis for the project – they describe what the customer wants and are used as a platform for the solution and the way in which that solution is provided. If requirements are not adequately determined and maintained, an excessive number of changes will be necessary and this will inevitably lead to cost and time over-runs.

Initially, the user requirements will be generated during the Concept phase. This will comprise a high-level view of the stakeholders' wants and will not necessarily describe what is actually needed. As the project moves into the Definition phase and more is known about the solution, the requirements will be revisited and refined to ensure that they are realistic and that they will be adequately satisfied by the solution.

During Implementation, the solution will be tested and the requirements will form a basis for these tests and finally during operations, the solution will be seen to satisfy the requirements.

Table 8.3 The requirements management process

Capture	Involves eliciting, structuring, and documenting the requirements and related Acceptance Criteria. This step is closely related to scope management, which is discussed in Chapter 5
Analysis and prioritization	Involves agreeing the priority of the requirements, taking into consideration benefits, business priorities, availability of resources and budget. The prioritized requirements should be evaluated to ensure that they meet the project objectives and will deliver the benefits that justify proceeding with the project
Testing	The structure and content of the documented requirements need to appeal to different people, with an expectation that testing of the requirements through reviews will be undertaken

Extracted from the *APM Body of Knowledge 5th Edition*, reproduced with the permission of the Association for Project Management

Table 8.4 Characteristics of requirements

Value	The size of the benefit associated with each requirement
Priority	Stakeholders agree the priority ordering of the requirements
Time	Business time imperatives drive the ordering of the requirements
Process	The way the solution is to be built; this is particularly important where subcontractors will be used to build some components

Extracted from the *APM Body of Knowledge 5th Edition*, reproduced with the permission of the Association for Project Management

The requirements should be documented and structured such that the value, priority, timescales and process (Table 8.4) are clear for each requirement.

Value represents the amount of benefit that will accrue from the requirement and could be used to assess its priority – how important is this requirement compared with the others. One method used to understand the importance that customers place on the delivery of a number of requirements is MoSCoW analysis. MoSCoW stands for:

- M – Must have this
- S – Should have this if it is possible
- C – Could have this if it does not affect anything else
- W – Won't have this now, but would like it in the future.

(The two 'o's are simply added to make the word pronounceable, which is why they are in lower case.)

The timescale associated with the requirement should reflect the timescales of the business, i.e. when must this requirement be satisfied if the business is to meet its strategic aims, and finally the process describes the means by which the requirements will be satisfied, i.e. the solution or project approach.

A common understanding of the requirements by all members of the Project Management Team is fundamental to ensuring that the wants and needs are captured and clearly articulated, and that solutions are developed to meet those needs.

8.6 QUALITY MANAGEMENT – EXERCISES

(Sample answers are provided in Appendix A for the first question within each section. Answers to the remaining questions can be assessed against the relevant section within the chapter.)

APMP topic 2.6

1 Explain when quality will be particularly relevant within a project lifecycle, making five relevant points.
2 Describe what is meant by quality management in a project environment.
3 Explain the purpose of five quality management tools and give examples of when each could be used.
4 Explain the differences between Quality Planning, Quality Assurance, Quality Control and Continuous Improvement.
5 Describe five benefits of project quality management.

APMP topic 4.1

1   State three elements of a requirements management process. Explain why requirements management is important.

2   Describe requirements management, making five relevant points.

Configuration management

9

9 Configuration management

9.1 PURPOSE

The purpose of this chapter is to describe a configuration management process and explain the reasons for requiring configuration management on a project (APMP topic 4.7).

9.2 DEFINITIONS

There are slightly different definitions of the key terms related to configuration management in PRINCE2 and the APM Body of Knowledge (Table 9.1).

9.3 PURPOSE OF CONFIGURATION MANAGEMENT

> Configuration management comprises the technical and administrative activities concerned with the creation, maintenance and controlled change of the configuration throughout the project lifecycle.
>
> Source: *APM Body of Knowledge 5th Edition*, with permission of the Association for Project Management.

The purpose of configuration management within the context of a project is to identify, track and protect the project's products. In other words:

- Identify – each product and each version of a product is uniquely identified
- Track – information is maintained for each product relating to its status, ownership and relationship with other products
- Protect – no product can be changed without authorized agreement.

Having the ability to identify, track and protect the project's product has a major part to play in enabling the project to deliver quality products. Without it, Project Managers have little control over the products being produced. Configuration management contributes towards the delivery of quality products by:

- Making the management of changes to products more cost effective and less error prone
- Helping to identify products that may be affected by problems or changes to related products

Table 9.1 Comparison of the definitions of key terms related to configuration management

	PRINCE2	APM Body of Knowledge
Configuration	A combined set of assets. The configuration of the final output of a project is the sum total of its products	Functional and physical characteristics of a deliverable (product) as defined in technical documents and achieved in the product
Configuration Management	A discipline, normally supported by software tools, which gives management precise control over its assets (for example, products of a project), covering planning, identification, control, status accounting and verification of the products	Technical and administrative activities concerned with the creation, maintenance and controlled change of configuration throughout the project lifecycle

The APM Body of Knowledge definitions are extracts from the *APM Body of Knowledge 5th Edition*, reproduced with the permission of the Association for Project Management

■ Checking that everyone is using the appropriate and authorized version of the product.

Configuration management is an essential element of any project that creates more than one version of a product.

9.4 CONFIGURATION MANAGEMENT PROCESS

Figure 9.1 illustrates the five activities (or functions) performed with a configuration management process (adapted from *APM Body of Knowledge 5th Edition*):

■ Planning
■ Identification
■ Control
■ Status accounting
■ Verification or audit.

Figure 9.1 Configuration management process

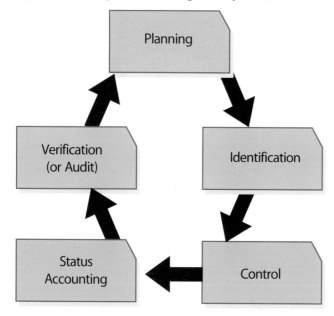

9.4.1 Configuration management planning

This involves deciding what level of configuration management will be required by the project and planning how this level will be achieved.

The level of control required will vary from project to project. A useful way of deciding on the appropriate level of control is to break down the project's end product into components, and then break down these further until the level is reached at which a component can be independently installed, replaced or modified. A Product Breakdown Structure (see Chapter 5) could fulfil this purpose.

Each project should produce a Configuration Management Plan to define:

■ How and where the project's products will be stored
■ What filing and retrieval security will be put in place
■ How the products and the various versions of these will be identified
■ Where responsibility for configuration management will lie.

Responsibility for producing this plan and performing configuration management may be delegated from the Project Manager to a Configuration Librarian.

9.4.2 Configuration identification

Configuration identification involves specifying and identifying all components of the final product.

Each product requires a unique identifier. As a minimum, a coding system should be used to identify:

■ The project in which the product is created
■ Type of product
■ Product title
■ Latest version number.

It is also useful for a Configuration Item Record to be maintained for each product within the project's configuration. In addition to the above, these records can be used to maintain information relating to:

- Owner of the product
- Person working on the product and date allocated
- Library or location where the product is kept
- Links to related products
- Status of the product
- Copyholders and potential users.

9.4.3 Configuration control

This involves having the ability to agree and baseline products and then to make changes to them only with the agreement of appropriate authorities.

A baseline, in configuration management terms, is a snapshot of a product and any component products, frozen at a point of time for a particular purpose. This purpose may be when a product is ready to be reviewed or when it has been approved. If the product that has been baselined is to be changed, a new version is created to accommodate the change, and the baseline version remains unchanged. Old baseline versions should never be discarded.

A related concept to a baseline is a release. This relates to a complete and consistent set of products that form a fixed reference point in the development of the end product. The most obvious release is when the final product of the project is handed over at the end of the project.

When a product is ready to be baselined, there should be a procedure for passing the product to the Configuration Librarian and for ensuring that the product cannot be changed without proper authority. Similarly, there should be a procedure for issuing products from the Configuration Librarian, which where practical, should entail only copies being issued and master copies being retained by the Configuration Librarian.

9.4.4 Configuration status accounting

This involves recording and reporting of all current and historical information concerning each product.

The Configuration Librarian may be asked to produce a Product Status Account, which is a report on the status of the project's products within defined limits. These limits could relate, for example, to a sub-set of the project's products or to a particular part of the project lifecycle.

Typical information provided within a Product Status Account will include:

- Date product was baselined
- List of related products
- Date when the product (or copy) was issued for change
- Planned date of next baseline
- Planned date of next release.

The Project Manager may call for a Product Status Account towards the end of a stage, at the end of the project, or as part of considering a request for change.

9.4.5 Configuration verification or audit

This involves undertaking a series of reviews to ensure that the actual status of all products matches the authorized state of products as recorded in the configuration management records.

These reviews audit the actual products against the Configuration Item Records, looking for any discrepancies. They also check that the configuration management process is being undertaken in accordance with the Configuration Management Plan.

The reviews are typically undertaken at the end of each stage and at the end of the project.

9.5 CONFIGURATION MANAGEMENT AND CHANGE CONTROL

The configuration management process must be closely aligned to the change control process within the project, as a key aspect of each is the ability to identify and control different versions of a product.

A product that has been baselined should only be changed under formal change control.

9.6 CONFIGURATION MANAGEMENT – EXERCISES

(Sample answers are provided in Appendix A for the first question. Answers to the remaining questions can be assessed against the relevant section within the chapter.)

APMP topic 4.7

1 Describe the linkage between change control and configuration management.

2 Explain a configuration management process. Make five relevant points.

3 Explain why configuration management is required on a project.

Change control and
issue management

10

10 Change control and issue management

10.1 PURPOSE

The purpose of this chapter is to describe the change control process (APMP topic 3.5) and issue management processes (APMP topic 3.8), and explain the importance of each to effective project management.

10.2 DEFINITIONS

There are slightly different definitions of the key terms related to change control and issue management in PRINCE2 and the APM Body of Knowledge (Table 10.1).

Within PRINCE2, change control is used as a common procedure to capture and record all Project Issues, whether they are Requests for Change or other types of issue. In this chapter, two separate processes are described to align to the approach taken in the APM Body of Knowledge.

10.3 CHANGE CONTROL

Change control is the process that ensures that all changes made to a project's baselined scope, time, cost and quality objectives or agreed benefits are identified, evaluated, approved, rejected or deferred.

Source: *APM Body of Knowledge 5th Edition*, with permission of the Association for Project Management.

The purpose of change control is to ensure that changes to the specification or scope of a project do not ruin the project. This is achieved by having a process in place that enables the project management team to:

■ Assess the impact, cost and importance of potential changes
■ Make a judgemental decision on whether or not to include them.

10.3.1 Change control process

The basic change control process consists of four steps (Figure 10.1).

Figure 10.1 Change control process

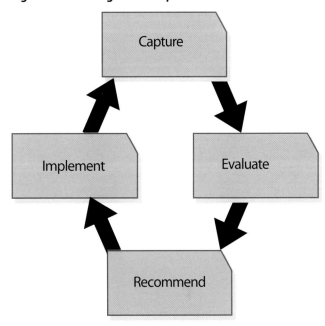

10.3.2 Capture

The first step in the process must be to capture all Requests for Change. These can be raised at any time during the project by anyone with an interest in the project.

To ensure that Requests for Change are captured effectively, anyone wishing to raise a Request for Change should be asked to complete a Request for Change form.

Table 10.1 Comparison of the definitions of key terms related to change control and issue management

	PRINCE2		APM Body of Knowledge
Request for Change	A means of proposing a modification to the current specification of a product. It is one type of Project Issue	Change request	A request to obtain formal approval for changes to scope, design, methods, costs or planned aspects of a project
Project Issue	A term used to cover any concern, query, Request for Change, suggestion or Off-Specification raised during the project. They can be about anything to do with the project	Issue	A threat to the project objectives that cannot be resolved by the Project Manager
Problem	Not defined. It is one type of Project Issue	Problem	In project management terms, these are problems which are concerns that the project manager has to deal with on a day-to-day basis
Change Control	The procedure to ensure that the processing of all Project Issues is controlled, including submission, analysis and decision-making	Change control	A process that ensures that all changes made to a project's baselined scope, cost, time and quality objectives are identified, evaluated, approved, rejected or deferred
		Issue management	The process by which concerns that threaten the project objectives and cannot be resolved by the Project Manager can be identified and addressed to remove the threats that they pose

The APM Body of Knowledge definitions are extracts from the *APM Body of Knowledge 5th Edition*, reproduced with the permission of the Association for Project Management

This form will typically capture information relating to:

- Date – when the Request for Change was first raised
- Reference number – a unique numerical reference to be provided for each Request for Change
- Status – could simply be 'Open' or 'Closed'
- Description – a full description of the Request for Change
- Author – the name of the person who has raised the Request for Change
- Impact – see below

- Priority assessment – based on the assessed impact
- Decision – whether to authorize, decline or defer
- Allocation details – details of to whom the Request for Change has been allocated.

On receipt of this form, a summary of this information is recorded in the project's Change Log. A copy of the Request for Change is returned to the author to acknowledge receipt and entry into the Change Log.

10.3.3 Evaluate

The next step is to evaluate each Request for Change by undertaking an impact analysis. An initial evaluation may be undertaken to consider whether it is worthwhile doing a detailed evaluation. The evaluation of Requests for Change consumes resources, which may itself cause a deviation from plan.

The detailed evaluation, if carried out, should consider the impact the Request for Change will have on:

■ The project objectives in terms of time, cost, quality and scope
■ The project Business Case, especially in terms of the impact on benefits
■ The project risk profile, i.e. the impact on the overall risk exposure of the project.

Based on this analysis, an assessment should then be made as to the priority of the Request for Change, e.g. is it considered to be a:

■ Must
■ Important
■ Nice to have
■ Cosmetic.

10.3.4 Recommend

The next step is for a decision to be taken on whether to authorize, reject or defer the Request for Change.

Requests for Change should be brought to the attention of the Project Board or Steering Group by means of an Exception Report. This report will contain information relating to:

■ Description of the Request for Change
■ Consequences of the Request for Change
■ Available options
■ Effect of each option on: the time, cost, quality and scope; the Business Case; and the risks

■ Project Manager's recommendation.

The Project Executive or Project Sponsor has ultimate authority to act on the recommendation. This decision must then be communicated to all interested parties.

10.3.5 Implement

Once a decision has been taken to authorize a Request for Change, all plans will need to be updated to reflect the change, and the necessary actions taken to implement the change. The Change Log is also updated to record the decision that has been made.

10.4 ISSUE MANAGEMENT

Issue management is the process by which concerns that threaten the project objectives and cannot be resolved by the Project Manager are identified and addressed to remove the threats they pose.

Source: *APM Body of Knowledge 5th Edition*, with permission of the Association for Project Management.

The purpose of issue management is to ensure that any threats to the objectives of the project, which cannot be resolved by the Project Manager, are escalated to the appropriate authority so that a resolution can be reached.

In the APM Body of Knowledge, a distinction is made between issues, problems and risks (Table 10.2).

The important distinction here is that Issues are outside the direct control of the Project Manager and must be escalated to the Project Executive or Project Sponsor for resolution, whereas problems are within the direct control of the Project Manager and can be managed without the need for escalation. Any Issues that remain unaddressed or unresolved may lead to project failure.

Table 10.2 Issues, problems and risks

Issues	Are threats to the project objectives that cannot be resolved by the Project Manager and the event has already occurred
Problems	Are concerns that the Project Manager has to deal with on a day-to-day basis
Risks	Are uncertain in that an event may or may not occur

Extracted from the *APM Body of Knowledge 5th Edition*, reproduced with the permission of the Association for Project Management

A similar process to that described for change control can be applied to Project Issues, but with extra steps to reflect the need for escalation (Figure 10.2).

Figure 10.2 Issue management process

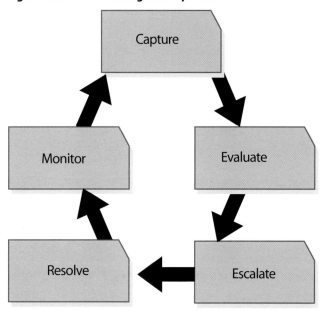

10.4.1 Capture

The first step in the process must be to capture all Issues. These can be raised at any time during the project by anyone with an interest in the project. To ensure that Issues are captured effectively, anyone wishing to raise an Issue should be asked to complete an Issue form.

This form will typically capture information relating to:

- Date – when the Issue was first raised
- Reference number – a unique numerical reference to be provided for each Issue
- Status – could simply be 'Open' or 'Closed'
- Description – a full description of the Issue
- Author – the name of the person who has raised the Issue
- Impact – possible consequences or impacts on the project
- Possible resolution – options for resolving the Issue
- Resolution owner – who is responsible for resolving the Issue
- Final outcome – how the Issue was eventually resolved
- Date closed.

On receipt of this form, a summary of this information is recorded in the project's Issue Log. A copy of the Issue is returned to the author to acknowledge receipt and entry into the Issue Log.

10.4.2 Evaluate

As with Requests for Change, the evaluation on an Issue should consider the impact that the Issue will have on:

- The project objectives in terms of time, cost, quality and scope
- The project Business Case, especially in terms of the impact on benefits
- The project risk profile, i.e. the impact on the overall risk exposure of the project.

The Issue Log will be updated with this evaluation.

10.4.3 Escalate

Issues need to be brought to the attention of the Project Board or Steering Group by means of an Exception Report. This report will contain information relating to:

- Description of the Issue
- Consequences of the Issue
- Available options
- Effect of each option on: the time, cost, quality and scope; the Business Case; and the risks
- Project Manager's recommendation.

10.4.4 Resolve

Once a decision has been taken as to how to resolve the Issue, the necessary actions should be undertaken by the Resolution Owner. The Issue Log is also updated to record the decision that has been made.

10.4.5 Monitor

Once an Issue is recorded in the Issue Log as open, it should be subject to regular monitoring, with the Resolution Owner being tasked to provide status reports on a regular basis. The Issue Log should be updated to reflect the results of this monitoring. The frequency of these reports will depend on the severity and urgency of the Issue.

10.5 ROLES AND RESPONSIBILITIES FOR CHANGE CONTROL AND ISSUE MANAGEMENT

The processes for dealing with Requests for Change and Issues should form part of the Project Initiation Document or Project Management Plan. (In PRINCE2 they would be described within the Project Quality Plan section of the Project Initiation Document.)

Within this, the roles and responsibilities for Change Control and Issue Management should be defined. These are likely to include:

- Project Executive or Project Sponsor – as the ultimate decision-maker on the Project Board or Steering Group
- Senior User – to represent the user community
- Senior Supplier – to provide input into the decision-making from a technical point of view
- Project Manager – to monitor and control all Requests for Change and Issues, and escalate them to the Project Board or Steering Group
- Change Authority – where the Project Board have decided to delegate the responsibility for making decisions on Requests for Change.

It may also be advisable to establish a separate Change Budget to pay for any approved changes.

10.6 CHANGE CONTROL AND ISSUE MANAGEMENT – EXERCISES

(Sample answers are provided in Appendix A for the first question within each section. Answers to the remaining questions can be assessed against the relevant section within the chapter.)

APMP topic 3.5

1 List five roles that are fundamentally involved in change control and describe the contribution of each role.

2 Explain five features of an effective change control process.

3 Explain why change control is required on a project.

APMP topic 3.8

1 Explain an issue management process, making four relevant points.

2 Explain the importance of issue management.

Stakeholder management and communication

11

11 Stakeholder management and communication

11.1 PURPOSE

The purpose of this chapter is to:

- Explain the importance of stakeholder management and describe a typical stakeholder management process (APMP topic 2.2)
- Explain the importance of effective communication, the typical barriers to communication and how these may be overcome, and describe the typical contents of a Project Communication Plan (APMP topic 7.1).

11.2 DEFINITIONS

There are slightly different definitions of the key terms related to stakeholder management and communication in PRINCE2 and the APM Body of Knowledge (Table 11.1).

11.3 STAKEHOLDER MANAGEMENT

> Stakeholder management is the systematic identification, analysis and planning of actions to communicate with, negotiate with and influence stakeholders. Stakeholders are all those who have an interest or role in the project or are impacted by the project.
>
> Source: *APM Body of Knowledge 5th Edition*, with permission of the Association for Project Management.

The purpose of stakeholder management is to maximize the positive influence and minimize the negative influence stakeholders can have on the success of the project.

Stakeholders have a key role in defining the success criteria used to judge the success of the project and their interests in and influence over the project need to be managed.

Stakeholders are individuals or groups who have an interest in or who will be impacted by the project. Stakeholders are people with feelings, perceptions, desires and influence. For any project there will be those who:

- Support it or oppose it
- End up gaining or losing
- See only a threat, perhaps convinced that they will lose despite all evidence to the contrary
- Are inherently indifferent to the project – they may become helpful or unhelpful, depending on how they themselves are managed and influenced
- May become either backers or blockers to the project depending on how and to what level they are engaged.

Project Managers need to think of stakeholder engagement not just as a system of tasks and managing 'things', but also as a way of achieving influence and positive outcomes through effective management of relationships. Project Managers need to understand that people need to be engaged with as more than resources to be used or obstacles to be removed. This will include considering matters of internal politics, and individual emotions and motivations. Good Project Managers take seriously the attitudes and agendas of individuals. They understand the challenges projects bring for people. Such Project Managers are likely to be more successful in influencing people around them, and in turning stakeholders from blockers into backers.

Table 11.1 Comparison of the definitions of key terms related to stakeholder management and communication

	PRINCE2	APM Body of Knowledge
Stakeholders	Parties with an interest in the execution and outcome of a project. They include business streams affected by or dependent on the outcome	The organizations or people who have an interest or role in the project or are impacted by the project
Stakeholder management	Not defined	The systematic identification, analysis and planning of actions to communicate with, negotiate with and influence stakeholders
Communication	Not defined	The giving, receiving, processing and interpretation of information. Information can be conveyed verbally, non-verbally, actively, passively, formally, informally, consciously or unconsciously
Communication Plan	Part of the Project Initiation Document describing how the project's stakeholders and interested parties will be kept informed during the project	A document that identifies what information is to be communicated to whom, why, when, where, how, through which medium and the desired impact

The APM Body of Knowledge definitions are extracts from the *APM Body of Knowledge 5th Edition*, reproduced with the permission of the Association for Project Management

11.4 STAKEHOLDER MANAGEMENT PROCESS

Stakeholder management is an ongoing process (Figure 11.1) through the lifecycle of a project, and accordingly the steps in the process need to be undertaken on a recurring and iterative basis.

11.4.1 Stakeholder identification

Stakeholder management begins with identifying all the stakeholders interested in or impacted by the project. Projects can have large numbers of individual stakeholders. It can therefore be useful to organize the project's stakeholders by category, such as:

- Users/beneficiaries
- Governance (management boards, steering groups, audit)
- Influencers (e.g. trade unions, the media)
- Providers (suppliers, business partners).

These high-level categories can be broken down further, or alternative groupings can be identified, in order to organize communication by shared interests. In this way, key messages can be targeted at and consultations undertaken with the relevant people.

Groupings should be practically identifiable rather than abstract; for example, 'employees based in the Dublin office' is a readily identifiable group, whereas 'members of the public who support human rights' is not. This exercise may identify the same individuals in different categories and groupings, therefore it is often a useful way of differentiating between stakeholders with multiple interests.

Figure 11.1 Stakeholder management process

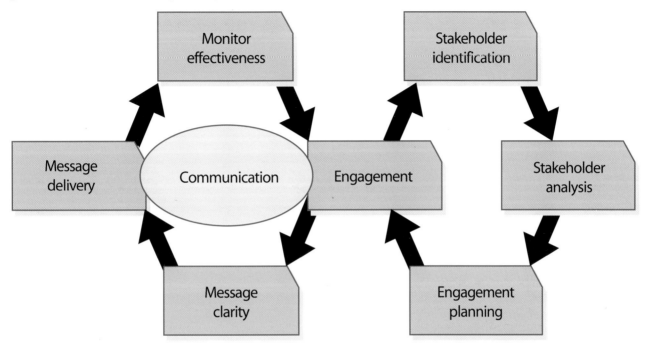

11.4.2 Stakeholder analysis

Various aspects of stakeholders need to be analysed, including their:

- Interests
- Influence/power
- Attitude.

A common means of analysing stakeholder interest is to produce a Stakeholder Map. This will show the different interest areas in the project. For example, some stakeholders will be concerned with how the project will affect their working environment whereas others will be concerned about how the project will change the way customers are handled. The Stakeholder Map in Figure 11.2 compares the various stakeholders against their interests in a project dealing with the construction of an international sports complex.

It is also useful to analyse the significance and potential influence of each stakeholder against their areas of interest to help:

- Prioritize stakeholder engagement
- Focus project resources to contribute the most towards successful outcomes
- Ensure communication channels are well exploited
- Align message content, media, frequency of engagement and level of detail to meet the relevant needs of the stakeholders.

There are several techniques for analysing stakeholders. One method is to consider each stakeholder in terms of their influence on the project and their potential interest in the project outcomes and 'plot' these on a map. The level of their importance to the project and its impact on them will determine the level and type of

Figure 11.2 Example Stakeholder Map of a sports complex

Stakeholders: \ Interest Areas:	Sports facilities	Transport infrastructure	Public Transport Service	City image/ prestige	Local economy	Housing	Hotel accommodation	Local environment	City taxes
Transport and Planning Department	✓	✓	✓		✓	✓		✓	
City Mayor	✓	✓	✓	✓	✓	✓		✓	✓
City Government	✓	✓	✓	✓	✓	✓	✓	✓	✓
Transport Department		✓	✓		✓				
Sports Minister	✓	✓	✓	✓			✓	✓	
National Government	✓	✓	✓	✓	✓	✓	✓	✓	✓
Local residents	✓	✓	✓		✓	✓		✓	
National Sports Council	✓						✓	✓	
Tourists	✓	✓	✓	✓			✓	✓	
Athletes	✓			✓			✓		
Rail company		✓	✓		✓				
Local business	✓	✓	✓	✓	✓	✓		✓	✓

stakeholder engagement the project should undertake with them. For example, in the project to construct an international sports complex illustrated in Figure 11.3, the Sports Minister will have 'high' importance to the project, and also 'high' influence upon it and so is a 'key player' and should be treated accordingly. However, the local residents, despite having a similarly high interest in the legacy of the sports complex, don't have so much direct influence on the project; hence the primary mode of engagement for these stakeholders is active consultation.

Another kind of analysis examines stakeholder attitude. An approach to help understand a stakeholder's position in relation to the project is a stakeholder attitude/influence map. See Figure 11.4 for an example. As with the above analyses, considering a stakeholder's position on this map will help to determine stakeholder engagement actions.

11.4.3 Engagement planning

Engagement is more active and embracing than communication. It covers aspects such as including stakeholders in decision-making and implementation, as well as consulting with them and informing them. The greater the change, the greater the need for clear communication about the reasons and rationale behind it, the benefits expected, the plans for its implementation and its proposed effects.

11.4.4 Engagement

The first two steps in the stakeholder management process, identification and analysis, engage stakeholders to some degree. Identification may well involve stakeholders in early workshops. The simplest and often most effective method of analysis is to ask the stakeholder and listen: 'First seek to understand, then to be understood.'

The next section of this chapter explores the topic of project communication.

Figure 11.3 Influence/interest map of a sports complex programme

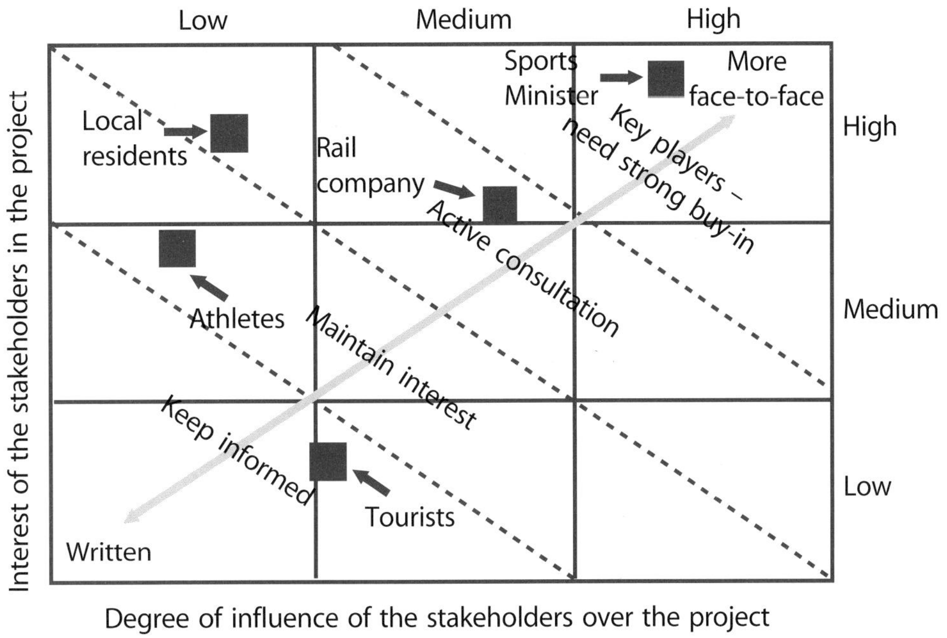

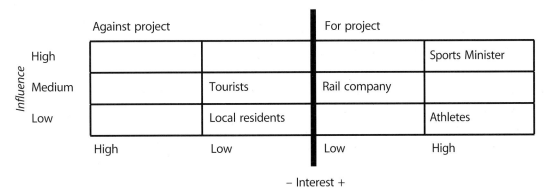

Figure 11.4 Influence/interest map of a sports complex programme (adapted from Figure 2.1 in APM Body of Knowledge 5th Edition)

	Against project		For project	
High				Sports Minister
Medium		Tourists	Rail company	
Low		Local residents		Athletes
	High	Low	Low	High

Influence (vertical axis)

– Interest +

11.5 COMMUNICATION

> Communication is the giving, receiving, processing and interpretation of information. Information can be conveyed verbally, non-verbally, actively, passively, formally, informally, consciously or unconsciously.
>
> Source: *APM Body of Knowledge 5th Edition*, with permission of the Association for Project Management.

The objectives of the communications process are to:

- Keep awareness and commitment high
- Ensure that expectations do not drift out of line with what will be delivered
- Explain what changes will be made and when
- Describe the desired future end state.

Successful communications will be judged on the ability to meet these objectives.

Successful communication requires the presence of four key elements:

- Message clarity and consistency, to ensure relevance and recognition and engender trust
- Stakeholder identification and analysis, to establish the target audience
- A system of message delivery, to ensure communications are delivered in a timely and effective manner
- A system of monitoring, to obtain feedback and assess the effectiveness of the communication process.

Messages must be consistent. Project Managers undermine their own credibility and risk hesitancy among stakeholders with inconsistent messages.

Messages should be few in number, simple, brief and derived from the project's objectives. It is useful to establish key phrases (touchstone statements, sound bites and word bites are alternative terms) as the foundation for more complex communications and then to repeat these throughout the project. This also ensures the project is seen to be speaking with one voice.

11.5.1 Message clarity

An essential element of ensuring message clarity is to allocate sufficient effort to the planning of communications. When producing a Project Communication Plan, the following topics should be considered, and should therefore form the main sections of a communication plan:

- Description of the key messages and other information to be communicated and the objectives for delivering these communications
- Responsibilities for delivering key messages and other information about the project
- Identification of the stakeholder audience for each communication
- Description of the channels to be used, including feedback mechanisms
- Process for handling feedback, including how objections will be identified and handled
- Schedule of communication activities, including target audiences for each.

11.5.2 Message delivery

Many different media can be used to communicate with the project's stakeholders. The main ones are:

- **Oral, face-to-face** – certainly the most successful form of communication, but it can be expensive and time consuming. It includes meetings, workshops and seminars. In any oral communication there are three main ways in which the communication is delivered:
  - Vocally, i.e. the actual words
  - Verbally, i.e. the way in which the words are spoken
  - Visually, i.e. the visual clues such as face and hand gestures

In terms of the importance of these aspects, research suggests that vocal accounts for 7%, verbal 38% and visual 55%.

- **Oral, not face-to face** – the most obvious form of this is the telephone. Whilst this can be a good form of communication it misses out on any visual impact.
- **Visual** – some communications can be delivered without the use of words. Examples could include displays, site exhibitions and the setting up of prototypes.
- **Electronic** – with the expanding use of the internet, there are ever more ways of communicating information electronically. Some methods (such as email) can be very limited, but websites can incorporate visual images as well as words, and web meetings are an excellent way of replicating face-to-face communication.
- **Written** – this can include letters, newsletters, notice boards and posters. This is often a cheap and quick way to communicate with a large audience, but the communication is limited to use of words and images.

11.5.3 Monitoring effectiveness

It is easy for the project management team to think that:

- 'Everybody who needs to know, knows'
- 'People are generally positive towards the change, and if they are not, they soon will be when they see the benefits being realized.'

Simple methods of checking perceptions include sampling stakeholder communities. One simple question early in the project might be: 'What are the project's success criteria?'

Communications specialists agree that people do not retain information until they have heard it several times. Feedback will reveal under-communication or miscommunication.

11.5.4 Barriers to communication

There are many barriers to effective communication. However, the majority of these barriers can be categorized as (Table 11.2):

- Psychological – related to the attitudes of the people involved and the personal characteristics of the people sending and receiving the communication, or
- Technical – related to the way in which the communication process is organized and structured.

Another form of barrier to effective communication is cultural. Cultural barriers tend to be more difficult to overcome, being caused by factors such as:

- Religion – if indifference is shown to a person's religious belief, it can cause withdrawal from the communication process
- Customs – in multi-cultural societies communication may fail if the appropriate customs are not recognized and respected
- Value systems – communication is likely to fail if it does not address an individual's value systems.

Table 11.2 The main barriers to communication

Barrier	Description and how it may be overcome
Psychological	
Perception	The way that people receive information will depend on their perception of its importance and relevance to them
	Accordingly, they are likely to relate to it better when the implications of the information are explained to them first
Dislike	If the receiver has a personal dislike of the sender, then the message is less likely to be listened to
	In this case, it may be necessary to arrange for another person to deliver the message
Lack of credibility	In a similar way, if the receiver does not respect the sender then again the message is unlikely to be well received
	It may be helpful to ensure that the expertise of the sender is made known before sending the message
Perceptual bias	The information received may be affected by a general impression of the sender. This may result in the receiver hearing what they want to hear and accordingly making misinformed judgements
	To avoid this it may be helpful to apply a systematic approach to decision-making that is information based
Defensiveness	When receiving information about ourselves we are likely to be defensive if that information does not accord with our own self-image. This can be particularly troublesome when the information appears to be subjective or judgemental
	One way to overcome this is by presenting factual information prior to stating any personal judgements
Neutrality	However, if the sender appears to be very clinical or detached, this may also produce a defensive response
	A balance needs to be achieved between presenting the cold facts and showing empathy
Dogmatism	This occurs when the sender does not appear to take any account of other people's opinions. In such cases the receiver is likely to be even less receptive to the message being sent
	So again, there is a need to show empathy with the receiver if the communication is to be effective
Bad news syndrome	No one likes to receive bad news and the receiver is likely to resent it, especially if the only news they receive is bad news
	A proven approach to providing feedback to individuals is to 'sandwich' any bad news between good news

Barrier	Description and how it may be overcome
Technical	
Lack of clarity	This can often result from the use of technical terms or jargon
	Wherever it is necessary to use such terms, then ensure that they are either already well known by the receiver or are explained within the communication
Lack of structure	Poor structure can lead to difficulties for the receiver in picking out the important points for them from the communication
	Ensure that the main messages of the communication are highlighted and if necessary repeated throughout the communication
Overload	If too much information is sent, there is a danger that none of it will be received as the receiver simply ignores it all
	Again, ensuring that the communication focuses solely on the key messages will help avoid this
Language	There is an obvious barrier when speaking another tongue, but this barrier can also be present when communicating with people from different disciplines or professions
	For a Project Manager working with multi-disciplined teams, it is important that they make an effort to understand the language and culture of these different disciplines.

11.6 STAKEHOLDER MANAGEMENT – EXERCISES

(Sample answers are provided in Appendix A for the first question within each section. Answers to the remaining questions can be assessed against the relevant section within the chapter.)

APMP topic 2.2

1 Explain the importance of stakeholder management, making four relevant points.
2 Explain a process that can be used to analyse stakeholder needs and expectations and the benefits of such a process. Make four relevant points and include a diagram that fully illustrates the use of the process.

APMP topic 7.1

1 State 10 factors that a Project Manager should consider to ensure that project communication is effective.
2 Describe the typical contents of a Project Communication Plan.
3 Explain why effective communication is important in a project environment, making five relevant points.
4 Describe five barriers to effective communication and suggest how these may be overcome.

Procurement **12**

12 Procurement

12.1 PURPOSE

The purpose of this chapter is to describe the process by which resources required by a project are acquired. The topics covered are:

- The procurement process
- The purpose and content of a Procurement Strategy
- Supplier selection
- Negotiation
- Types of contractual relationships
- Methods of supplier reimbursement.

The above topics will address the related subjects of Procurement (APMP topic 5.4) and Negotiation (APMP topic 7.5).

12.2 DEFINITIONS

The key terms related to procurement have been defined in the APM Body of Knowledge (Table 12.1).

12.3 PROCUREMENT PROCESS

Procurement is the process by which the resources (goods and services) required by a project are acquired. It includes development of the procurement strategy, preparation of contracts, selection and acquisition of suppliers, and management of the contracts.

Source: *APM Body of Knowledge 5th Edition*, with permission of the Association for Project Management.

A typical procurement process has several steps (Table 12.2). The steps are described in more detail in the following sections.

Table 12.1 Definitions of key terms related to procurement

	PRINCE2	APM Body of Knowledge
Procurement	No definition	The process by which the resources (goods and services) required by a project are acquired. It includes development of the procurement strategy, preparation of contracts, selection and acquisition of suppliers, and management of the contracts
Procurement Strategy	No definition	Sets out how to acquire and manage resources (goods and services) required by a project
Negotiation	No definition	A search for agreement, seeking acceptance, consensus and alignment of views. Negotiation in a project can take place on an informal basis throughout the project lifecycle, or on a formal basis such as during procurement, and between signatories to a contract

The APM Body of Knowledge definitions are extracts from the *APM Body of Knowledge 5th Edition*, reproduced with the permission of the Association for Project Management

Table 12.2 The procurement process

Step	Responsibility	Description
Procurement Strategy	Customer	Decision made to employ an external supplier to provide goods or services, and how these will be acquired
Invitation to tender (ITT)	Customer	Prepare an invitation to suppliers to tender or bid for the supply of specified goods or services
Tender	Potential suppliers	Prepare the tender, which is a document proposing to meet the specification in a certain way and at a stated price (or on a particular financial basis), an offer of price and conditions under which the supplier is willing to undertake the work for the customer. (The price stated in the tender is generally known as the bid)
Supplier Selection	Customer	Evaluate the various tenders and select the preferred supplier
Negotiation	Customer: Supplier	Reach agreement on all aspects of the relationship between the customer and the supplier
Contract	Customer: Supplier	Enter into a mutually binding agreement in which the contractor (supplier) is obligated to provide goods or services and the buyer (customer) is obligated to provide payment for them

12.4 PROCUREMENT STRATEGY

The Procurement Strategy should be prepared as part of the Project Initiation Document or Project Management Plan.

The approach to the acquisition and management of resources required by a project can and should vary to suit the particular objectives and nature of the project. Consideration should, however, be given to the organization's own Procurement Strategy.

In PRINCE2, the Project Approach addresses part of the Procurement Strategy, but other factors need to be considered in preparing a full Procurement Strategy (Table 12.3).

Other questions that may be useful in formulating a Procurement Strategy are:

■ What flexibility will the customer need to be able to change the nature and timing of the work to be undertaken by the supplier?

■ How well defined are the objectives of the project and the nature of the work to be undertaken?

■ What are the potential technical and commercial interfaces?

12.4.1 Invitation to tender

An invitation to tender signals to potential suppliers that the customer organization is prepared to be legally bound to another organization in a contract, but is not of itself a contract. Accordingly, it will typically contain much of the information that will eventually be included in the agreed contract. The main sections of the invitation to tender could include:

■ Statement of requirements
■ Technical specification
■ General terms of contract
■ Special terms of contract
■ Financial, insurance and payment terms.

Table 12.3 Factors impacting the Procurement Strategy (adapted from the *APM Body of Knowledge 5th Edition*)

Factors	Questions
Make or buy	What are the priorities in proposing to employ another organization to supply goods and services for the project? Could and should some of the work of the project be undertaken by the organization's own employees? What is the suitability and availability of the organization's own resources?
Single or multiple suppliers	How many separate suppliers should be employed? If more than one – are they best employed in parallel or in sequence?
Supplier relationships	Who is to be responsible for what is in the project? Who is best placed to own and manage the risks within the project?
Supplier selection	What procedure will be followed to enable competition between potential suppliers? Are there any rules or requirements that need to be met to ensure open competition?
Form of contract	Is it best to have one comprehensive contract, a sequence of contracts, parallel contracts or subcontracts?
Pricing and reimbursement	What payment terms will best motivate all parties to achieve the project objectives?

Alternatively, a customer can choose to issue only the statement of requirements and invite prospective suppliers to offer their technical and commercial proposals.

12.4.2 Tender

A tender signals to the customer organization that the prospective supplier is willing to be legally bound to that organization by a contract if the customer accepts the terms the tenderer is offering in its tender. This offer to do business can be withdrawn at any moment until a contract has been entered into, unless there is a separate agreement whereby the offer is to be kept open for a specified period. It is usual for tenders to state that the tender remains valid for a stated period of time; this is known as an option and cannot be withdrawn within the stated period without incurring some kind of penalty.

12.5 SUPPLIER SELECTION PROCESS

Suppliers should be selected on the basis of their capability, quality and price.

This process may begin before sending out invitations to tender by undertaking a pre-qualification stage. This assesses which potential bidders should be able and willing to carry out the work required under the proposed contract. The purpose here is to identify those potential bidders that have the required resources, financial standing, experience, managerial capability and quality assurance systems to undertake the work satisfactorily.

Pre-qualification should be undertaken systematically by considering various factors (such as those shown in Table 12.4) to avoid personal preferences and judgements having unbalanced influence.

Expected standards should be established for each factor and only those prospective suppliers that satisfy an essential minimum standard in every factor should be invited to tender.

A similar process can then be repeated once the tenders are received except that:

Table 12.4 Factors to consider in the pre-qualification stage

Factor	Indicated by
Organization	Size of company. Resource management structure. Presence of a quality management system. Membership of trade or professional associations
Financial	Form of ownership. Financial ratios, assets and liabilities. Credit and bank references
Experience	Types, size and location of similar work in hand and/or completed. Utilization of subcontractors, partners and other resources
Management	Experience, qualifications, and commitment of line managers. Formal training and development systems
Performance	Achievement of recent contracts. References from recent and current customers. Attitude to and recovery from service failures

- Additional factors will now be taken into consideration relating to the specific nature of the work to be undertaken
- Each factor should be weighted according to its importance to the objectives of the project
- Each factor is measured for each tenderer, ideally quantitatively and where this is not possible by judgement using numerical scales
- The measures for each factor are then aggregated to produce a total score for each prospective supplier.

Finally, these scores can be compared against the bid prices to establish the tender that represents best value for money.

12.6 NEGOTIATION PROCESS

Negotiation is a search for agreement, seeking acceptance, consensus and alignment of views. Negotiation in a project can take place on an informal basis throughout the project lifecycle, or on a formal basis such as during procurement, and between signatories to a contract.

Source: *APM Body of Knowledge 5th Edition*, with permission of the Association for Project Management.

The objective of most negotiations is to achieve an acceptable and agreed outcome for all participants – often referred to as 'win/win'. This does not mean that all parties will be equally happy with the result, but that the outcome is sustainable and does not lead to conflict in the future.

To conclude a successful negotiation that maintains or enhances the relationships between the people involved, the Project Manager should aim to understand and address the underlying motivation, wants and needs of all parties, and separate the different views from the people involved.

A structured process gives the negotiator a framework and some checks on progress. The main stages of any negotiation are preparation, discussion, proposals and bargaining, and closing. These are now briefly described.

12.6.1 Preparation

During the preparation stage it is important for the negotiators to prepare themselves for the meeting to follow. To do this they should:

- Understand the issue/problem by studying all relevant material
- Learn about opponents' objectives (if possible) – this should avoid any surprises
- Anticipate opponents' strategies

- Define their own objectives and priorities
- Agree their own negotiating strategy and allocate roles and responsibilities. This will include deciding which member of the team will lead the negotiation, the member who is to take notes and the member who will observe
- Establish what they are prepared to trade and establish their 'bottom line'. As well as deciding on their 'bottom line' the team should also anticipate the other party's 'bottom line' and areas of potential trade.

12.6.2 Discussion

The first step in the negotiation meeting should be to open up the discussions. This will involve:

- Trading information and checking any assumptions that have been made about the other party. At this point you may have to change your expectations in the light of some information gained from the other party.
- Looking for signals from the other party about interest points and areas that they will not discuss. Time spent at this step will assist the process later. This will involve the note taker in keeping notes of the discussions made, any phrases that may indicate that the other party is prepared to trade (e.g. 'normally ...', 'mostly we ...', 'there may be possibilities ...'). The observer should be concentrating on the responses of the other party to the statements made during the discussion.

It is often useful after this step to take a short break so that the information gathered by the negotiator, observer and note taker can be analysed and the negotiation strategy improved.

12.6.3 Proposals and bargaining

You should now be in a position to start making proposals and undertake some bargaining in respect of these.

- The opening bids should be made in the expectation of there being a counter bid. If your bids get rejected then you may have missed something in the discussion step, so go back. If a counter bid is made then you move into bargaining to get closer to a deal.
- Bargaining statements should always be made in format of 'If you ... then we ....' followed by counter-proposals, adjusting until you come to an acceptable agreement.
- During this stage it is again useful to break off to analyse the information gained by the team. This also stops hasty decisions being made and can lead to a better deal for all concerned.

12.6.4 Closing

It is important to confirm the agreement and record the results of the negotiation. This should be in the form of a written record that all parties can sign and leave the negotiating table with an accurate and complete record of the agreement achieved.

This is most important, as you want to avoid any comeback or misunderstandings later. When the agreement is written up, both parties should be prepared to scrutinize it carefully and make sure that the common agreement reached orally has been transcribed accurately into the written form. This may require some minor adjustments until the final document is agreed.

NB: Whilst negotiation has been described here as part of the procurement process, a project has many constraints such as time, cost and quality, and areas such as scope, requirements and technical aspects where people may have different agendas and interests. In all of these cases, the Project Manager may need to negotiate to reach agreement.

12.7 CONTRACT

12.7.1 Forms of contract

The number and scope of contracts used will affect how the relationship with the supplier will be managed. The main types of arrangement are:

- **Comprehensive Contract** – this is the simplest arrangement in which one supplier is responsible for everything required for the project. This is most appropriate where the customer wishes to place all responsibility with one supplier. The greatest risk to the customer with this arrangement is that the project depends upon the performance of one supplier. It also requires the customer having to define in detail what is expected of the supplier together with the parties' responsibilities and liabilities. However, the advantage is that the supplier has to manage all of the relationships between everyone who is supplying goods and services for the project.

- **Sequence of Contracts** – this involves having a sequence of two or more contracts stage by stage through the project. For example one supplier could be contracted for the design stage and a separate supplier for the construction stage. This is most appropriate where there is uncertainty about what is required and how it is to be delivered. This arrangement enables the customer to limit their commitment and risk at the start of the project and provides an opportunity at the end of each stage to review the viability of the project. The biggest downsides are that time has to be allowed for multiple contract negotiations and they provide less firm cost estimates.

- **Parallel Contracts** – this involves having separate contracts with each specialist supplier. This is most appropriate where individual suppliers have limited capabilities or know-how relative to the size or type of work needed for the project. This arrangement does mean that the customer has to manage the relationships with all suppliers.

12.7.2 Contractual relationships

In a similar way, there are various types of contractual relationships that need to be considered. The main types are:

- **Partnering** – this is often seen in manufacturing and construction industries where the customer invites bids for a contract on the basis that the customer and the supplier will work together to manage their contract and in particular plan to avoid and control problems and risks. The intention is that all parties should achieve their objectives to achieve a 'win-win'.

- **Alliancing** – this is similar to partnering except that rather than relating to a single contract it forms the basis for developing a successful series of contracts or a series of separate packages of work under one contract.

Partnering and alliancing are based on sharing ideas and information to improve all parties' performance during a contract or over a series of contracts. To succeed they require trust and a cultural change from adversarial attitudes – both between the parties to the contract and within their organizations. This is best achieved by establishing a single management team responsible to all the parties' senior managers. The intention to enter into partnering or an alliance is often stated in a 'framework agreement' established prior to entering into a contract for the work for the project.

- **Turnkey** – this is a form of comprehensive contract used in the construction industry in which the contractor is responsible for the complete supply of a facility, usually with responsibility for fitness for purpose, training operators, pre-commissioning and commissioning. It usually has a fixed completion date, a fixed price and guaranteed performance levels.

Table 12.5 Popular terms of payment

Firm Fixed Price Contract	A contract where the customer pays a set amount to the supplier regardless of that supplier's cost to complete the contract. In these contracts the customer knows the total price before entering into the contract; however, any variations to the contract can lead to claims from the supplier for extra time and payment. The supplier bears most of the risks associated with controlling costs
Cost Reimbursement Type Contract	A category of contract based on payments to a supplier for allowable estimated costs, usually requiring 'best efforts' performance standard from the supplier. In these contracts the customer pays ('reimburses') the supplier's costs of providing people and other resources to be used as directed by the customer. This enables: ■ A supplier to be chosen and to start work before what has to be done is well defined ■ The customer to vary the amount and speed of work ■ The customer to be responsible for the economical use of resources The customer bears most of the risks associated with controlling costs
Cost Plus Fixed Fee Contract	A type of contract where the customer reimburses the supplier for the supplier's allowable costs plus a fixed fee. A form of contract that combines the previous two types in which the customer has greater control over costs but bears most of the risks associated with these costs, but the supplier receives a fixed fee
Target Cost Contract	This is a development of the cost-reimbursement idea where both customer and supplier start by agreeing a target cost for an uncertain or high-risk project and agree that both will share savings and over-runs in the final cost relative to the target cost. Thus the customer and supplier share the risks associated with controlling costs. Target contracts are the best basis when partnering or alliancing are involved
Target Price Contract	This is similar to the Target Cost Contract but relates to the target price rather than the target cost. The target price relates to the negotiated estimated costs plus profit or fee
Cost Plus Incentive Fee Contract	A type of contract where the customer reimburses the supplier for the supplier's allowable costs and the supplier earns a profit if defined criteria are met. Traditionally, larger engineering and construction contracts have included terms for the reduction of payments to suppliers if the supplier is late in completing the work or if the specified performance levels are not achieved. These are referred to as 'liquidated damages' agreements in that the amount of the reduction is a demonstrably genuine pre-estimate of the damage likely to be suffered by the customer. (Any larger sum might be construed to be a penalty and as such would not be enforceable.) The Cost Plus Incentive Fee Contract is effectively the reverse of the liquidated damages approach

12.8 SUPPLIER REIMBURSEMENT

An important consideration as part of the contract is
what payment terms are most likely to motivate suppliers
to achieve the objectives of the project (Table 12.5).

12.9 PROCUREMENT – EXERCISES

(Sample answers are provided in Appendix A for the
first question within each section. Answers to the remaining
questions can be assessed against the relevant section
within the chapter.)

APMP topic 5.4

1 Explain a simple procurement process.
2 Explain the typical contents of a procurement strategy.
3 Describe a supplier selection process.
4 Describe five methods for supplier reimbursement.
5 Describe three different contractual relationships.

APMP topic 7.5

1 Explain four stages that an effective negotiation
should progress through.

People management

13

13 People management

13.1 PURPOSE

The purpose of this chapter is to describe some of the people management issues that are faced by Project Managers during the course of a project. The areas covered are:

- **Leadership** – explaining the principles and importance of motivation, describing typical leadership qualities and styles and also describing a situational leadership model (APMP topic 7.3)
- **Teamwork** – explaining the importance of team development and describing a team development model and a social roles model (APMP topic 7.2)
- **Conflict management** – describing the sources of conflict in the project lifecycle and describing a conflict resolution model (APMP topic 7.4).

As can be seen from the definitions in Table 13.1, the common theme across these areas is the creation, maintenance and working towards a common purpose or goal.

- Leadership creates and maintains the common purpose.
- Teamwork is about people working together to achieve that common purpose.
- Conflict management is about addressing any issues that could divert the team away from the common purpose.

13.2 DEFINITIONS

The key terms related to people management have been defined in the APM Body of Knowledge (Table 13.1).

Table 13.1 Key terms in relation to people management

	PRINCE2	APM Body of Knowledge
Leadership	Not defined	The ability to establish vision and direction, to influence and align others towards a common purpose, and to empower and inspire people to achieve project success. It enables the project to proceed in an environment of change and uncertainty
Teamwork	Not defined	The process whereby people work collaboratively towards a common goal as distinct from other ways that individuals can work within a group
Conflict management	Not defined	The process of identifying and addressing differences that if unmanaged would affect project objectives. Effective conflict management prevents differences becoming destructive elements in a project

The APM Body of Knowledge definitions are extracts from the *APM Body of Knowledge 5th Edition*, reproduced with the permission of the Association for Project Management

13.3 LEADERSHIP

> Leadership is the ability to establish vision and direction, to influence and align others towards a common purpose, and to empower and inspire people to achieve project success. It enables the project to proceed in an environment of change and uncertainty.
>
> Source: *APM Body of Knowledge 5th Edition*, with permission of the Association for Project Management.

An essential aspect of leadership is the ability to motivate others to achieve a common purpose by applying a flexible approach to the management of the team. In this section we consider the nature of motivation and then look at different styles of leadership.

Leadership should be exercised at all levels with the project, from the Project Board and the Project Manager through to the individual Team Managers. Thus, whilst leaders need followers, leaders must also be able and willing to follow.

13.3.1 Motivation

The performance of team members will depend on a combination of their ability and their motivation. Whereas ability can be taught, an individual's motivation will depend on a number of factors. Accordingly, it is important that a Project Manager understands what may motivate people in order to get the most out of them. There are a number of motivational theories, which will help this understanding.

Abraham Maslow – hierarchy of human needs

Maslow's hierarchy of human needs has, as its basis, the idea that the same person will be motivated by different factors or needs, according to the things that are preoccupying them at the time. This preoccupation is determined by what's going on in their life and is presented in the form of a pyramid (Figure 13.1).

- **Physiological needs** – at the lowest level, people are motivated by the need to survive, e.g. by the provision of food, drink and rest.
- **Safety or security needs** – if life is not under threat, then people are next motivated by the need for safety or security, e.g. by keeping their job or home.
- **Social needs** – once the physiological and safety needs are catered for, people then have a need for love, affection and belonging. People want to be part of a group or team and not to be isolated.
- **Esteem or egoistic needs** – once the lower three levels are satisfied, people begin to be motivated by things that are potentially more valuable to the organization that employs them, e.g. people in a professional environment who are motivated at this level will usually work hard to build and keep their reputation for competence and hard work.

Figure 13.1 Maslow's hierarchy of human needs

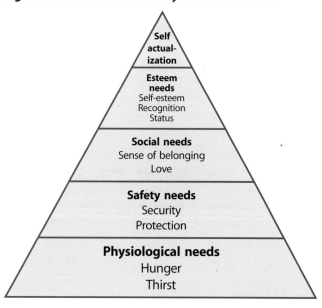

■ **Self-actualization needs** – the highest level is about self-fulfilment or realization of personal development. A person at this level is most likely to be concerned with the pursuit of personal excellence and the pursuit of the vision of what they, as an individual, want to be in their life.

Accordingly, a Project Manager can boost the project's chances of a positive outcome by ensuring that the three lowest levels of need are satisfied and by providing opportunities for individuals to fulfil their esteem/egoistic and self-actualization needs.

Frederick Herzberg – motivators and hygiene factors

Herzberg carried out research among 200 professional engineers and accountants, asking them what events in their work resulted in a marked increase or decrease in their job satisfaction and hence their motivation.

He found that motivation factors for these professional people could be categorized into positive and negative motivators (Figure 13.2).

■ **Positive motivators** are those which, when they are right, will increase motivation levels. Thus achievement, recognition and challenge can all increase job satisfaction and levels of productivity, quality and creativity.

■ **Negative motivators** (or hygiene factors) are those things which, when they are wrong, can de-motivate. Thus a lack of security, a poor working environment and insufficient money will reduce job satisfaction and motivational levels. However, people are unlikely to be motivated by improvements to the hygiene factors.

Figure 13.2 Herzberg's motivators

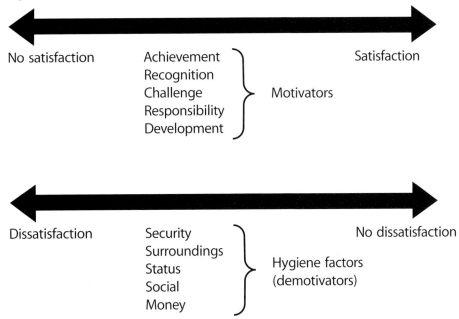

Thus, what motivates people tends to be the things they do and what de-motivates them is the environment in which they do it. Therefore a Project Manager should ensure that the hygiene factors are right first and then concentrate on the motivators.

13.3.2 Typical leadership qualities

In his book, *Organizing Genius*, Warren Bennis identifies a number of characteristics of great leaders:

- Must command respect and inspire trust
- Civility – not imposing your views on others
- A pragmatic dreamer – gets things done, but immortal longings
- Scientific minds with poetic souls
- Original vision – a dream of achievable greatness rather than a simple will to succeed
- Articulation of the vision – sharing the meaning of the goal, inspiring zeal and uniting the team
- Provider of freedom to be creative – using failure as a learning opportunity
- Willing to decide, but prefers to allow team to decide
- Protector – from undue outside influence or criticism, even enabling the team to draw strength and focus from opposition
- Passionate belief – seducing others into sharing the dream
- Facilitation rather than control
- Communicator – ensuring the right information gets to the right people
- Allowing people to discover their own greatness.

This list is particularly relevant to project leadership as Bennis' book is all about leading groups of talented people in an environment of 'collaborative meritocracy', rather than in a conventional 'functional bureaucracy'.

13.3.3 Leadership styles

Douglas McGregor

Scottish psychologist Douglas McGregor suggested that there were two extremes in the way that leaders perceived the people who worked for them, and that these perceptions strongly influence a leader's style of leadership.

McGregor called these extremes theory X and theory Y leaders.

- **Theory X leaders** believe that people must be made to do work, otherwise they will not do it. Such people have little ambition and dislike work. This leader will instruct, drive and monitor performance regularly, and is almost completely 'task focused', usually adopting an autocratic approach.
- **Theory Y leaders** believe that people enjoy work, respond to challenges, look for job satisfaction and are essentially self-motivated. This leader will allow people to be self-managing and is much more 'people focused', usually adopting a democratic approach.

Neither model is completely correct, but some project team members will exhibit predominantly theory X characteristics and others predominantly theory Y characteristics. Accordingly, a Project Manager may have to adapt their leadership style to the characteristics of the team members.

Based on the continuum from theory X to theory Y, McGregor defined three basic leadership styles:

- **Autocratic** (do it my way) – most appropriate where team members need direction, for example in an emergency situation
- **Democratic** (do it our way) – most appropriate where team members have something to contribute, for example in a meeting or brainstorming situation
- **Free rein** (do it your way) – most appropriate where team members are able to get on with the work at hand, for example where they are dealing with routine tasks with which they are very familiar.

John Adair

John Adair developed his concept of action-centred leadership at the British Army officer training college at Sandhurst. He believes that an effective leader needs to balance three separate and often incompatible needs (Figure 13.3):

- Task needs, i.e. the work that has to be done
- Team needs, i.e. building and maintaining an effective and productive team
- Individual needs, i.e. providing for the individual's need for attention and development.

Figure 13.3 Adair's action-centred leadership

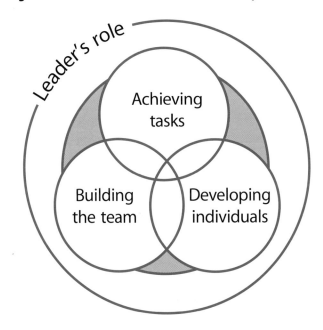

The Project Manager's aim should be to achieve an equal balance between these needs. To achieve this Adair defines five key actions that the Project Manager should perform on an ongoing basis:

- Define objectives
- Plan and discuss
- Brief and involve
- Support and monitor
- Evaluate.

Table 13.2 provides a useful checklist to help Project Managers give equal attention to the task, individual and team.

13.3.4 Situational leadership

Situational leadership relates to the need for leaders to adopt different leadership styles depending on the situation they are in. To a certain extent, most people will do this automatically, for example we will try to be more supportive towards someone who is new to a role than we are to someone who is very experienced; similarly we will chase up tasks issued to some people more frequently than others based on our experience of dealing with these different people. However, it is useful to have a simple model that can be applied for most situations in which Project Managers are likely to find themselves.

Such a model was developed in the late 1960s by Paul Hersey and Kenneth Blanchard, This model enables Project Managers to analyse the needs of the situation they are dealing with and then adopt the most appropriate leadership style.

Hersey and Blanchard characterized leadership style in terms of the amount of direction and of support that leaders give to their followers. This is depicted by a simple 2 × 2 grid that identifies four distinctive leadership styles (Figure 13.4).

These four leadership styles may be summarized as follows:

Table 13.2 Balancing the three needs (Adair's action-centred leadership)

Key actions	Task	Team	Individual
Define objectives	Identify task and constraints	Involve team and share commitment	Clarify objectives and gain acceptance
Plan and discuss	Establish priorities	Consult	Assess skills
	Check resources	Encourage ideas	Set targets
	Set standards	Develop structure	Delegate
Brief and involve	Brief the team	Answer questions	Listen and enthuse
	Check understanding	Give/receive feedback	
Support and monitor	Report progress	Coordinate effort	Advise and counsel
	Maintain standards	Handle conflict	Assist and reassure
			Recognize effort
Evaluate	Summarize progress	Recognize success	Assess performance
	Review objectives	Learn from failure	Appraise
	Re-plan if required		Guide and train

- **S1 – Telling**. This style is characterized by one-way communication in which the leader defines the roles of followers and tells them what, how, when and where to do various tasks and then supervises the tasks closely. Decisions are made by the leader and announced to the follower.

- **S2 – Selling**. With this style most of the direction is still provided by the leader, but the leader also attempts, through two-way communication and support, to get the follower to 'buy-in' to decisions that have been made.

- **S3 – Participating**. With this style the leader and the follower now share the decision-making through the use of two-way communication and facilitating behaviour from the leader.

- **S4 – Delegating**. This style involves the leader letting the follower manage their own work. The leader is still involved in decisions and problem solving, but control is with the follower, with the follower deciding when and how the leader will be involved.

Which style to use will depend largely on the person being led, i.e. the follower, with the leadership style being driven by the competence and commitment of the follower. Accordingly, Hersey and Blanchard extended their model to include a Development Level of the follower based on the level of competence and commitment.

- **D1 – Low Competence and Low Commitment**. The follower generally lacks the specific skills required for the job in hand, and lacks the confidence and/motivation to tackle it.

Figure 13.4 Situational leadership styles

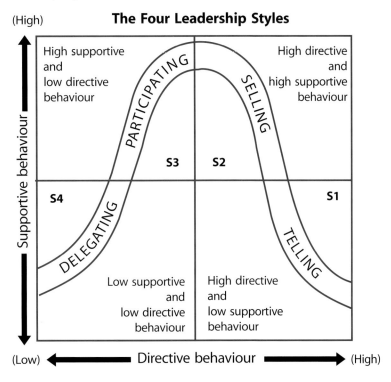

The Four Leadership Styles

(High)

High supportive
and
low directive
behaviour

PARTICIPATING

High directive
and
high supportive
behaviour

SELLING

S3   S2

S4   S1

DELEGATING

TELLING

Low supportive
and
low directive
behaviour

High directive
and
low supportive
behaviour

Supportive behaviour

(Low) ◄——— Directive behaviour ———► (High)

- **D2 – Some Competence and Low Commitment**. The follower has some relevant skills, but is unable to do the job without some help. The task or the situation may well be new to them.

- **D3 – High Competence and Variable Commitment**. The follower is experienced and capable, but may lack the confidence to go it alone, or the motivation to do it well/quickly.

- **D4 – High Competence and High Commitment**. The follower is experienced at the job, and is comfortable with their ability to do it well. Indeed, they may even be more skilled than the leader.

Accordingly, the leadership style adopted by the leader should correspond to the development level of the follower.

It must be noted, however, that the development levels are also situational in that a person may be well skilled, confident and motivated in their usual job, but would drop down to level D1 when faced with a task requiring skills that they do not possess.

13.4 TEAMWORK

Teamwork is when people work collaboratively towards a common goal as distinct from other ways that individuals can work within a group.

Source: *APM Body of Knowledge 5th Edition*, with permission of the Association for Project Management.

Teamwork is an essential aspect of project work. Project teams perform best when they consist of a number of people who are committed to a common goal that none can achieve alone, and where inter-relationships between tasks are managed by collaboration.

13.4.1 A team development model

When any team is brought together for the first time, such as in the case of a project team, the group of individuals will go through a number of phases until they form an efficient and effective team.

One theory of group dynamics (developed by Dr Bruce Tuckman) suggest that groups go through a series of four phases, the first two involving conflict, the last two involving cohesion. Understanding these phases and their impact on the team will enable the Project Manager to deal successfully with the problems that arise during the various phases. A structured teambuilding approach will help groups move more quickly through these phases.

By understanding and recognizing the symptoms and behaviours displayed during each phase, the Project Manager will be able to help reassure the team members that things are not going wrong and that what they are experiencing and feeling is a natural part of the team development.

These four phases are briefly described in Table 13.3.

A fifth stage is sometimes referred to as 'Adjourning' or 'Mourning', when the team disbands. This stage is about learning from experience, both from an individual and organizational perspective. This could include updating of CVs, some form of continuous professional development, or the maintenance of the organization's knowledge base. However, there can also be a significant sense of loss as the team disbands and the individuals struggle to move on. This will be more likely to happen where the team has been successful and the individuals have enjoyed being part of the team.

13.4.2 A social roles model

Individuals within a team will perform better if they are performing in a social role that plays to their strengths.

Meredith Belbin of the Henley Management Centre undertook research into teams and team roles over the course of 10 years. The result of this research was the identification of 'team roles', showing that different people have different strengths in different types of activity and that, in a given environment, some combinations of roles work better than others.

For each of the team roles, Belbin documented their typical features, positive qualities and allowable weaknesses (Table 13.4). An allowable weakness is one that facilitates the strength associated with a given team role and does not imply a need for correction.

It is believed that everyone has a preferred team role, and a secondary team role which they assume when someone exhibits their preferred role more dominantly. Everyone also has at least one team role that they should try to avoid.

Belbin concluded that successful teams require a balanced mix of all of these roles.

A team that is out of balance will under-perform. There may be too many people of the same or similar type, which can create too much competition among team members. A vital team role may not be represented, which can undermine the efficiency of the team. By assessing the team roles that are present within a team the Project Manager will be able to:

- Identify gaps in the composition of the team that will need attention
- Improve the self-insight of the team members
- Heighten understanding between colleagues of their respective team roles
- Provide a reference point to allow colleagues to agree how to divide work between them.

Table 13.3 Tuckman's phases of team development

Phase	Description	Potential Problems	Actions
Forming	When the team first comes together, people tend to be polite and true feelings are hidden Individuals are trying to get to know each other	Limited team identity Confusion and anxiety No common goal Aims and objectives go undiscussed Cliques form Frustration at lack of progress	Acknowledge individual attitudes and depersonalize them Manage expectations, explain context and nature of team task Help team reach consensus about its purpose
Storming	Individuals will now start to assert themselves and this results in debate or even arguments about the purpose of the team	Conflict arises People talk loudly and aggressively Others may be silent Some will think that the team is wasting time	Use brainstorming techniques to create the right environment Acknowledge uncertainty Share the vision and involve everyone Agree team objectives
Norming	The team shifts from competition to collaboration. Norms are established for the way the team will work together	Role conflict declines as individuals assume their respective roles 'Groupthink' emerges and any creativity is lost	Support the work being done Keep the team focused Give regular feedback Introduce fresh stimulus as needed Find time for fun
Performing	The team is in a dynamic state, sharing ideas, energy, understanding and commitment. Everyone is working towards achieving the agreed goals	Team becomes 'closed' and unapproachable	Keep focus on team performance Encourage communication Provide opportunities for team growth, challenge and training Act as team player Rely on commitment rather than control

Table 13.4 Social roles model: team roles

Team role	Description	Typical features	Positive qualities	Allowable weaknesses
Plant	The ideas person Provides solutions	Individualistic, serious-minded, unorthodox	Imaginative, creative, solves difficult problems	Too preoccupied to communicate effectively Disregards practical details, protocol
Resource Investigator	Explorer of opportunities Good at developing outside contacts	Enthusiastic, curious, communicative	Capacity for contacting people Explores opportunities Ability to respond to challenge	Liable to lose interest once the initial fascination has passed
Coordinator	Clarifies goals, coordinates, promotes decision-making	Calm, self-confident, controlled	Promotes decision-making, clarifies goals Strong sense of objectives	Can be seen as manipulative Delegates personal work
Shaper	Forces things along, shapes team's efforts Identifies relationships between issues	Outgoing, dynamic	Thrives on pressure, drive Ready to challenge inertia, ineffectiveness, complacency and self-deception	Prone to provocation, irritation and impatience
Monitor Evaluator	Analyser of options and good judge of things	Sober, prudent	Judgement, discretion, hard-headedness	Lacks inspiration Lacks ability to motivate others
Team worker	The diplomat Listens to all sides Calms the waters	Socially orientated, perceptive, diplomatic	Listens, builds, averts friction Promotes team spirit	Indecisiveness in crisis
Implementer	Good organizer who turns ideas into practical actions	Conservative, dutiful and predictable Disciplined, reliable and efficient	Organizing ability Common sense, hard-working	Lack of flexibility Slow to respond to new possibilities

Team role	Description	Typical features	Positive qualities	Allowable weaknesses
Complete Finisher	Looks after the detail, ensures nothing is missed	Painstaking, orderly, conscientious	Capacity to follow through Perfectionist, delivers on time	Can be a nit-picker Reluctance to delegate Inclined to worry unduly
Specialist	Specialist in a particular subject area	Single-minded, self-starting, dedicated	Provides knowledge and skill in rare supply	Contributes only on a narrow front Dwells on technicalities Overlooks the big picture

The Project Manager can also use this information to help improve the performance of the team by:

- Adopting a leadership style that suits the particular characteristics of the team
- Assigning tasks and responsibilities to team members that suit their strongest team role
- Encouraging team members to draw on the team role strengths of each other
- Coaching each team member on how to develop a secondary set of team roles in order to increase their personal versatility.

If achieved, getting the right balance will result in a number of benefits including:

- Fewer clashes between individuals competing for the same role
- More mutual appreciation and recognition
- A greater contribution to the whole team from each team member
- Insurance against the mistakes that can arise when an individual carries a heavy load of responsibility.

13.5 CONFLICT MANAGEMENT

Conflict management is the process of identifying and addressing differences that if unmanaged would affect project objectives. Effective conflict management prevents differences becoming destructive elements in a project.

Source: *APM Body of Knowledge 5th Edition*, with permission of the Association for Project Management.

There are always likely to be differences of opinion expressed during the life of a project. In most cases these can be resolved through discussion and negotiation. However, when agreement cannot be reached, the differences must be resolved through the use of conflict management.

The role of the Project Manager can be broken down into three main functions:

- Conflict identification – recognizing the potential sources of conflict which may impact on the project
- Conflict reduction – reducing the likelihood or potential impact of the conflicts that have been identified
- Conflict resolution – handling a conflict that has occurred.

13.5.1 Conflict identification

Conflict can arise among individuals, teams and stakeholders, or at an organizational level. Conflict may also occur internally within the project or externally, affecting the project.

Table 13.5 shows the typical sources of conflict that may arise during the project lifecycle.

13.5.2 Conflict reduction

Clearly, the best way to deal with conflict is to deal with it before it becomes destructive and has a detrimental impact on the project objectives. As with the sources of conflict, reduction techniques can be adopted throughout the project lifecycle (Table 13.6).

In addition to the above, many potential conflict situations can easily be reduced by the use of an effective communication process throughout the life of the project:

- Outward communication can be used to ensure that the various aspects of the project are clearly communicated to the project stakeholders
- Inward communication can be used to help identify where conflict situations are starting to arise, e.g. where communication is being avoided, is becoming aggressive or informal methods are starting to be used. These could all be indicators of potential conflict situations.

(For more guidance on effective project communication see Chapter 10.)

Table 13.5 How conflicts may arise in a project's lifecycle

Lifecycle phase	Potential source of conflict
Concept	■ Differences of view about the need for the project
	■ Competition between sponsors of competing projects
Definition	■ Differences of view about the objectives of the project
	■ Differences of view about the scope of the project
	■ Disagreements about task or project requirements in terms of time, cost and quality
	■ Differences of view about how the project will approach the overall project solution
	■ Conflict among the project team members as they go through the 'Forming' phase of team development
Implementation	■ Conflict resulting from miscommunication between participants on responsibility, task handover, support, timescale, cost, payment arrangements
	■ Differences of view in relation to the justification, approval and implications of changes to the project
Handover and Closeout	■ Differences of opinion on the extent to which the project deliverables have been achieved
	■ Disagreements about the point at which responsibility is transferred from the project team
	■ Conflict within the project team as a result of uncertainty or apprehension about the effect of the project coming to a close

Table 13.6 Reducing potential conflicts in a project's lifecycle

Lifecycle phase	Approaches to reducing potential conflict
Concept	▦ Using proven and objective project selection processes to ensure the organization takes on the appropriate number and type of projects which can be supported and resourced
	▦ In a PRINCE2 environment, the appropriate use of the Starting up a Project (SU) process can help avoid potential conflict
Definition	▦ Creating a clear and agreed definition for the project before moving into the implementation phase
	▦ Using PRINCE2, this would start with the Project Brief as a key output of SU and culminate with a commitment by all stakeholders to the Project Initiation Document (or Project Management Plan) as the key output of the Initiating a Project (IP) process
	▦ Using frameworks such as the Tuckman team development model and the Belbin team roles to help create a cohesive team
Implementation	▦ Using techniques such as Responsibility Matrices to clarify roles and responsibilities for the work to be undertaken
	▦ In PRINCE2, the use of Work Packages can help to achieve clarity around the work required to be undertaken
	▦ Involving those with the relevant experience in the detailed planning of each stage in the Implementation phase to help achieve agreement to cost and duration estimates
Handover and Closeout	▦ Defining clear Acceptance Criteria during the definition phase and as part of the Project Initiation Document can help to avoid many areas of conflict as the project approaches closure

13.5.3 Conflict resolution

Where conflict situations occur, they need to be addressed. Thomas and Kilmann developed a useful model for considering the options available in such situations. This model maps two elements:

- **Assertiveness** – the ability and intent to achieve an outcome suitable to the Project Manager's needs
- **Cooperativeness** – the ability and intent to achieve an outcome suitable to the needs of the third party.

When mapped as shown in Figure 13.5, this generates five broad options for dealing with conflict. Each one of these options can be a valid approach, depending on the circumstances surrounding the conflict. The use of this model can help the Project Manager to consider the pros and cons of each approach when dealing with a particular conflict, rather than simply reverting to their natural style of conflict resolution.

The options and their implications are:

- **Avoiding** (low assertiveness, low cooperativeness) – this involves ignoring or retreating from the conflict situation. This may be appropriate where the conflict is:
  - Minor and unlikely to escalate
  - Personal, and withdrawal is feasible
  - Getting worse and people need time to cool off
  - Best resolved by an arbitrator or other third party.

Figure 13.5 Thomas and Kilmann's conflict options model.

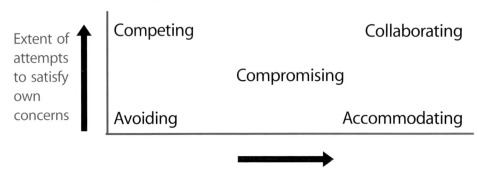

- **Competing** (high assertiveness, low cooperativeness) – this involves insisting on a resolution that meets the Project Manager's needs. This may appear aggressive but would be appropriate where the conflict is:
  - Putting the Project Manager in a situation where they have much to lose and they are in a position of power
  - In relation to a health, safety or other legal requirement
  - Such that there can only be a win-lose outcome.
- **Accommodation** (low assertiveness, high cooperativeness) – this involves acceding to the other person's view. Although this may appear as if the Project Manager is giving ground too easily, this approach may be appropriate where:
  - The other party makes a better case
  - The other party is in a position of power, authority or expertise
  - Acceding will help build longer-term relationships
  - The issue is minor and this will provide the quickest resolution.
- **Compromising** (medium assertiveness, medium cooperativeness) – this involves each party conceding some aspect of their needs in order to reach an agreement. This is probably the most frequently and

appropriately used form of conflict resolution, but care should be exercised as this approach may result in a suboptimal solution. It is most appropriate where:
- It is important for all parties to 'save face'
- There is a range of issues across which compromises can be traded
- Power is evenly balanced between the two parties.
- **Collaborating** (high assertiveness, high cooperativeness) – this involves searching for a solution, which will meet all parties' needs to a large extent. This may not always be possible, and even where it is possible, arriving at a solution may take a considerable amount of time. However, it may be appropriate where:
  - The issue is of high importance to all parties
  - Other options threaten the project objectives
  - There is scope to consider alternative options
  - The situation is unfamiliar to all parties.

13.6 PEOPLE MANAGEMENT – EXERCISES

(Sample answers are provided in Appendix A for the first question within each section. Answers to the remaining questions can be assessed against the relevant section within the chapter.)

APMP topic 7.2

1 Explain how a team develops over time.
2 Explain the importance of team development.
3 Describe a social roles model.

APMP topic 7.3

1 Explain the difference between motivators and hygiene factors.
2 Describe five leadership qualities.
3 Explain the principles and importance of motivation, making five relevant points.
4 Describe how a situational leadership model may be applied as a team develops.

APMP topic 7.4

1 Explain the impact of avoiding conflict and not resolving it, making five relevant points.
2 Describe five sources of conflict in the project lifecycle.
3 Explain five different approaches that could be used in a conflict situation and give an example of when each approach would be relevant.

Exercise solutions

Appendix A: Exercise solutions

This section contains sample answers and guidance on structuring good answers to typical APMP examination questions.

CHAPTER 2 PROJECT MANAGEMENT CONTEXT

APMP topic 1.1

Question 1: *Explain five differences between projects and business-as-usual.*

A project introduces change into an organization whilst business-as-usual (BAU) manages the operational process. When a project delivers (or hands over) its final product, be that a new building, an IT system or an organizational process, the business will change dramatically – a step change in the way that things are done. On the other hand BAU optimizes the way things are done – the operational process – and any changes are introduced relatively slowly.

Projects deliver products into the business as described above, after which the project is usually disbanded. The BAU on the other hand uses the products of the project to realize the benefits. It is unusual for projects to deliver any benefits into the organization during their implementation (unless there is some form of phased roll-out). The task of Benefits Realization belongs to the BAU, and it is fundamental to the success of the project that this task is given priority and that benefits are realized.

Project Managers manage time whereas BAU managers optimize time. In a project the Project Manager has to deliver the products within an appropriate timescale and will take action to make sure the products are delivered on time – this may result in other elements of the project

such as cost suffering. The BAU manager must optimize the timescale within which his/her repetitive tasks are undertaken to drive out inefficiencies within the business.

Projects are inherently risky and Project Managers need to be risk aware and manage the risk, reducing it to an acceptable level. No risk means 'no or little change' and on occasion the Project Manager will take risks to get things done on time and on cost. The BAU manager on the other hand generally looks to reduce risk to its lowest practical level and is often risk averse, and limits change by concentrating on standard production techniques.

BAU often uses a process of continual improvement to increase the quality of the service or the product in question. The Project Manager is responsible for producing products that conform to a specified standard and whilst he or she will look to improve the quality of the process, it is the quality of the output that is the prime concern. The Project Manager should prevent the team from continually trying to improve the product if the customer has not specified this, whilst the BAU manager will see continual improvement as part of their daily routine.

APMP topic 1.2

Question 1: *Explain five typical responsibilities of the Programme Manager throughout the programme lifecycle.*

■ **Planning**. The Programme Manager is responsible for planning the programme. This will start at the beginning of the programme by identifying a list of contributing projects and then having the Project Managers produce a plan and schedule for their work. The Programme Manager takes the outputs from the projects and, in conjunction with the Project Managers, identifies the relationships between the projects and their interdependencies. This will result in a programme plan that can be put into action.

- **Monitoring and controlling the plan**. The Programme Manager is responsible for ensuring that the projects produce their outputs on time, on cost and to the appropriate standard. The Programme Manager will authorize the projects to proceed after each stage of work and will accept the completed products. Any problems must be addressed and appropriate action taken. The Programme Manager must manage the interdependencies between the projects. This may include starting new projects, stopping projects and accelerating projects.
- **Managing communications**. The Programme Manager must make sure that communications to the programme stakeholders are completed in a timely manner and that all information required is collated and issued. This not only includes external stakeholders but also includes those in the programme team and in the projects themselves.
- **Managing risks and issues**. Risks at project level may well have knock-on effects at programme level because they cause problems for other projects. As such it is important that the Programme Manager ensures that the Project Manager escalates all risks within the project that might affect the programme. This enables the Programme Manager to assess these project risks along with any specifically programme-related risks identified in the normal manner. The risk management process in terms of assessment and action is largely the same at both levels, although the impacts may be greater at programme level.
- **Benefits management**. A key responsibility of the Programme Manager is to ensure that benefits are realized as a result of the outputs from the projects being implemented within the business. At the end of each tranche of the programme the manager must make sure that the outputs are accepted by the business and a formal Benefits Realization Plan is in place. The Programme Manager must make sure that the Benefits Realization Plan is developed before the outputs are delivered.

APMP topic 1.3

Question 1: *Explain the principles of portfolio management, making four relevant points.*

In its simplest form, an organization would have a single portfolio containing one or more programmes that support the strategic vision and intent of the company. Each programme is then broken down into its constituent projects, all of which will be undertaken in addition to the normal operations of the organization. Management of the relationships between the programmes, projects and business-as-usual (BAU) is normally the responsibility of a senior management team within the organization concerned.

Key tasks for the senior management team will be to monitor the resource requirements across the three strands, to ensure that the programmes continue to support the global strategy and vision, and to ensure that benefits are realized. In particular the portfolio management team will be concerned with the interdependencies between programmes and projects in terms of scarce resources, balance within the portfolio of risks and returns, timing of the outputs and managing capacity bottlenecks where more than one project requires the same resource(s) at the same time.

It is probable in many large organizations that whilst there might be an overarching strategy each function may have its own portfolio. For example, the Sales and Marketing Department may have a number of programmes running which support its strategic sales vision, each spawning a number of projects whilst the department continues to manage the BAU.

At the same time the Operations Department may have a similar portfolio to manage. This portfolio may be centred on the business cycle (such as the company's financial year). The challenges for the Operational Manager are to implement a number of projects within his or her budget constraints for people and money. Typically, this will involve trade-offs between the day-to-day BAU activities and delivering the projects and prioritizing those projects that must be undertaken. At the operational level the manager will also have the added challenge of implementing new initiatives from other strategies.

APMP topic 1.4

Question 1: *Explain why it is important to consider a project's context, making four relevant points.*

A project cannot operate as an island. It will be affected by the environment in which it is being undertaken. It is therefore important to understand that environment, as this is likely to influence the way in which the project is managed.

A SWOT analysis is one way of understanding the environment. Such an analysis will help the Project Manager understand both the internal strengths and weaknesses and the external opportunities and threats faced by the project. This will help the Project Manager to consider the most appropriate approach to take for managing the project.

Undertaking a PESTLE analysis will help to identify the risks facing the project and the main areas of risk. This will help the Project Sponsor and Project Manager decide who is best placed to own and tackle the risks. It will also indicate how much of the risk should be escalated to the programme or strategic level.

Finally, the results of a PESTLE analysis may well identify the options that could be used to satisfy the reasons for the project. These options can be used as a basis for the Business Case. Careful considerations of these options will ensure that the Business Case is robust and valid before major commitment is made to the project in terms of both time and money.

Failure to consider any of the above factors will significantly increase the chance of project failure, poor public perception and de-motivated teams.

APMP topic 6.1

Question 1: *Describe five benefits of splitting a project into phases.*

Splitting the project will assist with the overall planning of the project. It is very difficult to accurately plan timescales in excess of say, three to six months. By splitting the project into smaller chunks the entire project can be planned at high level and the detail required for the day-to-day management can be planned in detail for three to six months. This gives greater control over the monitoring and control of the project.

The risks inherent in any project can be managed better if the project is split into phases. For example a high-risk project would have more phases; at the end of each phase, a decision is made on whether or not to continue. More frequent decision points allow for gathering information on risks and making sure they are under control before authorizing spend on the next phase. This limits the exposure of the project to risk.

Phases enable the payment profile to be managed as it becomes easier to set the appropriate milestones or decision points related to payments. This is associated with the point made above about planning. Smaller stages planned in greater detail make it easier to plan payments and ensure they are geared to actual progress and delivery of key milestones.

Stages or phases assist the Project Manager to predict the resource requirements, improving utilization of resource and its availability. If the plan is made on a rolling basis of, say, 100 days, the plan can be rolled forward every few weeks and the ongoing need for resources predicted. This will enable costs to be kept to a minimum.

A final and most important benefit of splitting a project into phases or stages is that it allows each phase or stage to be assessed before any further work takes place. The Business Case, risks and overall progress of the project can be assessed by the Sponsor and Steering Group before funds and resources are committed to the next stage or phase. Again this helps to reduce the risk of spending money on a project that has ceased to have any benefits.

APMP topic 6.9

Question 2: *Explain the advantages and disadvantages of using a structured method, making five relevant points.*

Advantages

A structured method brings rigour and discipline to the management of projects within an organization and provides a common language for project management terms. If the method is adopted across the organization, all of the members of the organization will understand the responsibilities associated with their role in the project.

The method will establish common documentation formats and all parties will know where to find the relevant information, e.g. some organizations have a Project Definition Document that clearly describes the project and its objectives and includes many elements normally included in the Project Management Plan.

Disadvantages

In some organizations the method can be implemented with too much rigour and instead of being a means to an end the method becomes a means in itself. This is particularly apparent on smaller projects where the need for rigour and discipline is much less than is needed for a larger project, but the same methods and processes are applied, which makes the project process heavy.

Staff are not adequately trained in the method and its use. For a method to be effective, all staff should understand how it must be applied. This is often not the case,

particularly at senior management level. This can lead to people being unsure of their responsibilities, with confusion and ensuing failure.

Training in the method does not necessarily mean that people understand the techniques of project management such as scheduling, resourcing, risk management. As these basic points are missed, projects continue to fail, and the method is blamed and ceases to be used.

CHAPTER 3 BUSINESS CASE

APMP topic 5.1

Question 1: *Describe the typical contents of the business case.*

The Business Case will typically contain the following sections:

- **Background and reasons** – describes the business setting of the project and the problem that is to be solved, or the opportunity that is to be grasped. The reasons are distinct from the benefits, which describe the improvement that will be gained when the project's products have been implemented.
- **Goals and objectives** – states the key objectives in terms of time, cost and quality for the project and the ultimate goal that will be achieved when the project is closed.
- **Options** – states the options that have been considered, and the selected option and the reasons for its adoption.
- **Key deliverables** – the main products of the project are described here.
- **Scope** – describes the main work areas of the project and the outputs of the project that will form the key deliverables. Will also state what is not being done. Most important as otherwise the readership tends to assume these things are included.

■ **Benefits and outline realization plan** – this is a key section of the Business Case as it is the benefits that justify the expenditure in terms of time and cost that is proposed. The benefits should be tangible and financially biased, and they must outweigh the costs and risks if the business case is to be viable.

■ **Stakeholder analysis** – provides a view of the backers and their role in the project. Also identifies any negative stakeholders and their likely reactions to the project.

■ **Organization structure** – based on the stakeholder analysis this indicates who is taking the key roles in the project, particularly the Sponsor, Steering Group and Project Manager.

■ **Assumptions** – states what has been assumed about the project during the preparation of the business case and what will need to be tested.

■ **Risks** – a list of the major threats and opportunities raised during the preparation of the Business Case.

■ **Issues** – a list of issues requiring resolution.

■ **Dependencies**. A list of things on which the Business Case is dependent.

■ **Constraints**. Those things that the project must work within, such as time, cost, safety, technology, legal, etc.

■ **Investment appraisal**. This states the financial aspects of the business case. This could include discounted cash flow, net present value, internal rate of return and return on investment figures.

■ **Evaluation**. This final section provides a summary of the Business Case and evaluates the investment appraisal.

APMP topic 2.1

Question 1: *Explain the differences between success criteria and success factors.*

Success criteria are those things which, if met, will indicate that the project has been successful. Specifically these revolve around time, cost, quality/performance and the customer's requirements. Of these the last is particularly important. Budgets and timescales are often set in advance, and the customer's requirements and associated acceptance criteria can be difficult to pin down.

What makes the product/deliverable acceptable to the customer? Indeed sometimes the question 'Who is the customer?' needs to be answered.

Examples are:

■ The project completes within four weeks of its target date.

■ The project completes within 10% of the agreed budget.

Success factors are those things that contribute to the achievement of the success criteria. Research has indicated that there are five key factors that can be established against which success can be measured:

■ **Project Objectives**: must be clearly identified within the project plans and kept to throughout the work.

■ **Project Personnel**: the Project Manager and the project team must be competent.

■ **Support from Above**: the project must be supported by top management.

■ **Resources**: time, money, material and people must be sufficient to do the job.

■ **Communication and Control**: communications channels up, down and across the project are established with clear mechanisms for feedback on reports, deliverables and quality. Control such as milestones, plans, approvals, reviews etc. must be in place and used. Contractors must be responsive to their clients.

CHAPTER 4 ORGANIZATION AND GOVERNANCE

APMP topic 6.7

Question 1: *Explain the strengths and weaknesses of managing a project in a matrix type of organizational structure. Make five relevant points.*

Many organizations use this form of organizational structure to manage their projects, as business-as-usual and project work can coexist and be undertaken by the same workforce. Projects can draw on the entire resources of the organization. Resources can be 'shared' by a number of projects. In theory, a matrix organization attempts to support effective project management by formalizing the informal links between projects and the organization's specialist functions. This facilitates communication at the operational level.

As all projects within the organization are managed using the matrix there is a common understanding of the need to share staff between the project and the business. Personnel within the business (or function) are able to enhance their technical expertise whilst getting experience of working on a range of projects. This provides greater variance in job role, gives individuals a wider career path and is often seen as motivational.

As each project has different objectives and technical needs the organization can be tailored to meet the needs of the project, whilst maintaining a single point of responsibility for the project, facilitating a rapid response to client needs. However, this can lead to difficulties as the individual team members may have divided loyalties between the function and the project.

Dual reporting can also be a problem in matrix organizations. Members of the team have to report to the Project Manager on project matters, and often have to report the same thing to their Functional Manager. This, of course, increases the individual's workload and can be de-motivating.

Sharing resources can lead to conflict between the functions that need the resources to undertake business-as-usual and the project that needs the resources at specific times in order to meet time constraints. In addition, projects may compete for the same resource, and functional departments may be reluctant to surrender their best personnel to projects.

APMP topic 1.5

Question 1: *Explain the typical responsibilities of the Project Sponsor in the Concept, Definition, Implementation and Handover and Closeout phases of the project lifecycle.*

Concept phase

During Concept the Project Sponsor (PS) should establish, with the Project Manager (PM), the context of the project. This will include consideration of the political, economic, social, technical, legal and environmental aspects of the project. This will help the PM to design the team, which the PS should confirm. The PS should also make sure that adequate resources are made available. During Concept the Business Case for the project must be prepared and this will require the PS to state the benefits and contribute to its production. On completion the PS will sign off the Business Case and make application to the corporate body for agreement to proceed into the Definition phase. The PS owns the Business Case and is accountable for delivering the benefits to the organization.

Definition phase

During Definition the Project Management Plan (PMP) will be produced and this will incorporate fundamental decisions on risk, plans, budgets and stakeholder management. The PS will make these decisions and provide guidance throughout. It is very important that the PS is involved and 100% committed to the project; this will be demonstrated by his or her involvement during Definition. At the end of Definition, the PS will make an application to the corporate body for the funding to cover the project and sign off the PMP.

Implementation phase

During Implementation the PS will receive the regular progress reports, resolve issues, chair Steering Group meetings, and provide advice, guidance and support to the PM throughout. If the project is staged, the PS will be required to authorize the PM to proceed with the work in the next stage of the implementation phase. Another important facet of the PS involvement in implementation will be making decisions about change requests received and analysed by the PM. Finally, the PS must make sure that arrangements are made to realize the benefits, and that the benefits are benchmarked during the Implementation phase.

Handover and Closeout phase

In this final phase of the project the PS must accept the project's deliverables after checking and being confident that they have met their acceptance criteria. The PS must ensure that she or he understands the amount of outstanding work and the arrangements that have been made to have it completed. During this phase the PS must complete the arrangements for benefits realization with the business areas concerned. The PS must take part in the Post-Project Review and sign off the final project reports.

APMP topic 6.8

Question 1: *Explain the main responsibilities of five key project management team roles.*

Project Sponsor

The PS owns the project's Business Case and is the primary risk taker. Representing the business, the PS is primarily concerned with value for money. Throughout the project the sponsor is the key decision-maker and will hold the budget for the project. The PS will chair the Steering Group. Ultimate accountability for the success or failure of the project will lie with the PS. Other responsibilities include:

- Decisions on change matters
- Issue resolution
- Ensure agreed risk management activities are implemented.

Steering Group

This group is made up of key stakeholders and chaired by the Project Sponsor. Its role is to provide guidance on all aspects of the project, particularly with regard to strategic direction, risk management decisions and issue management.

Project Manager

The PM is responsible for the day-to-day management of the project on behalf of the PS and the Steering Group. The PM will ensure that:

- The Project Management Plan is produced
- The project schedule is accurate and reflects realistic estimates
- The Statements of Work are written and issued
- The work is monitored and controlled in an appropriate manner
- Management reports are issued in a timely manner and accurately reflect the situation.

Project support office

The project support office or PSO will provide administrative support to the PM throughout the project. This will include preparing minutes of meetings, logging issues and risks, receiving progress reports from the teams and updating the schedule accordingly, bringing matters of concern to the attention of the PM. The PSO will often consist of subject matter experts on matters such as risk and planning software.

Team Manager

The Team Managers will run the teams of people who are undertaking the work itself. Their responsibilities include scheduling the teams' work, making sure the work is to the required standard, motivating the teams, liaising with the PM, receiving work instructions (statements of work), managing team level risks, reporting progress to the PM and taking corrective action at team level if required.

APMP topic 1.6

Question 1: *Explain the role of a project office, making four relevant points.*

In all but the smallest of projects there will be a significant amount of administration to be undertaken. Without any support this falls to the PM to complete and can easily result in one of two outcomes – the administration is left whilst the PM concentrates on day-to-day management, or the PM gets the administration done at the expense of the day-to-day management. Alternatively, the PM works lots of overtime!

This is where the role of the basic project office comes in. It can be administrative support, perhaps two or three days a week, and the person taking the role assists the PM with administration, completion of minutes of meetings, maintaining the schedule, receiving and analysing reports. In a small project, this is often a part-time function and can be difficult to justify in terms of headcount and the resources available. For this reason many organizations have established a formal PSO function.

A PSO is a group of five or six staff who support several projects between them. As the peak demand for administration varies the staff are able to cross project boundaries and assist where required.

Typical responsibilities of a PSO include:

■ Operate a filing system for several projects
■ Operate a configuration management system

■ Be a centre of expertise for:
  • Estimating techniques
  • Planning and control software
  • Risk analysis methods and software
■ Preparation of plans
■ Project reporting
■ Assurance of the process
■ Maintain logs for risks, issues and changes.

In some organizations the PSO functions are combined with a Programme Support Office, becoming a Programme and Project Support Office (PPSO). At the programme level, the role is often expanded to cover the governance of the project, and staff in these units often act as 'deputy' managers.

APMP topic 6.10

Question 1: *For two distinct principles of governance of project management, explain the possible effects of not practising them.*

■ **Principle**: The project Business Case is supported by relevant and realistic information that provides a reliable basis for making authorization decisions.

The Business Case is the driver of a project as it provides the business justification for the project and states why the forecast time and effort is worth the expenditure. It must contain tangible business benefits that can be accurately measured and realized post project. If this is not done, the money spent on the project will be wasted as the reason and benefits for the project are lost over time.

The Business Case is also used to continually align the project with the business. It also provides a focus for the ongoing justification of the project and will be used at key decision points to decide whether the project should continue. If this is not done the project becomes a 'mastermind' project – 'I've started so I'll finish!' Again the effort and costs are wasted.

■ **Principle**: There are clearly defined criteria for reporting project status and for the escalation of risks and issues to the levels required by the organization.

For any project to succeed it is essential that the risks faced by the project are identified, analysed and appropriate actions taken to mitigate the threats or maximize the opportunities. This often requires escalation to the PS and/or Steering Group. If the escalation process is not defined these decisions will not be made, opportunities will be missed and risks will occur, increasing project costs and timescales, and ultimately leading to project failure.

Similarly, issues require immediate action. If they are not resolved they will become 'showstoppers' and the project will fail. Clear lines of escalation are required and all parties need to be clear about, and accept, their responsibilities.

Finally, if clear reporting lines are not in place senior project staff, the PS and Steering Group will not have the right level of information to make decisions and this leads to extensive delays.

CHAPTER 5 PLANNING

APMP topic 3.1

Question 1: *Explain how a Work Breakdown Structure will be constructed and its purpose in a project.*

A Work Breakdown Structure (WBS) is a hierarchical breakdown of the activities that are required to produce the products described in the product breakdown structure. It is not strictly necessary to have a Product Breakdown Structure available before the WBS is constructed but it will help. If this is the case then each product will have a breakdown of activities beneath it.

This is shown in Figure A.1. To produce the site description five tasks are required as shown.

Whilst the top level remains as a product the subsidiary level contains activities.

Each element of the WBS is numbered and this numbering will remain constant throughout the project.

Figure A.1 Example of a Work Breakdown Structure

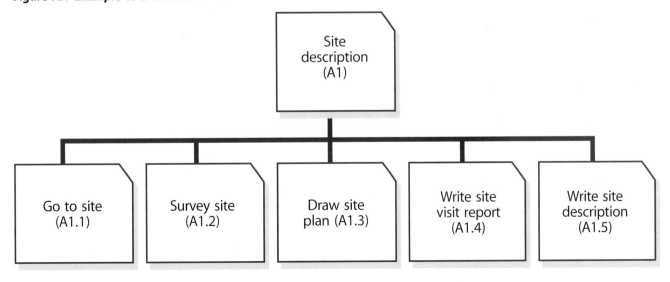

The key purposes of the WBS are to:

- Help define the scope of the project
- Force the team to think through the production process
- Form the basis for precedence networks and estimating
- Define the work content
- Assist in the preparation of Statement of Works
- Form the basis of Earned Value calculations by defining the base data for effort, materials and other resources.

Once a WBS has been completed it will become necessary to assign the work to the teams or personnel responsible for undertaking the work. This results in a Responsibility Assignment Matrix that is produced by cross-referencing the work and organization breakdown structures.

APMP topic 3.2

Question 1: *Using the information given in Table 5.9 draw a network (Figure A.2), and identify the critical path, total and free floats. Use the network to draw a Gantt chart (Figure A.3). Indicate the free and total floats on the chart.*

APMP topic 3.3

Question 1: *Using the information given in Table 5.10 draw a network (Figure A.4), and identify the critical path, total and free floats. Use the network to draw a Gantt chart (Figure A.5). Indicate the free and total floats on the chart.*

Derive a resource histogram (Figure A.6) and cumulative resource curve ('S'-curve) (Figure A.7) from the Gantt chart. Table 5.10 gives the resources per activity.

What could be done to reduce the peak resource demand on day 9?

Table 5.9 Estimates of duration for each activity

Activity	Predecessor	Duration (weeks)
A	–	2
B	A	4
C	A	6
D	C	3
E	D	3
F	B	1
G	F	4
H	G and E	6
J	H	3
K	H	2
L	K	4
M	J and L	2

Table 5.10 Resources per activity

Activity	Predecessor	Duration (weeks)	Resources
A	–	3	3
B	–	4	2
C	A	2	4
D	C	1	4
E	B	4	1
F	E	5	2
G	E	2	3
H	D	3	3
J	G and F	1	2
K	J and H	4	4
L	J	6	1
M	L and K	3	3

Figure A.2 Network Diagram

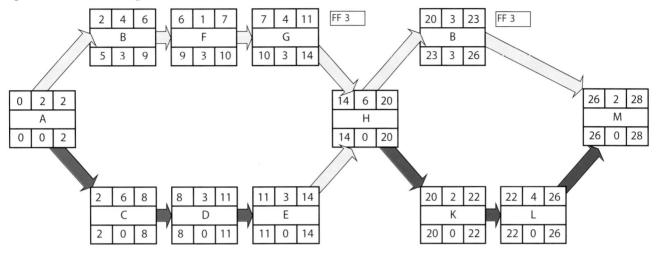

Critical Path = A – E and H – K – L – M   G and J have Free Float = 3 weeks

KEY

ES Earliest Start Time
EF Earliest Finish Time
LS Latest Start Time
LF Latest Finish Time
D Duration
TF Total Float

| FF 2 | Free Float (2 units)

Arrow indicates critical path

Figure A.3 Gantt chart

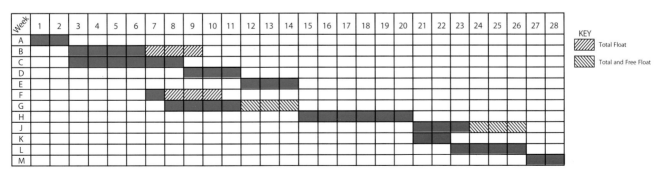

Figure A.4 Network Diagram

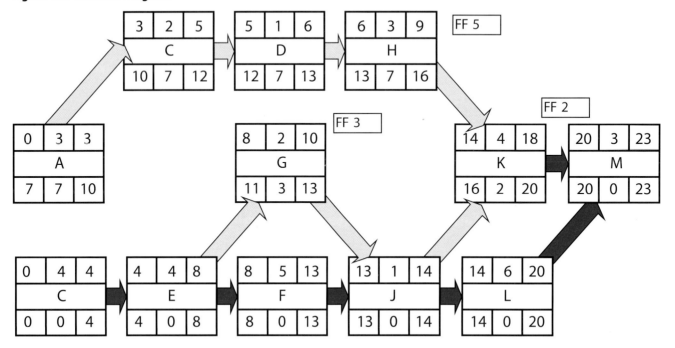

Figure A.5 Gantt chart

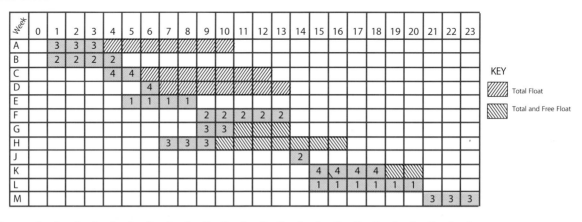

Figure A.6 Resource histogram

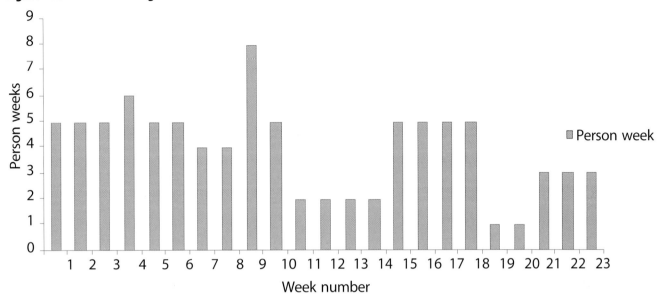

Figure A.7 Cumulative 'S' curve

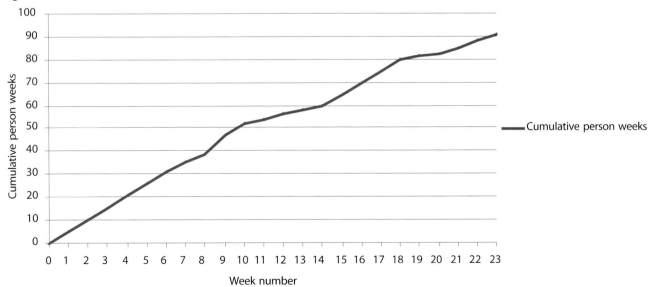

Figure A.8 Cumulative 'S' curve

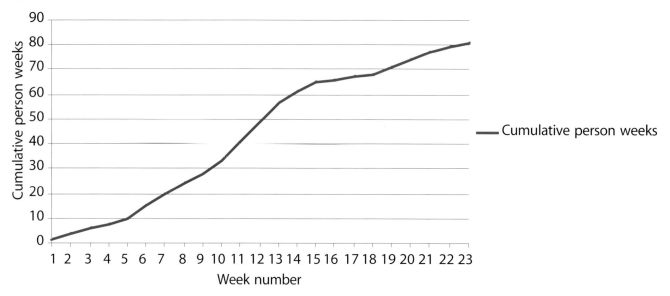

The resource numbers have been entered onto the task bars on the chart in Figure A.5 so that the resources per day can be calculated by addition down the week column and the cumulative resources calculated by simple addition. The inclusion of 'week 0' is not required by the answer (it is used to make the 'S'-curve start at the origin by the spreadsheet package).

By delaying the start of Task G by one week the resource demand for day 9 will reduce from 8 to 5; the resources required on day 11 will increase from 2 to 5. This will use one week of free float of Task G (and its total float will also decrease by one week).

APMP topic 3.4

Question 1: *Explain the difference between commitment and accrual and state four benefits of cost management.*

In a cash accounting environment, entries are made into the accounts when funds are paid or received for the goods/services in question.

This gives a simple picture of the state of the project's finances but does not indicate any commitment or accrual that is relevant.

In an accrual-based environment, the entries are made into the project's accounts when the goods or services are received. This means that the liability to pay for the goods/services has already been made and the accounts will reflect the state of the project's finances assuming all has been paid. This helps the Project Manager to accurately forecast cash flow for the project.

In a commitment-based environment the entries are based when the contract is let or the order made. In other words, the funds for that set of goods or services are effectively withdrawn from the project's accounts and put in reserve so that the commitment can be honoured at a future date. This means that the cash flow must be carefully managed as the funds in the accounts may not actually be available for use between the commitment and the actual date the payment is made.

Benefits of cost management include the ability to:

■ Accurately forecast cash flow, so that borrowing or financing requirements are known, understood and controlled.

■ Ensure payment milestones are placed in a manner that supports the schedule of work, reducing negative balances to a minimum.

■ Maximize the opportunities to receive advance payments that can be used to finance future work, reducing the borrowing requirement and maximizing profits.

■ Reduce risks associated with payments and costs, thereby affording the opportunity to reduce the contingency allowances within the project budget.

APMP topic 4.3

Question 1: *Explain bottom-up estimating. Include a diagram to illustrate your answer.*

Bottom-up estimating is an estimating technique based on making estimates for every work package (or activity) in the Work Breakdown Structure and summarizing them to provide a total estimate of cost or effort required. This technique uses the project work breakdown structure derived to a level of detail that allows estimates of cost and time for the project activities to be provided. Once estimates for each work package (or activity) have been agreed, these can be totalled together and the overall project estimate can be established.

In the example given in Figure A.9, the site description is completed when the activities below it are completed. The cost of the description is a summation of the costs of all the subsidiary activities and amounts to £1,950. The summation of the time required for each of the activities will give the total effort required of 9.5 days.

However, in this example it is likely that tasks A1.4 and A1.5 will happen concurrently and the others will be sequential. Thus the elapsed time is actually 6.5 days, not the 9.5 days.

Figure A.9 Example – bottom-up estimating

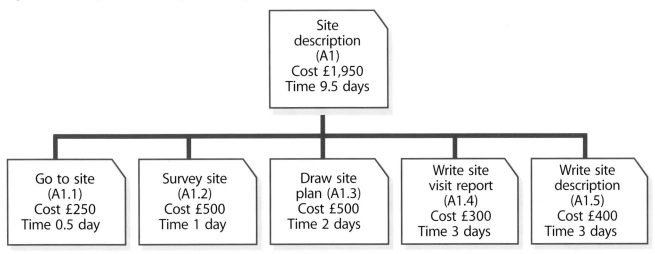

CHAPTER 6 CONTROLS

APMP topic 2.4

Question 1: *List and briefly describe 10 fundamental parts of the Project Management Plan.*

- **Work Breakdown Structure** (WBS) – this will show the tasks that must be completed in the project in order for the products to be built. It will help all concerned to see the amount of work required and define the scope of the project.
- **Monitoring and control methods** – this section will define the reporting structure for the project (monitoring) and the way in which decisions will be made (control); it will also include an exception process for escalating issues and define the way the project will be phased (or staged) to give senior management control over the progress of the project.
- **Risk management strategy** (or plan) – this will define the project's approach to risk, the processes to be used to identify, analyse and select mitigating actions including the timing of the analysis, and the way in which mitigating actions should be managed.
- **Stakeholder management strategy** – used to define the process for identification and analysis of stakeholders and resultant management.
- **Procurement strategy** – will define the organization's approach to procurement in the project, e.g. is it formal or informal.
- **Health and Safety plan** – used to document the results of the Health and Safety risk analysis that has been undertaken and the resultant actions.
- **Change Control procedure** – fundamental part of project control and will document how change is to be managed, the person(s) responsible for accepting changes, or otherwise and the limits of their authority.
- **Configuration Management Plan** – will define the way in which the products of the project will be controlled, baselined, issued for change and released to the customer. It will include the method of identification to be used and note the name of the responsible person or group.
- **Project Schedule** – this defines the high level view of the project in terms of key milestones and major deliverables. It may be in the form of a high level Gantt chart.
- **Project Budget** – this will reflect the estimated time and cost associated with the project's WBS and schedule.

APMP topic 3.6

Question 1: *Consider a project with a budget of £1 million (BAC). It has a planned duration of 18 months. Table 6.12 shows the reported figures after 10 months.*

Calculate the CPI, CV, SPI, SV, Final Cost, Final Planned Duration and Percentage Complete. Comment on the figures you have calculated.

Table 6.12 Reported figures after 10 months

Cost type	Amount
Planned Costs	£600,000
Actual Costs	£500,000
Earned Value	£460,000

Formulae

CPI = EV/AC

SPI = EV/PC

CV = EV – AC

SV = EV – PC

EAC = BAC/CPI

ETC = OD/SPI

% complete = (EV/BAC) × 100

CPI: 0.92

SPI: 0.77

CV: −40

SV: −140

Final Cost: £1,087,000

Final Planned Duration: 23 months

% complete: 46%

A CPI value less than 1, or a negative CV, indicates that the project will be over budget. This is supported by the Final Cost calculation indicating a budget over-run of just under 9%.

An SPI value less than 1, or a negative SV, indicates that the project will be late. This is supported by the Final Planned Duration figure of 23 months.

The project is less than half finished (% complete = 46%) and is going to be late by 5 months in an 18-month project, based on performance to date and assuming nothing changes. This is perhaps more worrying than the cost over-run as this is less than a potentially acceptable 10% overall.

APMP topic 3.6

Question 2: *Consider a project with a budget of £1.6 million (BAC). It has a planned duration of 24 months. Table 6.13 shows the reported figures after 10 months.*

Table 6.13 Reported figures after 10 months

Cost type	Amount
Planned Costs	£700,000
Actual Costs	£800,000
Earned Value	£850,000

Calculate CPI, CV, SPI, SV, Final Cost, Final Planned Duration and Percentage Complete. Comment on the figures you have calculated.

CPI: 1.06

SPI: 1.21

CV: 50

SV: 150

Final Cost: £1,506,000

Final Planned Duration: 20 months

% complete: 53%

A CPI value greater than 1, or a positive CV, indicates that the project will be under budget. The Final Cost calculation indicating a budget under-spend of about 10% supports this.

An SPI value greater than 1, or a positive SV indicates that the project will be completed ahead of schedule. This is supported by the Final Planned Duration figure of 20 months.

The project is more than half finished (% complete = 53%) and is going to be early by four months in a 24-month project, based on performance to date and assuming nothing changes.

APMP topic 3.6

Question 3: *Complete Table 6.14, calculating the Earned Value (EV), the Efficiency and the % Complete for weeks 4, 8, 12, 16 and 20. What can you conclude from the results?*

Table 6.14 Calculating the Earned Value (EV), Efficiency and % Complete
(all figures for Budget and Actual Costs in man/hours)

Activity	Budget	Week 4				Week 8				Week 12				Week16				Week 20			
		% Complete	Actual Costs	EV	Efficiency	% Complete	Actual Costs	EV	Efficiency	% Complete	Actual Costs	EV	Efficiency	% Complete	Actual Costs	EV	Efficiency	% Complete	Actual Costs	EV	Efficiency
A	300	20	65	60	92.3%	30	85	90	105.9%	50	130	150	115.4%	80	180	240	133.3%	100	240	300	125.0%
B	400	15	70	60	85.7%	25	120	100	83.3%	40	180	160	88.9%	60	250	240	96.0%	100	420	400	95.2%
C	500	10	90	50	55.6%	20	200	100	50.0%	50	450	250	55.6%	70	600	350	58.3%	90	750	450	60.0%
D	200	5	12	10	83.3%	10	23	20	87.0%	20	45	40	88.9%	50	110	100	90.9%	70	155	140	90.3%
E	350	0	0	0		5	20	17.5	87.5%	15	58	52.5	90.5%	40	150	140	93.9%	50	180	175	97.2%
F	240	0	0	0		5	14	12	85.7%	10	30	24	80.0%	30	90	72	80.0%	40	115	96	83.5%
TOTALS	1,990	9%	237	180	75.9%	17%	462	339.5	73.5%	34%	893	676.5	75.8%	57%	1,380	1,142	82.8%	78%	1,860	1,561	83.9%
BAC	1,990																				

The solution is Table 6.14 completed.

Calculations used:

■ **At task level:**

EV = % complete × Budget (for the task)

Efficiency = CPI × 100% = (EV/AC) × 100%

■ **At project level**:

EV total = sum of EV for the week

% complete = EV Total/BAC

Efficiency = CPI × 100% (for the week)
= (EV total/AC total) × 100%

In all control mechanisms the important factor is to look for trends, and when using Earned Value data such as this, it is the trend that is important.

If one assumes that the optimum performance is 100% ± 20% then the following is clear from the data:

■ Activity A has gone very well with a month-on-month increase in performance. It would be worth investigating the cause of the increased efficiency as perhaps it could be applied elsewhere in the project.

■ Activity B has completed within the parameters set.

■ Activity C has problems – the staff on the task have consistently under-performed and a trend such as this should be ringing alarm bells. In the first instance the Project Manager should have got to grips with the situation at week 4 and certainly by week 8. There must be a reason – perhaps there are unapproved changes taking place, perhaps there is a claim to be made for delays elsewhere. In any event action is required now.

■ Activity D is performing satisfactorily.

■ Activity E is performing satisfactorily.

■ Activity F is performing within limits, but at the lower end. Some investigation could be undertaken to look at improving the efficiency.

APMP topic 3.7

Question 1: *Explain the purpose of archiving project documentation. Make five relevant points.*

Archiving project documentation is vital as it provides a repository for historic records. This may be important for legal reasons including perhaps the provisions of the Data Protection Act.

The records provide an audit trail of the project and will facilitate a future audit of the project's performance. It is often required that these records are kept for seven to 10 years for this purpose. Whilst necessary in all cases, it is particularly important when projects have not gone as well as expected and a major review is required. An example would be the enquiry into the Scottish Parliament Project.

Project records will (should) record original and final estimates for each of the tasks. This provides vital information for an organization and enables it to improve its forecasting and estimating capability.

The records will record that which went well, that which went badly and that which would be done differently in future. Often noted in a lessons learned report, this information is important for both Project Managers and the organization if his/her/its ability to implement projects is to improve. This information should be made available for all parties to review and share throughout the organization.

As the information is to be shared with many people every effort should be made to capture experience in a form that they can use. Often this is achieved through the use of a company intranet and in some cases it is open to a wider audience through the internet.

APMP topic 6.5

Question 1: *Explain five benefits of formally closing a project.*

■ **Clear handover.** Formal closure will ensure that the products of the project are formally handed to the customer and that the customer accepts the outputs. Similarly, the products must be handed to, and accepted by, the operational and maintenance area that will look after the products in service. This avoids the tendency to drift into operational life with no clear demarcation between the project and the business. Handover at this point may be qualified in that there may be some remedial work to complete.

■ **Provides an opportunity to take stock of achievement.** It is important that members of the project management team have some time to take stock of what has, and has not, been achieved. This forms part of the Post-Project Review and it is important to cover the operational aspects of the project in terms of the way it was managed and also to collect and distribute the lessons learned focusing on what went well, what went badly and what would be done differently. It is important that this information is not lost.

■ **Prevents loss of focus.** Often one of the main difficulties at the end of a project is that both the client and the contractor/supplier 'lose' interest. This is due to a variety of emotional responses. Often supplier staff are becoming concerned over their future – what happens when the project finishes, what shall I do? On the client side, the focus has been lost and they are working towards the next initiative, before the current one is completed. By maintaining a focus on the end of the project, the need for a formal handover ensures that the Project Manager (PM) motivates all concerned to make that extra effort and make sure all is completed and managed appropriately.

- **Financial control**. At the end of a project there will be a number of financial aspects to be completed. These include payment of final contractor invoices, payment of expenses, finalizing the project's accounts and closing the cost centres down. The last is most important and the PM must make sure that all claims are received before the cost centre is closed – if not then getting the funds can be difficult. It is also important to make sure that project staff do not continue to book time and expense to the project when it has been completed. This can occur if the project is not formally closed.
- **Focus for benefits realization**. Finally a formal closure ensures that there is commitment from the business to the Benefits Realization Process. Benefits realization is often difficult to achieve, as many people seem to 'find something better to do'. Formal closure should include a process to ensure that a realization plan is in place, signed off by the sponsor and that such a plan has the commitment of the business. This could include these objectives in Personal Development Plans, on performance- or bonus-related criteria.

APMP topic 6.6

Question 1: *Describe five types of project review.*

Project Evaluation Review

These reviews are additional to the normal monitoring and control points within a project. They are often undertaken by some form of assurance function and their purpose is to discover whether the project is being managed correctly. They should be included in the project schedule by the Project Manager and they will use the Project Management Plan as their base document.

Gate Reviews

Typically undertaken at the end of a phase, a gate review is a point where the senior management in an organization assures itself that the project is worthwhile. It will concentrate on the viability of the project based on the work to date, the outcome of the project evaluation reviews and any other relevant organizational standards.

Audits

Normally undertaken by an independent body, internal or external to the organization, an audit is similar to a Project Evaluation Review. Its objective is to provide (senior) management with assurance that the project is being managed correctly. Audits can be undertaken by a project support office, should one exist.

Post-Project Reviews

These are an operation review of how well the project was managed. It should be concluded prior to formal closure of the project. It can be considered as the final Project Evaluation Review, except that it has an historical perspective.

It should focus on how the project performed in terms of cost, schedule adherence and delivery of specification. Its report should be widely distributed; recipients may include:

- Project Sponsor
- Project Manager
- Project Team
- Key stakeholders.

The essential outcome is to make lessons learnt available to all.

Benefit Realization Review

Between three and six months after the project has been closed a formal review should be undertaken to determine whether the project has met its stated objectives or is on course to meet them. It is important that the review is considered from the differing viewpoints of the various stakeholders involved.

The benefits review will probably be initiated by the Project Sponsor and should result in action plans for improvement where necessary and help in the achievement of the benefits if they have not been realized already.

CHAPTER 7 MANAGEMENT OF RISK

APMP topic 2.5

Question 1: *Explain how a probability impact grid can be used to assess the importance of a risk to a project. Make four relevant points and include a diagram that fully illustrates the use of the technique.*

A probability impact grid such as that shown in Figure A.10 has a number of uses. However, before it can be used it must be quantified. The scales of 'Very Low' to 'Very High' must be established as per the example in Figure A.11.

The placing of the lines that denote red, amber and green risks must be done for each project. A red risk is one that must be responded to and its probability, impact or both reduced (for threats) so that the assessment goes into the amber or green area.

An amber risk is one that need not necessarily be responded to but must be reviewed regularly in case its probability or impact increases, in which case it must be responded to. Risks falling into the green area can be accepted and monitored in case their probability or impact changes.

Figure A.10 Probability impact grid

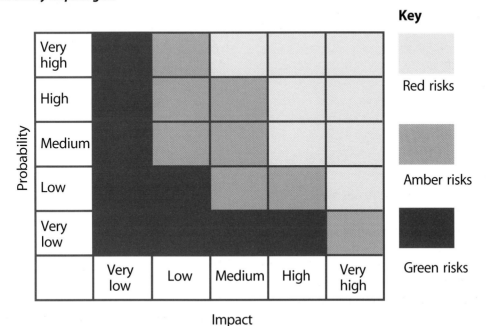

Figure A.11 Sample scales of probability/impact grid

Scale	Probability	Impact on Project		
		Timescale (months)	Cost (% Increase)	Performance
Very low	< 10%	< 1	< 5%	Failure to meet a minor criterion
Low	10–30%	1–2	5–10%	Failure to meet more than one minor criterion
Medium	30–50%	3–4	10–15%	Shortfall in meeting acceptance criteria
High	50–70%	5–6	15–30%	Significant shortfall in meeting acceptance criteria
Very high	> 70%	> 6	> 30%	Failure to meet acceptance criteria

It is possible that placing the lines may be different for time, cost and quality. If this were the case then it may be preferable to have three probability impact grids, one for each impact type. An example of this would be the Olympic Stadium, where it is likely that tolerance of risks adversely affecting time must be mitigated giving a large area of the grid in the 'red' area, whereas cost may not be a major driver and the red risk area could be smaller.

Whether one or three grids are used the process is the same. The risk is assessed using the scales, for example a risk could have a high probability, with a low time impact, a high cost impact and a very high quality impact – the last two assessments would take the risk into the 'red risk' area. At this point the risk can be responded to.

The grid can also be used as a reporting tool; all the risks can be plotted on the grid and the overall level of risk to the project reviewed. Clearly if there were many red risks, it may indicate that the project should not be undertaken.

Values can also be allocated to the Probability and Impact scales, the fields cross-multiplied to give a 'score'. Typically, values for probability would be 0.1, 0.3, 0.5, 0.7 and 0.9; for impact values may be 0.05, 0.1, 0.2, 0.4 and 0.8. This scale weights the result towards impact.

APMP topic 2.7

Question 1: *Explain four specific duties of employers or employees regarding the Health and Safety at Work Act.*

Duties of employers:

1 Provide and maintain a safe workplace, plant and equipment.

It is important that the employer makes sure that the workplace is safe and that any plant and equipment in use is suitably maintained in accordance with the manufacturer's recommendations. This ensures that any risks associated with the work are reduced to a reasonable level, i.e. as low as reasonably practicable (ALARP).

2 Provide the information, instruction, training and supervision necessary so that employees endanger neither themselves nor their colleagues.

The employer must make sure that all staff are given the appropriate training and so forth when they are recruited and when there are changes to working practices. This will make sure that all understand the procedures, and assuming the employee plays their part will ensure that the work proceeds in a safe manner.

Duties of employees:

1 To take reasonable care while at work for his or her own health and safety and for that of persons who may be affected by his or her acts or omissions at work.

The employee must make sure that they understand the hazards in the workplace, attends safety briefings, does not take risks with procedures or equipment and act in a responsible manner to ensure the work is undertaken in a safe manner. Where the employee sees something that affects the safety of the operation they should bring this to the attention of the employer. The employee should also be aware of others in the workplace and their safety.

2 To cooperate with the employer on safety matters.

Attending safety briefings, notifying the employer of safety issues and behaving responsibly ensures that the risks in the workplace are reduced to the lowest practical level.

CHAPTER 8 QUALITY MANAGEMENT

APMP topic 2.6

Question 1: *Explain when quality will be particularly relevant within a project lifecycle, making five relevant points.*

- **Concept**: at the start of the project it is necessary to establish the Acceptance Criteria for the project, in other words, a list of measurable criteria that determine what will make the project's final product acceptable to the customer. These criteria must be measurable and examples are: delivery date, development cost, elements of functionality, running costs, reliability, mean time to repair, mean time between failures. The Project Sponsor must agree the criteria.

- **Definition**: based on these criteria a quality plan for the project should be prepared and included in the Project Management Plan. This document will state the Acceptance Criteria and quality responsibilities and describe the processes to be used for testing the product. For example, an IT system would include: module testing, integration testing, system testing, user testing and operational testing. It could also include reference to standards to be used.

- **Implementation**: Once the project has been given the go-ahead the products must be described, either as a product description, or as the output of a task or activity and described in a statement of work. The description of the product will include a list of quality criteria that are pertinent to the product. This will ensure that the product is produced 'right first time' because the producer will know exactly what is required.

As the project progresses the quality tests and checks (quality control) will be planned into the schedules to reflect the process described in the project quality plan. These checks will test the products against the product's quality criteria which if achieved will ensure that the project's Acceptance Criteria are met. It is important at these points to record the results and watch for trends – particularly of poor performance.

● **Handover and Closeout**: at the end of the project it is likely that there will be a final inspection or test that will demonstrate the quality of the final product. Based on this the product will be handed over to the customer and accepted. The customer will assess the product against the initial Acceptance Criteria and if it is found to be acceptable will sign for and take responsibility for the project's products.

APMP topic 4.1

Question 1: *State three elements of a requirements management process. Explain why requirements management is important.*

1 *Capture* – where requirements are discovered, and structured and documented along with any relevant Acceptance Criteria.
2 *Analysis* – where they are assessed and prioritized in accordance with the needs of the business and the project's priorities.
3 *Testing* – where the views of different stakeholders need to be considered and the requirements tested against them to ensure that they are comprehensive and accurate and if met will satisfy the diverse stakeholder groupings.

Requirements are the basis for the project – they describe what the customer wants and are used as a platform for the solution and the way in which that solution is provided. If requirements are not adequately determined and maintained, an excessive amount of changes will be necessary and this will inevitably lead to cost and time over-runs.

Initially, the user requirements will be generated during the Concept phase. This will comprise a high-level view of the stakeholders' wants and will not necessarily describe what is actually needed. As the project moves into the Definition stage and more is known about the solution the requirements will be revisited and refined to ensure that they are realistic and that they will be adequately satisfied by the solution.

During Implementation the solution will be tested and the requirement will form a basis for these tests and finally during operations the solution will be seen to satisfy the requirements.

The requirements should be documented and structured such that the value, priority, timescales and process are clear for each requirement.

Value represents the amount of benefit that will accrue from the requirement and could be used to assess its priority – how important is this requirement compared with the others.

The timescale associated with the requirement should reflect the timescales of the business, i.e. when must this requirement be satisfied if the business is to meet its strategic aims, and finally the process describes the means by which the requirements will be satisfied, i.e. the solution or project approach.

CHAPTER 9 CONFIGURATION MANAGEMENT

APMP topic 4.7

Question 1: *Explain the linkage between change control and configuration management.*

Once the individual components of the project have been identified they are brought under control. This means that nothing moves and nothing changes unless it passes through the change control process and the associated link to change control.

The Configuration Librarian will often be responsible for maintaining the change log, and if not, he or she must maintain a close relationship with the group that does.

When products are produced they are baselined, and if they need to be amended then a change request must be raised. Once the request has been through the change process and been agreed the Configuration Librarian will take a copy of the product (NB: the master is never changed) and give it a new version number, ideally indicating that this is a draft product that is being worked on. Typically this is undertaken by adding a lower case letter after the version number, e.g. v1.6a.

This product is issued to the appropriate team for updating and when the product is completed and signed off it will be returned to the Configuration Librarian. The librarian baselines the product, taking away the lower case letter, and archives the old baseline. Copies of the new product are released and the old version is recalled and destroyed.

If multiple changes to a product are required then they should be sent as a group of changes with the product to one person to undertake so that one change does not undo another.

Finally the system should maintain a link between the product and the change request that caused the change to the product.

CHAPTER 10 CHANGE CONTROL AND ISSUE MANAGEMENT

APMP topic 3.5

Question 1: *List five roles that are fundamentally involved in change control and describe the contribution of each role.*

- **Project Manager**. The Project Manager (PM) will be responsible for ensuring that the change requests are logged and that the Change Log is kept updated throughout the project. (Often this will be delegated to the project support office.) Once the change request is received, the PM will have to analyse the change, asking a range of questions to establish what

is actually required, how much it will cost, the effect of the change on the schedule and budget, and the benefits and risks associated with the change. Once this analysis is complete the PM will pass on the change to the body authorized to agree the change, or otherwise.

- **Project Executive/Sponsor**. The sponsor will be the focal point for decision-making on change issues. He or she will sign off the change control process and will often take the role of authorizing body. In any event the sponsor will chair the Steering Group. The sponsor will discuss the change with the user and decide whether the change can be justified. It is likely that the sponsor will control the change budget.

- **Project Board/Steering Group**. Often the Steering Group will act as a change control board. This forum has the authority to accept or reject changes (or put them on the pending pile). Chaired by the sponsor, the board will examine the PM's analysis of the situation and make decisions about the change.

- **Senior User**. The user community will often be the prime source of change requests. They will be required to justify the change and provide the benefits information so that the PM can evaluate the cost–benefit balance when he or she has obtained the costs for the change.

- **Senior Supplier**. The supplier can raise change requests although these are likely to be 'internal' and raised to correct problems during the 'build' process and therefore not chargeable to the customer. The supplier will also examine customer change requests and provide the time and cost information required by the PM as part of his or her analysis. Income from change requests can form a key part of the supplier's profit and care must be taken to ensure that the costs obtained are fully justified. This risk could be limited by asking the supplier to include a schedule of rates within their bid.

APMP topic 3.8

Question 1: *Explain an issue management process, making four relevant points.*

An Issue is something that threatens the project objectives and cannot be resolved by the Project Manager. An example could be a risk that has happened and the result requires senior management intervention.

Step 1

There must be a log in which the Project Manager can record all project issues that are raised. (It is also possible that there may be a corresponding issue form.) The log would contain information such as:

Issue number, Author, date raised, description, analysis, date escalated, action taken, status, owner and date cleared. Once the issue has been logged and given a number the author should be advised and given the number so that he or she can enquire about the progress of the issue.

Step 2 (analysis)

The issue must be reviewed to establish the cause and exact details of the problem, its effect on the time, cost, quality, scope, risks and benefit objectives. This information can be used to establish the best possible course of action so that a recommendation can be made to the Sponsor/Steering Group. An owner of the issue should also be established. This would be the person who is responsible for its resolution.

Step 3

Escalate the issue to the sponsor and steering group for action. This senior management body is then responsible for agreeing, or otherwise, the Project Manager's recommendation and ensuring that the owner is aware of the situation and has agreed to take action to resolve the issue. The Project Manager is informed of the decision and the Issue Log updated.

Step 4

Once escalated the Project Manager should ensure that the agreed actions are happening and having the desired effect.

Step 5

All outstanding issues should be monitored on a regular basis. Information on the issue status should be included in the reports, and given to both senior management and the team. In the event of an Issue not being resolved, further escalation to the sponsor will be required. If issues continue to be raised and older ones are left unresolved then the project is out of control.

CHAPTER 11 STAKEHOLDER MANAGEMENT AND COMMUNICATION

APMP topic 2.2

Question 1: *Explain the importance of stakeholder management, making four relevant points.*

- **Risk management**. Once stakeholders are identified and analysed it will help with the management of risks within the project, including their identification and assessment. For example, if there are a significant number of negative stakeholders, or if a key stakeholder is found to be negative, the risk in the project will be high. Once this is established it can be mitigated and reduced.

- **Communications planning**. Not everybody needs to know everything, but everybody needs to know something. The results of the analysis will define these key requirements. This is especially true if the key interests of the stakeholders have been gathered in terms of time, cost, quality, scope and benefits. Not only can the appropriate level of information be ascertained but also where the information will come from and how it will be transmitted, for example, by email, monthly traffic light reports (showing red, amber, green status), intranet communications or internet communications.

- **Team formation**. Knowing which stakeholders are key players, need active consultation, need their interest maintained or need to be kept informed, will help to define whether or not they need a place on the team. Certainly those seen as key players will have a key role as suppliers and members of the Steering Group depending on their interests and level of seniority.

- **Management actions**. Once stakeholders are identified, it is possible to conduct further stakeholder analysis to develop a strategy for dealing with the stakeholders concerned. Basically for each stakeholder, or group, the following information should be defined:
  - Their goal
  - Past reactions
  - What to expect
  - Positive/negative impact
  - Possible reactions to the project.

  This information is used to develop a number of strategies to deal with the reactions of the stakeholder.

APMP topic 7.1

Question 1: *State 10 factors that a Project Manager should consider to ensure that project communication is effective.*

- Clearly define the requirements of all stakeholders to make sure that all stakeholders are known, their position understood, and their needs noted in the communications plan.

- Agree the communications plan with the stakeholders to ensure that their needs have been correctly understood and recorded.

- Build a feedback loop into the communications process so that communications can be evaluated to see that they are meeting the need.

- Assess the appropriateness of the information, for example is it too much or too little? If it is too much it will not be read, if it is too little it will be ignored.

- Assess the method of communication to be used, for example electronic/hard copy/internet/intranet. If using electronic communication, do not send large multi-megabyte files – do not assume everybody has broadband. It is also very easy to fill someone's inbox, and again this will devalue the communication.

- Make sure the style of communication is appropriate for the audience. A freeform chatty style may not be appropriate for senior management. Similarly, formal communications may not be appropriate for the team members.

- Make sure the language is appropriate for the audience. This is most important if dealing with teams from different countries and cultures. Ensure that the language does not cause offence. Do not use colloquialisms as these may not be understood, or may be misunderstood.

- Make sure regulatory requirements are covered. In some projects formal representation to government bodies may be required.

- Ensure configuration management is in place. If more than one version of a document is required, there should be some form of version control and a formal process for issuing the updated versions and disposing and archiving of old versions.

- Do not use technical jargon and acronyms in communications. Many people do not know what they mean but are afraid to ask. If jargon and acronyms must be used make sure they are defined.

CHAPTER 12 PROCUREMENT

APMP topic 5.4

Question 1: *Explain a simple procurement process.*

The basic steps involved in a simple procurement process are given below. The procurement of a new hotel kitchen has been used to explain the process.

1 **Establish the user's need**. In the first step the users (the chefs) would be consulted and a list of requirements developed. These requirements may be in the form of a 'wish list' at this stage, and it may not be possible to achieve them all. This expectation should be clearly set at this stage.

2 **Survey the market place**. Taking the list to market will enable you to answer questions such as: how much the kitchen is likely to cost; is it possible to get this type of technology; how long will it take to be delivered; are there any constraints; what are the likely maintenance costs.

3 **Specify a realistic requirement**. Having got some preliminary information you can now engage the chefs in the debate, and a realistic set of requirements can be generated taking into account the information discovered in Step 2.

4 **Seek tenders for supply**. The information agreed in Step 3 is converted into a specification that is issued with an invitation to tender (ITT) or request for proposal (RFP) to a number of suppliers. It is likely that these suppliers have been pre-qualified by this stage. I will also have prepared a list of assessment criteria for the tenders, including weighting of requirements, cost, support terms etc.

5 **Assess tenders and choose supplier**. When the tenders are received they will be assessed against the assessment criteria. It is likely that a shortlist will be established and interviews undertaken to clarify points of detail. Following this the supplier will be appointed.

6 **Accept the goods into service (commissioning)**. The supplier will build the kitchen, commission the systems and hand over the completed kitchen to the customer – the chefs. After a final inspection the kitchen will be accepted into service and the final invoices paid.

7 **Support the equipment during use** (storage, maintenance, repair, training etc.) This part of the process covers the ongoing maintenance and support of the kitchen. This may include regular servicing of appliances, repair activities and upgrades during its useful life.

8 **Decommission and dispose of redundant equipment**. In this final stage the kitchen will come to the end of its useful life and will be replaced.

APMP topic 7.5

Question 1: *Explain four stages that an effective negotiation should progress through.*

Preparation

During the preparation stage it is important for the negotiators to understand the issue/problem, study relevant material and learn about opponents' objectives (if possible), and this should avoid surprises, anticipate opponents' strategies, define their own objectives and priorities, define their own negotiating strategy and allocate roles and responsibilities. This will include deciding which member of the team will lead the negotiation, the member who is to take notes and the member who will observe. The team should establish what it is prepared to trade and establish its 'bottom line'. As well as deciding on the 'bottom line' the team should also anticipate the other party's bottom line and areas of potential trade.

Discuss

Trade information and check any assumptions you have made about the other party. At this point you may have to change your expectations in the light of some information gained from the other party. You should also be looking for signals from the other party about interest points and areas that they will not discuss. Time spent at this step will assist the process later. This will involve the note taker in keeping notes of the discussions made, any phrases that may indicate that the other party is prepared to trade (e.g. 'normally', 'mostly we ...', there may be possibilities'). The observer should be concentrating on the responses of the other party to the statements made during the discussion. It is often useful after this step to take a short break so that the information gathered by the negotiator, observer and note taker can be analysed and the negotiation strategy improved.

Propose and bargain

The opening bids should be made in the expectation of a counter bid. If they get rejected then you have missed something in the discuss step, go back. If a counter bid is made then you move into bargaining to get closer to a deal. Opening and later bids should always be formatted as 'If you ... then we ....' followed by counter-proposals, adjusting until you come to an acceptable agreement. During this stage it is again useful to break off to analyse the information gained by the team. This also stops hasty decisions being made and can lead to a better deal for all concerned.

Closing

It is important to confirm the agreement and record the results of the negotiation. This should be a written record that all parties can sign and leave the negotiating table with an accurate and complete record of the agreement achieved. This is most important, as you want to avoid any comeback or misunderstandings later. When the agreement is written up, both parties should be prepared to scrutinize it carefully and make sure that the common agreement reached orally has been transcribed accurately into the written form. This may require some minor adjustments until the final document is agreed.

CHAPTER 13 PEOPLE MANAGEMENT

APMP topic 7.2

Question 1: *Explain how a team develops over time.*

Effective team working develops over time. During that period a lot of learning and development takes place and the team collectively goes through a number of developmental phases, classically referred to as Forming, Storming, Norming and Performing.

Stage 1: Forming

This initial stage establishes the foundations upon which the team is 'constructed' or developed. Typically, team members are unsure of both their individual objectives and the overall team objectives. They therefore look to each other and the leader for direction and guidance.

Stage 2: Storming

During this stage team members begin to understand the task, and may perhaps realize that it is more difficult than they imagined. They are likely to be uncertain about their own individual objectives and become defensive. If not well managed, competition between team members may give rise to conflict.

Stage 3: Norming

During this third stage, team members begin to identify with the team and reconcile their differences. They begin to realize that if the team succeeds they all succeed and if the team fails they all fail. As a result, competitive relationships become more cooperative and team members begin to learn from each other.

Stage 4: Performing

At this stage, team members have reconciled most of their differences and communicate openly within the team. They should now be committed to one another and their objective. As a result, a lot of work gets done, quickly and efficiently (i.e. the sum is now greater than the parts).

APMP topic 7.3

Question 1: *Explain the difference between motivators and hygiene factors.*

The first three levels of Maslow's hierarchy are concerned with 'extrinsic factors', that is, the working environment and not with the content of the work. Herzberg called these 'hygiene factors' and they have the following attributes:

- They are not a potent source of satisfaction
- Their absence is the cause of dissatisfaction
- Their impact on attitudes is relatively short-lived
- They are 'inflationary'.

This is why the 'carrot and stick' approach does not work for very long.

Factors predominantly associated with satisfying 'higher order needs' tend to be 'intrinsic factors', that is, those concerned with the content of the work. They have the effect of motivating higher performance.

Herzberg called these 'motivators' and they have the following attributes:

- Their absence is less likely to cause complaint or dissatisfaction
- Their absence causes a lack of satisfaction which leads to apathy and lack of interest and initiative
- Their presence is likely to be highly motivational.

Herzberg suggests the need for a two-pronged approach that: first, removes factors that distract from performance such as discriminatory promotion policies, unfair salary systems, poor working conditions and poor management; and, next, seeks out ways that enable employees to get more recognition, challenge, self-fulfilment and satisfaction from their work.

APMP topic 7.4

Question 1: *Explain the impact of avoiding conflict and not resolving it, making five relevant points.*

If conflict is avoided then it can lead to:

- An escalation of the conflict situation between the parties concerned – as the conflict escalates it will become progressively more difficult to deal with and may result in drastic action being taken. For example, if there was some dissatisfaction among the labour force and this was not resolved it could escalate into strike action.

- Team formation going backwards – if conflict within a team is avoided then the team will move back through the model to the storming stage. This will lead to inefficiencies, poor team motivation and increased stress to all concerned, which could have the potential for sickness absences and increased costs and delays.

- Increased costs – avoidance of conflict may mean that the project is being undertaken in an inefficient manner because the team leader or Project Manager is not prepared to tackle the situation. This will ultimately lead to failure and poor team motivation compounding the situation further.

- Loss of respect – by not tackling a problem or conflict situation the Project Manager or team leader is likely to lose the respect of their team. This will make it difficult to complete the project in a satisfactory manner and could lead to further conflict throughout the project lifecycle.

- Removal from the team – avoidance of conflict often leads to its escalation and it becomes more difficult to resolve. The final option may well be to remove the persons concerned from the project team entirely. This affects the individuals concerned and the rest of the team members, who, in many cases, have 'taken sides'. This is going to make resolution and further team building as the personnel are replaced that much more difficult.

APMP syllabus
– 3rd edition

B

Appendix B: APMP syllabus – 3rd edition

Table B.1 Project management in context

Title	Topic coverage	Learning outcomes
1.1 Project management	▓ Compare and contrast projects versus business-as-usual type activities within an organization.	A. Distinguish between project management and business-as-usual.
	▓ The benefits of using project management.	B. Explain the benefits of project management.
	▓ The challenges of using project management within an organization.	C. Explain the challenges that organizations face when using project management.
	▓ The difference between project management processes as used throughout the project (such as starting, defining, monitoring and learning) and the phases of the project lifecycle.	D. Distinguish between project management processes and the phases of the project lifecycle.
1.2 Programme management	▓ The characteristics of programme management.	A. Distinguish between programme management and project management.
	▓ The differences between project management and programme management.	B. Describe the role and typical responsibilities of the programme manager.
	▓ Programme management and its links to strategic change.	C. Explain the benefits of programme management.
	▓ The role and responsibilities of a programme manager.	D. Explain the challenges that organizations face when using programme management.
	▓ The benefits of using programme management.	
	▓ The challenges in using programme management within an organization.	
	▓ The differences between programme management and portfolio management.	

Table B.1 *continued*

Title	Topic coverage	Learning outcomes
1.3 Portfolio management	■ How portfolio management assists in the prioritization of projects.	A. Distinguish between portfolio management and project management.
	■ The characteristics of portfolio management.	B. Explain situations where portfolio management would be appropriate.
	■ Risk versus return in relation to why projects are prioritized.	
	■ Recognize that the capacity of an organization to undertake projects is linked to its available resources and how it forms part of portfolio management.	
	■ Situations where the use of portfolio management is appropriate.	
1.4 Project context	■ The need to understand a project's context.	A. Describe what is meant by a project's context.
	■ The need to consider the internal and external context (environment) of a project.	B. Explain a tool or technique for ascertaining a project's context.
	■ The use of tools and techniques such as PESTLE and SWOT.	
1.5 Project sponsorship	■ The role and responsibilities of the project sponsor (executive) and how it changes through the project lifecycle.	A. Describe the role and typical responsibilities of the project sponsor (executive) across a project lifecycle.
	■ Why effective project sponsorship is important to project management.	B. Explain the importance of project sponsorship in project management.
	■ The relationship between the Project Sponsor (Executive) and the Project Manager.	
1.6 Project office	■ The role of the project office.	A. Describe functions that project offices often perform.
	■ Different types and functions of project office, some acronyms include project support office (PSO), project and programme support office (PPSO), programme management office (PMO), enterprise programme management office (EPMO).	B. Explain the benefits of a project office.
	■ The benefits of using a project office linked to its type and function such as PSO, PPSO, PMO, EPMO.	
	■ The role of project support in project management.	

Table B.2 Planning and strategy

Title	Topic coverage	Learning outcomes
2.1 Project success and benefits management	■ Success criteria and key performance indicators (KPIs) and their uses in defining and measuring project success.	A. Distinguish between success criteria and success factors.
	■ The importance of success factors to project management.	B. Explain the relationship between success criteria and KPIs.
	■ Benefits management and how benefits should be realized.	C. Describe benefits management.
2.2 Stakeholder management	■ A stakeholder management process (such as identification, analysis, communications planning, ongoing management).	A. Describe a stakeholder management process.
	■ Tools and techniques that can be used in stakeholder analysis such as suitably labelled axes on a 2 × 2 or 4 × 2 grid.	B. Explain the importance of stakeholder management.
	■ Why stakeholder management should be undertaken.	
2.3 Value management	■ NOT INCLUDED IN THE APMP SYLLABUS	NOT INCLUDED IN THE APMP SYLLABUS
2.4 Project Management Plan	■ The typical contents of the Project Management Plan (PMP).	A. Explain the purpose of a PMP.
	■ The PMP as the why, what, how, how much, who, when and where for a project.	B. Describe typical contents of a PMP.
	■ Authorship, approval and audience for the PMP.	C. Describe the authorship, ownership and audience of a PMP.
	– Who should develop the PMP.	
	– Who should own and update the PMP.	
	– Who needs to read and understand the PMP.	
	■ The PMP as a baseline document.	
	■ The use of the PMP throughout the project lifecycle.	

Table B.2 *continued*

Title	Topic coverage	Learning outcomes
2.5 Project risk management	▦ A risk management process such as that described in the APM's *PRAM Guide 2nd edition* excluding quantitative analysis, i.e. initiate, identify, assess, plan responses, implement responses and the overarching management process.	A. Describe a project risk management process.
	▦ Risk as threat and opportunity.	B. Explain each stage of a project risk management process.
	▦ Tools and techniques for risk identification such as brainstorming, SWOT analysis, assumptions analysis, constraints analysis, prompt lists, checklists, interviews.	C. Explain the benefits of project risk management.
	▦ The use of a probability and impact grid (matrix) to assess risks.	
	▦ How risk ownership should be determined and managed.	
	▦ Basic responses to threats, i.e. avoid, reduce, transfer and accept.	
	▦ Basic responses to opportunities, i.e. exploit, enhance, share and accept.	
	▦ The use of a risk log (register).	
	▦ Benefits and costs of risk management.	
2.6 Project quality management	▦ Quality planning, quality assurance, quality control and continuous improvement	A. Describe project quality management.
	▦ The need to manage the quality of the deliverables (products) or service that a project delivers.	B. Explain the differences between quality planning, quality assurance, quality control and continuous improvement.
	▦ The need to manage the quality of the project management process.	C. Explain benefits of project quality management.
	▦ Techniques used in quality planning and assurance such as quality plans, audit, procedures/checklists.	
	▦ Techniques used in quality control and improvement such as inspection, Ishikawa Diagrams, Pareto Analysis, Control Charts.	

Title	Topic coverage	Learning outcomes
	▦ The importance of acceptance criteria for each work package.	
	▦ Benefits and costs of project quality management.	
2.7 Health, safety and environmental management	▦ Purpose of health, safety and environmental (HSE) regulations.	A. Explain the importance of project health and safety management.
	▦ Examples of generally applicable health and safety regulation/guidance such as COSHH, management standards for tackling stress at work, preventing slips and trips at work.	B. Explain the importance of project environmental management.
	▦ Duty of care for a Project Manager and team member in health and safety.	
	▦ Responsibilities of a Project Manager regarding health and safety.	
	▦ Health and safety risk assessment as applicable to project management.	
	▦ Environmental legislation as applicable to project management such as noise and statutory nuisance and waste including pollution.	

Table B.3 Executing the strategy

Title	Topic coverage	Learning outcomes
3.1 Scope management	■ The need for effective scope definition and management.	A. Explain scope management.
	■ An example of:	B. Describe Product Breakdown Structure (PBS).
	— Product Breakdown Structure (PBS).	C. Describe Work Breakdown Structure (WBS).
	— Work Breakdown Structure (WBS).	D. Describe Cost Breakdown Structure (CBS).
	— Cost Breakdown Structure (CBS).	E. Describe Organizational Breakdown Structure (OBS).
	— Organizational Breakdown Structure (OBS).	F. Explain the reasons for using a Responsibility Assignment Matrix (RAM).
	■ Responsibility Assignment Matrix (RAM) and how it is constructed.	
	■ Features of a work package.	
	■ The scope baseline.	
	■ The link between the WBS and project scheduling.	

Title	Topic coverage	Learning outcomes
3.2 Scheduling	▓ The scheduling process and the use of project schedules.	A. Explain how a project schedule is created and maintained.
	▓ The precedence (Activity-on-Node) diagramming technique including different types of logical dependencies (links) such as finish to start, start to start and finish to finish.	B. Demonstrate the use of different techniques for scheduling projects.
	▓ Basic Critical Path Analysis (only using finish to start dependencies).	C. Explain advantages and disadvantages of using software tools for scheduling.
	▓ The use of Total and Free Float in scheduling.	
	▓ The use of Gantt (bar) charts.	
	▓ Durations estimating (overview).	
	▓ Updating project schedules.	
	▓ Program Evaluation and Review Technique (PERT) as a method for estimating activity durations. The PERT formula should be understood but there is no need to calculate values.	
	▓ Milestones and milestone progress charts.	
	▓ Software tools used to create and manage schedules. No particular software tools need to be known.	

Table B.3 *continued*

Title	Topic coverage	Learning outcomes
3.3 Resource management	■ Types of resources such as replenishable and re-usable.	A. Describe resource management.
	■ Resource estimating (overview).	B. Distinguish between resource smoothing (time-limited scheduling) and resource levelling (resource-limited scheduling).
	■ Resource allocation.	C. Demonstrate the use of different resource management techniques.
	■ Resource smoothing (time-limited scheduling) and resource levelling (resource-limited scheduling).	
	■ The concept of splitting activities to assist in resource smoothing and levelling.	
	■ Resource histograms and cumulative S curves.	
	■ Software tools used to manage resources. No particular software tools need to be known.	
3.4 Budgeting and cost management	■ The link between cost estimating and budgeting and cost management (overview).	A. Explain budgeting and cost management.
	■ Planned expenditure.	B. Explain the benefits of budgeting and cost management.
	■ Commitments and accruals.	
	■ Actual expenditure.	
	■ Cash flow forecasts.	
	■ Forecast out-turn cost.	
	■ Cost monitoring and control and cost reporting.	

Title	Topic coverage	Learning outcomes
3.5 Change control	▓ A change control process.	A. Describe a change control process.
	▓ Change the requests and change request forms.	B. Explain each stage of a change control process.
	▓ The use of a change log (register).	C. Explain the reasons for requiring change control on a project.
	▓ The importance of change control in preventing scope creep or requirements creep.	
	▓ Why does change occur and what are the different types of change.	
	▓ The increasing cost of making changes through the project lifecycle.	
	▓ The concept of a change freeze.	
	▓ Responsibilities in change control such as Project Sponsor (Executive), Project Manager, change control board.	
	▓ Links between change control and configuration management.	

Table B.3 *continued*

Title	Topic coverage	Learning outcomes
3.6 Earned Value management	■ The principles of Earned Value management (EVM).	A. Describe Earned Value management (EVM).
	■ Planned Costs (Budgeted Cost of Work Scheduled – BCWS).	B. Explain the advantages and disadvantages of EVM.
	■ Actual Costs (Actual Cost of Work Performed – ACWP).	C. Perform earned value calculations and interpret earned value data.
	■ Earned Value (Budgeted Cost of Work Performed – BCWP).	
	■ Cost Variances (CV) and Schedule Variance (cost) (SV). As defined in BS6079-1:2002.	
	■ Trends and Indices; Cost Performance Index (CPI) and Schedule Performance Index (cost) (SPI). As defined in BS6079-1:2002.	
	■ CPI as a measure of efficiency.	
	■ Derive earned value curves from basic data.	
	■ Using earned value analysis to forecast out-turn costs and durations.	
	■ Why use EVM and what are its advantages and disadvantages.	
	■ The link between cumulative resource S curves and planned costs.	
	Note: examination candidates will not be required to provide definitions of earned value terms. Only the wording, Planned Costs, Actual Costs and Earned Value will be used in examinations.	

Title	Topic coverage	Learning outcomes
3.7 Information management and reporting	▓ An information management system (such as collection, storage, dissemination, archiving and appropriate destruction of information).	A. Explain information management.
	▓ Project reporting and reporting requirements.	B. Explain project reporting.
	▓ A typical project reporting cycle including the gathering of data and dissemination of reports.	
	▓ The principles of reporting by exception.	
3.8 Issue management	▓ An issue management process (such as identification, escalation, monitoring/reporting, resolution).	A. Describe issue management.
	▓ The use of an issue log (register).	B. Explain the importance of issue management.
	▓ The importance of issue management.	

Table B.4 Techniques

Title	Topic coverage	Learning outcomes
4.1 Requirements management	▪ A requirements management process (such as capture, analysis and prioritization, testing).	A. Describe requirements management.
	▪ Factors used to structure requirements.	B. Explain the importance of requirements management.
	▪ The importance of requirements management and links to scope management and project quality management.	
4.2 Development	NOT INCLUDED IN THE APMP SYLLABUS	NOT INCLUDED IN THE APMP SYLLABUS
4.3 Estimating	▪ Estimating through the project lifecycle.	A. Describe practical problems of estimating across the project lifecycle.
	▪ The changing accuracy of estimates through the project lifecycle and the concept of the estimating funnel.	B. Explain bottom-up estimating.
	▪ Estimating methods such as bottom up, comparative, parametric.	C. Explain comparative estimating.
	▪ Estimating durations, resources and costs.	D. Explain parametric estimating.
	▪ The importance and practical difficulties of estimating.	E. Explain three-point estimating.
	▪ Three-point estimating and its links to PERT (see scheduling).	
4.4 Technology management	NOT INCLUDED IN THE APMP SYLLABUS	NOT INCLUDED IN THE APMP SYLLABUS
4.5 Value engineering	NOT INCLUDED IN THE APMP SYLLABUS	NOT INCLUDED IN THE APMP SYLLABUS
4.6 Modelling and testing	NOT INCLUDED IN THE APMP SYLLABUS	NOT INCLUDED IN THE APMP SYLLABUS
4.7 Configuration management	▪ A configuration management process (such as planning, identification, control, status accounting, audit, closeout)	A. Describe a configuration management process.
	▪ The principle of a configuration item.	B. Explain reasons for requiring configuration management on a project.
	▪ Similarities between configuration management and version control.	
	▪ Links to change control.	

Table B.5 Business and commercial

Title	Topic coverage	Learning outcomes
5.1 Business Case	The purpose of the Business Case.	A. Explain the purpose of a Business Case.
	The typical contents of the Business Case.	B. Describe typical contents of a Business Case.
	The Business Case as the 'why' for the project.	C. Describe the authorship and ownership of a business case.
	Authorship and ownership of the Business Case.	D. Explain the use of payback, Internal Rate of Return (IRR) and Net Present Value (NPV) as investment appraisal techniques.
	Importance and use of a Business Case during the project lifecycle.	
	The use of investment appraisal techniques such as payback (using non-discounted figures), Internal Rate of Return (IRR), Net Present Value (NPV). Excluding the need to explain formulae or to calculate values.	
5.2 Marketing and sales	NOT INCLUDED IN THE APMP SYLLABUS	NOT INCLUDED IN THE APMP SYLLABUS
5.3 Project financing and funding	NOT INCLUDED IN THE APMP SYLLABUS	NOT INCLUDED IN THE APMP SYLLABUS
5.4 Procurement	Procurement in project management.	A. Describe procurement.
	The purpose and content of a procurement strategy.	B. Explain the typical contents of a procurement strategy.
	Processes for supplier selection.	C. Explain a supplier selection process.
	Different methods of supplier reimbursement, such as firm fixed price contract, contract target cost, contract target price, cost plus fixed fee contract, cost reimbursement type contract, cost plus incentive fee contract.	D. Distinguish between different methods for supplier reimbursement.
	Types of contractual relationship such as partnering, alliancing, turnkey contract.	E. Distinguish between different contractual relationships.
5.5 Legal awareness	NOT INCLUDED IN THE APMP SYLLABUS	NOT INCLUDED IN THE APMP SYLLABUS

Table B.6 Organization and governance

Title	Topic coverage	Learning outcomes
6.1 Project lifecycles	▪ The project lifecycle.	A. Describe a project lifecycle.
	▪ Project phases such as Concept, Definition, Implementation, Handover and Closeout.	B. Explain why projects are split into lifecycle phases.
	▪ The relationship between phases and stages.	C. Explain the differences between a project lifecycle and an extended lifecycle.
	▪ Why split projects into phases, e.g. end of phase reviews, go/no go decisions, high-level planning.	
	▪ The extended lifecycle.	
6.2 Concept	NOT INCLUDED IN THE APMP SYLLABUS	NOT INCLUDED IN THE APMP SYLLABUS
6.3 Definition	NOT INCLUDED IN THE APMP SYLLABUS	NOT INCLUDED IN THE APMP SYLLABUS
6.4 Implementation	NOT INCLUDED IN THE APMP SYLLABUS	NOT INCLUDED IN THE APMP SYLLABUS
6.5 Handover and Closeout	▪ Typical activities involved in Handover and Closeout such as preparation, testing and acceptance of deliverables.	A. Describe the activities involved in Handover and Closeout.
	▪ Handover to the client, customer, operations, business user.	B. Explain the importance of project handover.
	▪ Formally closing the project.	C. Explain the importance of project closeout.
	▪ The importance of handover.	
	▪ The importance of closeout.	
6.6 Project reviews	▪ Different types of reviews, including project evaluation reviews, gate reviews, audits, post-project reviews, benefits realization reviews.	A. Describe project evaluation reviews.
	▪ Importance of project reviews.	B. Describe gate reviews.
	▪ The need to learn lessons throughout the project.	C. Describe audits.
	▪ Benefits of performing reviews.	D. Describe post-project reviews.
		E. Describe benefit realization reviews.
		F. Explain the benefits of project reviews.

Title	Topic coverage	Learning outcomes
6.7 Organization Structure	▪ Different types of organization structure (functional, matrix, project).	A. Distinguish between functional, matrix and project organization structures.
	▪ The advantages and disadvantages of different types of organizational structure.	B. Explain the advantages and disadvantages of a functional organization structure.
	▪ The types of projects suited to each type of organization.	C. Explain the advantages and disadvantages of a matrix organization structure.
	▪ Links between organization structure, the Organizational Breakdown Structure (OBS) and the Responsibility Assignment Matrix (RAM).	D. Explain the advantages and disadvantages of a project organization structure.
6.8 Organizational roles	▪ Roles and responsibilities of the Project Manager, Project Sponsor (Executive), users, project team members and the project Steering Group (Project Board).	A. Explain the role and typical responsibilities of the Project Manager.
	▪ The relationship between the different roles.	B. Explain the differences between the role and typical responsibilities of the Project Manager and the Project Sponsor (Executive).
		C. Describe the role of users.
		D. Describe the role of project team members.
		E. Describe the role of the project Steering Group (Project Board).
6.9 Methods and procedures	Methods and procedures as a means to maintain consistency of project management practice within an organization.	A. Describe the typical contents of a structured method.
	Development and maintenance of methods and procedures.	B. Explain the advantages of adopting a structured method.
	Typical contents of a structured method.	
	The advantages of using a structured method.	
	Awareness of publicly available methods including PRINCE2.	
	Links to governance of project management.	

Table B.6 *continued*

Title	Topic coverage	Learning outcomes
6.10 Governance of project management	Use *Directing Change, a Guide to Governance of Project Management* as a guide to why governance of project management is important and what principles should be used.	A. Explain governance of project management.
	The principles of the governance of project management.	B. Describe the principles of governance of project management.

Table B.7 People and profession

Title	Topic coverage	Learning outcomes
7.1 Communication	▓ The contents of a communication plan.	A. Describe the typical contents of a project communication plan.
	▓ The importance of effective communication.	B. Explain the importance of effective communication in project management.
	▓ Methods and media that can be used for communication within a project.	C. Explain the typical barriers to communication and how they may be overcome.
	▓ The need for two-way communication.	
	▓ Barriers to communication.	
	▓ Links between the communication plan and information management and reporting.	
7.2 Teamwork	▓ Differentiate between groups and teams.	A. Describe a team development model.
	▓ The concept of teamwork.	B. Explain the importance of team development.
	▓ Team development models such as Tuckman or Katzenbach and Smith.	C. Describe a social roles model.
	▓ Features of a high performing team.	
	▓ Social roles in teams such as Belbin or Parker.	
7.3 Leadership	▓ Impact of leadership on team performance.	A. Describe typical leadership qualities.
	▓ Leadership qualities of a Project Manager.	B. Explain the principles and importance of motivation.
	▓ Motivational theories such as Maslow or Herzberg.	C. Describe a situational leadership model.
	▓ A situational leadership model such as Hersey and Blanchard.	
7.4 Conflict management	▓ Sources of conflict in the project lifecycle.	A. Describe sources of conflict in the project lifecycle.
	▓ Conflict resolution models such as Thomas and Kilmann or Russo and Eckler.	B. Explain a conflict resolution model.

Table B.7 *continued*

Title	Topic coverage	Learning outcomes
7.5 Negotiation	■ The process and stages of negotiation such as preparation, face-to-face meeting, follow-up.	A. Describe a negotiation process.
	■ The importance of preparing for a negotiation.	B. Explain each stage of a negotiation process.
	■ When will a Project Manager need to negotiate, including negotiations with suppliers or contractors, users, resource providers, team members and the Project Sponsor.	
7.6 Human resource management	NOT INCLUDED IN THE APMP SYLLABUS	NOT INCLUDED IN THE APMP SYLLABUS
7.7 Behavioural characteristics	NOT INCLUDED IN THE APMP SYLLABUS	NOT INCLUDED IN THE APMP SYLLABUS
7.8 Learning and development	NOT INCLUDED IN THE APMP SYLLABUS	NOT INCLUDED IN THE APMP SYLLABUS
7.9 Professionalism and ethics	NOT INCLUDED IN THE APMP SYLLABUS	NOT INCLUDED IN THE APMP SYLLABUS

Mapping of guide to APMP syllabus

Appendix C: Mapping of guide to APMP syllabus

PURPOSE

This appendix shows the alignment of the chapters in this guide to the APMP syllabus knowledge areas and provides a brief explanation for this alignment.

Table C.1 Mapping of guide to APMP syllabus (reproduced from the *APMP Syllabus 3rd Edition*)

Chapter		Syllabus knowledge areas	Explanation
2	Project management context	1.1; 1.2; 1.3; 1.4; 6.1; 6.9	Describes all of the forms of management that influence projects
3	Business Case	2.1; 5.1	Describes the key issues that affect the realization of benefits
4	Organization and governance	1.5; 1.6; 6.7; 6.8; 6.10	Describes all of the organizational aspects of project management
5	Planning	3.1; 3.2; 3.3; 3.4; 4.3	Describes all of the techniques required to produce plans
6	Controls	2.4; 3.6; 3.7; 6.5; 6.6	Describes controls from the start, middle and end of the project
7	Management of Risk	2.5; 2.7	Describes risk and health and safety as a specialist form of risk
8	Quality management	2.6; 4.1	Describes both quality and requirements management
9	Configuration management	4.7	Describes the configuration management process
10	Change control and issue management	3.5; 3.8	Describes these two very closely related topics
11	Stakeholder management and communication	2.2; 7.1	Describes these two very closely related topics
12	Procurement	5.4; 7.5	Describes negotiation as it forms part of the procurement process
13	People management	7.2; 7.3; 7.4	Describes the related topics of Teamwork, Leadership and Conflict Management

Further reading **D**

Appendix D: Further reading

APM publications

APM Body of Knowledge 5th Edition (2006). APM Publishing Ltd, High Wycombe.

APMP Syllabus 3rd Edition (2006). APM Publishing Ltd, High Wycombe.

Directing Change: A Guide to Governance of Project Management (2004). APM Publishing Ltd, High Wycombe.

Earned Value Management: Guidelines for the UK CD-ROM (2002). APM Publishing Ltd, High Wycombe. Revision to be published in 2008.

Project Risk Analysis and Management Guide 2nd Edition (2004). APM Publishing Ltd, High Wycombe.

Contract Strategy for Successful Project Management (1998). APM Publishing Ltd, High Wycombe.

Project Management Pathways (2002). APM Publishing Ltd, High Wycombe.

TSO publications

Managing Successful Projects with PRINCE2 (2005). The Stationery Office, London.

Managing Successful Programmes (2007). The Stationery Office, London.

Management of Risk: Guidance for Practitioners (2007). The Stationery Office, London.

Other publications

Adair, John (2005). *How to Grow Leaders: The Seven Key Principles of Effective Leadership Development*. Kogan Page.

Belbin, Meredith R. (1996). *Team Roles at Work*. Butterworth-Heinemann.

Hersey, Paul H., Blanchard, Kenneth H. and Johnson, Dewey E. (2008). *Management of Organizational Behavior*. Prentice Hall.

Index

Index

Page numbers in *italics* denote figures. Page numbers in **bold** denote tables.